W9-BUN-602

THE LAST DAYS OF THE ROMANOVS

ALSO BY HELEN RAPPAPORT

No Place for Ladies
Joseph Stalin
Queen Victoria
An Encyclopaedia of Women Social Reformers

Dark Hearts of Chicago
(with William Horwood)

THE LAST DAYS OF THE ROMANOVS

TRAGEDY AT EKATERINBURG

Helen Rappaport

St. Martin's Press ✹ New York

www.stmartins.com

Library of Congress Cataloging-in-Publication Data

Rappaport, Helen.
   The last days of the Romanovs : tragedy at Ekaterinburg / Helen Rappaport.—1st U.S. ed.
        p. cm.
   Includes bibliographical references and index.
   ISBN-13: 978-0-312-37976-6
   ISBN-10: 0-312-37976-5
   1. Nicholas II, Emperor of Russia, 1868–1918—Family.   2. Nicholas II, Emperor of Russia, 1868–1918—Assassination.   3. Emperors—Russia—Biography.   4. Russia—History—Nicholas II, 1894–1917.
   DK258 .R35 2009
   947.08'30922—dc22
   [B]

                                                                    2008038733

First published in Great Britain as *Ekaterinburg: The Last Days of the Romanovs* by Hutchinson, an imprint of The Random House Group Limited

First U.S. Edition: February 2009

10 9 8 7 6 5 4 3 2 1

For my daughters, Dani and Lucy

Contents

Acknowledgements

The Ural Mountains are a very long way from home – or so they seemed to me back in October 2006 when I began this project. I knew that I simply could not write the story of the Romanovs in Ekaterinburg without going to the city where it all happened. Despite my apprehensions, it proved to be a most wonderful, memorable experience; the one moment I shall never forget is standing among the thousands of worshippers at the all-night vigil held at the Church on the Blood to commemorate the murder of the Romanovs on the night of 16–17 July. Here at last I got a sense of the power of the story and its continuing impact on Russian history and culture, and realised why Russia, its history and its people have always been and will remain a consuming passion in my life.

During my stay in Ekaterinburg there were several people without whose kindness and good company it might have been a lonely research trip. First and foremost, Alex Kilin of the History Faculty of the Urals State University proved an irrepressibly good companion and guide through two hot days in July walking the streets of Ekaterinburg from north to south and east to west. I am deeply grateful for his time, his energy and his lively discourse on the city, and for the fact that he spoke no English – it made me work very hard at my Russian.

Valentina Lapina of the British Council offices at the Belinsky Library was kind and welcoming from my very first day and offered the use of internet and email, as well as providing endless cups of tea with her wonderful home-made jam, and inviting me out to her family dacha near Lake Baltysh. Valery Gafurov gave up time to meet and talk with me and drive me round the city. He also kindly set up my meetings with Professors Alekseev and Plotnikov. Professor Venyamin Alekseev found time in a very busy schedule as Vice-President of the Urals Branch of the Russian Academy of Sciences to talk to me about his long-standing research on the Romanov murders. Irina Bedrina of the Ural State Law Academy accompanied me across Ekaterinburg to visit Professor Ivan Plotnikov (about whose outstanding contribution to Romanov studies see Note on Sources). Despite being in frail health, Professor Plotnikov generously gave of his time to talk to me about his many fascinating theories. Konstantin Brylyakov of the Ekaterinburg Guide Centre arranged my trip to Ganina Yama with guide Nadezhda Sokolova, who provided a vivid non-stop Russian commentary on the Romanov story. Princess Svetlana Galitzine of Oxford, while visiting family in Ekaterinburg, kindly met up with me to talk about the city.

My thanks also must go to the many nameless worshippers I talked to at the Church on the Blood and the Voznesensky Cathedral in Ekaterinburg about the Romanovs and their Orthodox faith. A special word of thanks is due to Irina Chirkova, a volunteer at the Voznesensky Cathedral, who out of the goodness of her very warm Russian heart gave me her own treasured copy of Gleb Panfilov's film *Romanovy – Ventsenosnaya Sem'ya* (2000), which I had not been able to locate anywhere. Her gesture was typical of the warmth and kindness I met everywhere in Ekaterinburg, down to the delightful reception staff at the Park Inn who made my stay such a pleasure and were so complimentary about my Russian.

Back home in England I am hugely grateful to the specialist knowledge and help of Phil Tomaselli, an outstanding expert on British Secret Service and Russian-related Foreign Office and War Office records at Kew for the period. Phil helped me dig out the fascinating reports from Ekaterinburg sent by Sir Thomas Preston, as well as a wealth of other valuable material. Frank Swann, a legal forensics and wounds ballistics expert found time for a very long lunch with me, during which he took me through a fascinating analysis of the likely forensics of the basement murders. Peter Bull at York University was a most entertaining guide through the intriguing body language of the official and unofficial Romanov family photographs. Rosemary Matthew, archivist for the Bible Society Library at Cambridge, located the Belusov letter about conditions in Ekaterinburg in 1918. Marie Takayanagi at the Parliamentary Archives helped me access Sir George Buchanan material in the Lloyd George papers. Gillian Long arranged for my access to the Bernard Pares archive at the School of Slavonic and East European Studies in London; Annie Kemkaran-Smith did her best to locate the Sidney Gibbes Collection, now part of the Wernher Collection, but sadly in storage, awaiting a new home and unavailable to researchers at present.

My good friend Michael Holman, former Professor of the Department of Russian and Slavonic Studies at Leeds, put me in touch with Jonathan Sutton, the present incumbent, who provided several useful suggestions and contacts in Ekaterinburg. I owe special thanks, too, to James Harris of Leeds University's School of History – himself an expert on Urals regional history of the period – for putting me in touch with Alex Kilin in Ekaterinburg. At the Brotherton Library I worked in the incomparable

Leeds Russian Archive and am particularly grateful to Richard Davies for his help in making material available and to the Liddle Collection and the Leeds Russian Archive for allowing me permission to quote from it. Roger Taylor alerted me to the wonderful Galloway Stewart photographs at Bradford, and Brian Liddy kindly made available all 22 volumes for me to see. Nick Mays at News International Archive allowed access to the papers of the *Times* correspondent Robert Wilton, part of the Geoffrey Dawson papers, and I am grateful to News International Limited for permission to quote from them; Professor John Rohl at the University of Sussex provided some valuable insights on Kaiser Wilhelm and Melanie Ilic at the University of Gloucestershire passed on numerous valuable bibliographic suggestions.

Elsewhere in England, Princess Olga Romanoff welcomed me into her wonderful home in Kent and shared her photographs and memories of the Romanov ceremonials in St Petersburg in 1998. Sonya Goodman and her husband Philip offered the hospitality of their home in Kensington and Sonya talked vividly about her Kleinmichel ancestors' connections at the Russian imperial court. Colleagues from the Crimean War Research Society Hugh Small and Bill Curtis offered information on pistols and machine guns. In Oxford, Professor Harry Shukman at St Anthony's College entertained me to lunch and gave much advice on Russian sources for the period and his full encouragement in the project. I could not, however, end this particular list without mentioning the wonderful facilities of my second home, the Bodleian Library, Oxford, and its always helpful and obliging staff.

It was a joy to discover, during the writing of this book, that I lived but a five-minute walk from the place of worship of the Russian Orthodox community of St Nicholas the Wonderworker, founded in 1941 by Father Nicholas, formerly Charles Sidney Gibbes, the Tsarevich's tutor. Its members gave me a most warm welcome at their services and I would like to take this opportunity to commend their work in the Russian Orthodox community in Britain.

From the United States, Joshua Wearout at Wichita State University kindly sent photocopies of the material and photographs gathered in Siberia by Paul James Rainey. Ronald M. Bulatoff at the Hoover Institution sent photocopies of the papers of Riza Kuli Mirza (Commander of the Ekaterinburg Garrison 1918–19) from the Vera Cattell collection. John Jenkins at the Spark Museum provided information on telegraphs and telephonograms and David Mould at Ohio University also answered questions about Russian telecommunications. In New York I enjoyed the wonderful facilities of the Yivo Institute for Jewish Research on 16th and 5th (now part of the Center for Jewish

Studies), where I studied the extensive and greatly undervalued archive of Herman Bernstein (see Note on Sources). At Yivo, Jesse Aaron Cohen helped me locate Bernstein's Siberian photographs as well as those taken by the US Expeditionary Force in Siberia. Gunnar M. Berg graciously ferried large numbers of files back and forth from the Bernstein collection and photocopied much reference material for me. Finally, my trip to New York would not have been such a joy without the good companionship and support of my friend John Reiner.

In the wider community of the World Wide Web, I must express my gratitude for the wonderful work in making available material by and about the Romanovs carried out at the Alexander Palace Time Machine website and in particular its enormously interesting, lively and informative discussion list. This list is populated by hundreds of amateur enthusiasts, many of whom have made a lifetime's study of the Romanov family. Here I drew on a wealth of interested and informed opinion and recommend the list most heartily to anyone wishing to learn more. See www.alexanderpalace.org/palace/.

During the writing of this book I greatly appreciated the love and support of my family – especially my brothers Christopher and Peter Ware who helped me in the construction of my website and were a continuous source of encouragement, as too was my dear friend Christina Zaba. William Horwood offered insightful comments and constructive criticism on some key passages. At Hutchinson, my commissioning editor, Caroline Gascoigne, offered lively support and enthusiasm for the book, as too did my wonderful publicist Cecília Durães. My thanks too must go to my picture researcher Elaine Willis and my copy editor Jane Selley.

Finally, but most importantly, I owe an enormous debt of gratitude to my agent, Charlie Viney. When he first mooted the idea of a book about the Romanovs to me I groaned, insisting there was nothing left to say. But with his encouragement, I went away and looked at the story again, from different perspectives, and came up with the tight 14-day scenario. Thereafter, Charlie cajoled and praised and guided me to the right way of writing this book, involving as it did a major rethink of how, till then, I had approached history writing. I am profoundly grateful to him for his patience, support and belief in this project and for all his hours of hard work. Without him, *Ekaterinburg* simply would never have happened.

Helen Rappaport
Oxford
September 2008

List of Illustrations

Section One

1. Tsar Nicholas II with his wife the Tsaritsa Alexandra shortly after their marriage, c. 1895. (Photo Popperfoto/Getty Images)

2. The four Romanov Grand Duchesses in an official photograph, 1915. Standing from left-right, the Grand Duchesses Maria, Anastasia and Olga and seated Grand Duchess Tatiana (Photo Popperfoto/Getty Images)

3. Tsar Nicholas II of Russia with his wife, Alexandra and their five children. Alexandra holds the baby Tsarevich, Alexey, surrounded by the Grand Duchesses Olga, Tatiana, Maria and Anastasia.(Photo Hulton Archive/Getty Images)

4. Nicholas enjoying a cigarette on board the Imperial yacht, the *Shtandart* (Photo Rex Features)

5. Empress Alexandra in her wheelchair at Tsarskoe Selo, 1917 (Photo Underwood & Underwood / Library of Congress)

6. Alexandra seated on Nicholas's desk, taken during the war years, 1916. (Photo from *The End of the Romanovs* by Victor Alexandrov, translated by William Sutcliffe (English translation, Hutchinson, 1966))

7. Prince Edward (later briefly King Edward VIII) with Tsar Nicholas II, Tsarevich Alexey and George, Prince of Wales (later King George V), at Cowes in 1909 (Photo Keystone/Getty Images)

8. Alexey with his pet cat and his King Charles Spaniel Joy, at Army HQ in 1916 (Photo Roger Violet / Topfoto)

9. The Tsaritsa with her two oldest daughters, Olga and Tatiana, in their nurses' uniforms, with Maria and Anastasia in civilian dress (Photo David King Collection)

10. Members of the Czech Legion standing by the obelisk outside Ekaterinburg marking the boundary between Europe and Asia (Photo from *The Lost Legion 1939* by Gustav Becvar (Stanley Paul, 1939))

11. Dr Evgeny Botkin, the Romanov family's physician (Photo from *Thirteen Years at the Russian Court* by Pierre Gilliard (Hutchinson, 1921))

12. Exterior of Ipatiev House showing the first palisade erected just before the Romanovs' arrival at the end of April 1918. American Expeditionary Forces in Siberia album (Photo YIVO Institute for Jewish Research)

13. The Commandant's room on the first floor of the Ipatiev House occupied by Avdeev and after him, Yurovsky. American Expeditionary Forces in Siberia album (Photo YIVO Institute for Jewish Research)

14. The dining room in the Ipatiev House where the Imperial Family shared their simple meals with their servants (Photo YIVO Institute for Jewish Research)

15. View of Voznesensky Prospekt c. 1900s showing the Ipatiev House in the bottom left hand corner (Photo Author's Collection)

16. View of Ekaterinburg showing the bell tower of the Voznesensky Cathedral in distance on right (Photo Prokudin-Gorskii, Sergei Mikhailovich / Library of Congress)

Section Two

17. Filipp Goloshchekin in exile in Turukhansk, Siberia with Yakov Sverdlov, with Joseph Stalin third from left, back row (Photo David King Collection)

18. Lenin in his study in the Kremlin, 1918 (Photo AKG images)

19. Pavel Medvedev, head of the Ipatiev House guard, on the left, with a fellow Bolshevik, Larin (Photo David King Collection)

20. Yurovsky's family, taken in Ekaterinburg c. 1919. Yurovsky is standing on the back right (Photo from *The Murder of the Romanovs* by Captain Paul Bulygin (Hutchinson, 1935))

21. The Tsar and Tsaritsa's bedroom on the corner of Voznesensky Prospekt and Voznesensky Lane (Photo from *The End of the Romanovs* by Victor Alexandrov, translated by William Sutcliffe (English translation, Hutchinson, 1966))

22. Main entrance of the Novo-Tikhvinsky Convent in Ekaterinburg (Photo Sergey Prokudin-Gorskii / Library of Congress)

23. The US journalist Herman Bernstein in Siberia (Photo YIVO Institute for Jewish Research)

24. Thomas Preston, British Consul in Ekaterinburg in 1918 (Photo Telegraph Group)

25. Lieutenant Colonel Mariya Bochkareva of the 1st women's Battalion of Death (Photo George Grantham Bain Collection / Library of Congress)

26. President Woodrow Wilson, who reluctantly ordered US intervention forces into Russia in the summer of 1918 (Photo Library of Congress)

27. The coded telegram sent by Aleksandr Beloborodov to Moscow confirming that all the Romanov family had been killed (Photo Topfoto)

28. The Grand Duchesses' bedroom in the Ipatiev House, showing remains of a fire in which the personal effects of the Romanovs were burned. (Photo from *The End of the Romanovs* by Victor Alexandrov, translated by William Sutcliffe (English translation, Hutchinson, 1966))

29. Petr Ermakov, one of the Romanovs' killers (Photo David King Collection)

30. One of the complex of churches at Ganina Yama in the Koptyaki Forest outside Ekaterinburg commemorating the Romanov family (Author's photograph)

31. The opening of the mine-working in the clearing known as the 'Four Brothers' in the Koptyaki Forest where the Romanovs were first buried on 17 July (Photo from *The End of the Romanovs* by Victor Alexandrov, translated by William Sutcliffe (English translation, Hutchinson, 1966))

32. The Church on the Blood in Ekaterinburg, built on the site of the Ipatiev House in 2003 (Author's photograph)

33. A 1900s view of the Voznesensky Cathedral located across the road from the Ipatiev House (Photo Author's Collection)

34. The Amerikanskaya Hotel on Pokrovsky Prospekt, headquarters of the Ekaterinburg Cheka, c. 1900s. (Photo Author's Collection)

35. One of many modern day icons celebrating the Romanovs as saints in the Russian Orthodox calendar (Photo Author's Collection)

36. The Scent of Lilies. The 'Four Brothers' burial site today, covered with arum lilies on the anniversary of the murders in July. (Author's photograph)

Don't you forget what's divine in the Russian soul—and that's resignation.

—Joseph Conrad, *Under Western Eyes,* 1911

The Red Urals

On the evening of 29 April 1918, a special train stood in a siding at the remote railway halt of Lyubinskaya on the Trans-Siberian railway line, not far from the city of Omsk. It was abnormally well guarded. Inside its first-class carriage sat Nicholas Alexandrovich Romanov, former Tsar of All the Russias, and his German-born wife Alexandra.

Stripped of all privileges, a captive awaiting trial or exile, Nicholas was being moved after 13 months under house arrest with his family, first at the Alexander Palace in St Petersburg and latterly at Tobolsk in Western Siberia. If he did not know it already, some of those around him most certainly did: the Tsar was making his final journey. But even those who guessed what might happen to their former monarch could not possibly have imagined the true, appalling horror of what was to come.

Nicholas had been in good spirits till then, but his hopes of a safe refuge were brutally dashed when he and his wife discovered they were not being taken to Moscow, or to exile out of Russia, as they had hoped.

The train they were on was heading for the very last place Nicholas wished to be sent. Ekaterinburg.

'I would go anywhere at all, only not to the Urals,' he is reported to have said that night as the train slowed in its approach to the city. Having regularly read the local papers whilst at Tobolsk, he was well aware that the mood among workers in the Urals was 'harshly against him'. He had good reason to dread being forcibly taken to such a place, among such people – whether as deposed monarch or as a loving family man with a sick wife, four vulnerable daughters, and an ailing, haemophiliac son. Ekaterinburg was violently anti-tsarist and, as the historic hub of Russia's old penal system, had been a point of transit to places and horrors from which there was no return.

★

Outside Ekaterinburg there once stood a stone obelisk in a lonely forest glade, its plaster facing pitted and worn by the harsh Russian climate. On one side was inscribed the Cyrillic word *ЕВРОПА* – Europe – and on the other, *АЗИЯ* – Asia – for this monument marked the symbolic boundary between European and Asian Russia. Straddling the Great Siberian Highway, Ekaterinburg had been Imperial Russia's gateway to the East since the city's foundation in the early eighteenth century, and beyond it the original post road stretched 3,000 miles to the Manchurian border.

The natural boundary was formed by the Ural Mountains, a 1,700-mile-long range which split Russia from north to south. To the east lay the arctic wastes of the Siberian plain, stretching like a vast sea and ending, as the writer Anton Chekhov observed, 'the devil knows where'. But the Great Siberian Highway was no grand thoroughfare. For two centuries or more this 'brown streak of road running like a thread' right across Russia was better known as the Trakt. From Ekaterinburg, convoys of exiles and criminals, after being transported by steamboat and barge to Tyumen from the central prisons in Moscow, would tramp along its narrow, meandering gravel path – in columns of dust in the dry summer months and in the arctic snowstorms of winter, their legs in clanking fetters.

During their two-year forced march into imprisonment or exile, hundreds of thousands of men, women and children passed this way during the worst years of Tsarist oppression. Their arrival at the Ekaterinburg obelisk marked a Dantesque point of transition, the portal to a Russian kind of hell beyond which unfortunates abandoned all hope of seeing homes and families again. Stopping briefly here, they would look their last on European Russia before venturing into the pagan wilderness beyond. Many would kiss the obelisk in a final farewell; others scratched their names on the plasterwork. Most would never pass this way again.

Pronounced *Ye-ka-tyer-in-boorg*, the city has an oddly Western-sounding name, but Asia is all around. Nestling on the eastern slopes of the Urals, the low horizon lies open to expanses of swampy *taiga*, the forests of pine, birch and larch extending far to the north and east, where wild bears, elk, wolves and mountain cats roam. The climate here is unforgivingly Siberian, with spring not arriving until mid-May. Even then snow is on the ground, the lakes are still under ice and the earth is muddy from spring floods. Accompanied by swarms of mosquitoes, summer makes a brief appearance in June, bringing with it the brief idyll of the midnight sun, as well as fierce thunder and lightning storms sparked by the rich mineral deposits in the hills. But late August sees the return of frosts and the cycle tightens its grip once more.

Given its name in 1723 after Peter the Great's second wife, Ekaterinburg started as a distant outpost of empire – little more than a wooden fortress built to protect the valuable iron-smelting works established there. Despite its remoteness, it was to grow in importance as an economic, scientific and cultural centre, eventually becoming wealthy as a city of mining engineers, merchants and bankers and home to the Russian Imperial Mint. Ekaterinburg's prosperity was founded on the vast mineral resources of the Urals; the semi-precious stones which decorated Russia's imperial palaces and cathedrals were mined here, their deep hues seen in exquisite inlay work, in columns of jasper, porphyry and lapis lazuli and the distinctive dark green of the superb urns, vases and tables of malachite that graced the great palaces of the tsars. The mountains here held an abundance of diamonds, amethysts and emeralds, as well as warm, rosy rhodonite and the rare and fascinating alexandrite with its ever-changing hues of red and green. Supplied to the Imperial Lapidary works in Ekaterinburg and St Petersburg, these gemstones provided much of the raw material for the fantastically elaborate jewellery and *objets d'art* created by craftsmen such as Karl Fabergé, the Romanovs' court jeweller.

The Urals were equally rich in precious metals. Gold had been discovered here in 1814, platinum five years later. Indeed, there was gold in such abundance that the locals claimed that 'where it has not been found, it has not been looked for'. By the time revolution came, Ekaterinburg was supplying 90 per cent of the world's platinum, and a profusion of luxury goods, perfumes and furs of the finest quality – beaver from Kamchatka, sable, ermine, mink, black and grey fox, bearskin rugs – were all to be found in the city, brought in from all over Siberia. But the city's real wealth lay in iron ore and the pig iron produced from it. By the beginning of the nineteenth century, with the Urals now the biggest iron producer in the world, Ekaterinburg was building the new industrial plants of modernising Russia. But by the end of the century the once dominant ironworks of Ekaterinburg were being outstripped by a powerful new metallurgical industry in the Don basin in the south, powered by vast resources of coal. Industry began to stagnate, only to be rescued by an intensive period of modernisation and the construction of the Trans-Siberian Railway.

Passing through Ekaterinburg in 1890, Chekhov found it dull and provincial, only being taken by 'the magnificent, velvety' sound of its many church bells ringing out in the crisp spring air during Lent. Seeking refuge in the comforts of the Amerikanskaya Hotel, the 30-year-old playwright retreated to his room and kept the blinds down in order not to have to look out on what seemed to him an alien world. All night long he had heard the distant thud-thud of machine presses. You would need a head of cast iron not to be driven mad by them, he wrote. As for the inhabitants of this semi-Asiatic city, he found them inscrutable, intimidating even. They inspired in him 'a feeling akin to horror with their prominent cheekbones, large foreheads, tiny eyes and utterly enormous fists'. Stunted by heavy labour, brutalised by the appalling climate, Ekaterinburgers were 'born in the local iron foundries and brought into the world not by midwives, but mechanics'.

By the 1900s Ekaterinburg had mushroomed from an eighteenth-century settlement of single-storey log houses into a powerful regional city with armies of peasants labouring in its iron-smelting factories, flour and paper mills, soap works and tanneries. Legions of tsarist officials had settled here to run the Ural Mining Industry and Imperial Mint. There was a large foreign contingent too, at the British-owned Hubbard candle works, the Tait mechanical works and the Sysert iron foundry, as well as a strong diplomatic presence, the British Consulate having opened its imposing premises on Voznesensky Prospekt in 1913. French, Swiss, American, German, Swedish and Danish consulates soon were operating nearby. Framed by linden trees, Ekaterinburg's broad, stone-paved boulevards were grand and airy in the all too brief summer, its parks and ornamental gardens glowing with flowers. The city had its own 'millionaire's row' of fine houses, a museum of natural history, two theatres that were visited by tours from the Moscow Art Theatre, and an imposing opera house where Chaliapin came to sing. It offered several comfortable and grandly named hotels such as the Eldorado and the Palais Royal. Heartily recommended by Baedeker, the Amerikanskaya Hotel was undoubtedly the best in town and comparatively clean by Siberian standards; it also provided good dinners for less than four roubles.

Many travellers arriving here after weary weeks on the road were captivated by the city's beauty. It was a welcome sight after the sombre, bleak wastes of Siberia – the first 'really cultivated place' they had seen since leaving Shanghai. Ekaterinburg had much to offer: stone-built, stuccoed houses of classical architectural beauty, a skyline of golden-domed churches and the cream and turquoise baroque beauty of its Voznesensky and Ekaterininsky cathedrals. Crowning the three-mile-long Voznesensky Prospekt, which intersected the heart of the old city, the Rastorguev-Kharitonov House, a finely proportioned Palladian mansion built by Ekaterinburg's platinum king, looked down on a regional city flexing its industrial power and basking in its economic prosperity. Ekaterinburg was in the vanguard of a rapidly modernising

Russia: a place with street lighting, telephones, electric trams and a substantial rail depot at the junction of seven railway lines, through which the Trans-Siberian Railway powered its way into the East.

But the October Revolution of 1917 brought seismic changes to the city. In November, the 'agitators' arrived and with the support of local railway workers staged a Bolshevik *coup d'état*. This was swiftly followed by industrial and financial crisis as the city fell into debt and bankruptcy. Then followed arrests, shootings, confiscations and fear. Russia's fifth largest city had become one of its most forbidding strongholds of conflicting political forces and a major hub of Bolshevik activity. Of its population of about 100,000, a large proportion was workers and soldiers, many of them tough young militants notorious for their radical political line.

It was into this menacing hotbed of revolutionary fervour that Public Enemy No. 1, Citizen Nicholas Alexandrovich Romanov, arrived on 30 April 1918. It seemed poetic justice that he should end up in a city through which so many of those condemned into political exile by the old tsarist system had passed on their own journey into Siberia.

But how had one of the world's most wealthy, powerful autocrats found himself here, in the notorious 'Red Urals'? And how had this devout, insistently dull and dogmatic little man, whose primary interest was family life, come to be demonised as the repository of all that was corrupt, reactionary and despotic about the Romanov dynasty?

Tsar Nicholas II was not the first monarch to have kingship unexpectedly thrust upon him, nor was he the first to be emotionally and politically unprepared for its onerous responsibilities. As a man of limited political ability and vision, Nicholas had done what came naturally. He had assiduously maintained the autocratic rule of his father whilst blindly resisting all political innovation and condoning the suppression of the empire's turbulent minorities. His stubborn belief in his role as God's anointed representative made him turn a blind eye to increasingly anxious calls for political change. But political and social unrest, fanned by revolutionary activity among the urban workforces of St Petersburg and Moscow, had finally forced Nicholas into token gestures of constitutional reform in 1905. The democratic powers of the newly inaugurated Duma were, however, greatly circumscribed and Nicholas routinely subverted its activities, refusing any real concessions to representative government, and condemning moves to modernise, as he had since the day he ascended the throne, as mere 'senseless dreams'. He retreated instead into domesticity; playing contentedly with his children, closeted away at the Alexander Palace at Tsarskoe Selo outside St Petersburg and seeing only a small inner circle of family and friends.

Nicholas's increasing invisibility from public view and his continuing resistance to reform rapidly set in motion the inexorable collapse of an already moribund political regime, despite a degree of economic recovery and growth in the years between 1907 and 1914. The process of collapse was accelerated after Russia's enthusiastic entry into the First World War in August 1914. The initial euphoria of national solidarity, which Nicholas could and should have capitalised on politically, rapidly crumbled in the face of catastrophic losses. By September of the following year continuing gross ineptitude in both the conduct of the war and the supply of materiel, coupled with serious territorial losses to the Germans in Galicia, finally dragged Nicholas away from family preoccupations to assume supreme command at the front. But by now, despite the presence of its *batyushka* – 'little father' – at the head of the army, Russia was engaged in a war of attrition, fuelling unprecedented desertion rates in its demoralised, ill-equipped and starving peasant army. After centuries of unquestioning loyalty, the long-suffering conscript had begun to ask what he was fighting for. The Tsar, it seemed, only wanted him to plough, and fight, and pay taxes. And so Nicholas's peasant army began deserting in their thousands.

Back in Petrograd (as St Petersburg had been renamed in August 1914), Nicholas's deeply unpopular wife, Alexandra, had been left in effective political control at a time when she was increasingly spellbound by Grigory Rasputin, the charismatic but hugely manipulative 'holy man' who had demonstrated an inexplicable ability to control her haemophiliac son Alexey's attacks of bleeding. Alexandra's intimacy with Rasputin had thrown her into hysterical conflict with government ministers and fuelled unbridled and increasingly virulent gossip about the true nature of their relationship. Meanwhile, Nicholas ignored the repeated and increasingly urgent warnings from members of his government about the escalating situation in Petrograd. He would not even listen to his devoted uncle, Grand Duke Nikolay, whom he had relieved of supreme command of the army, when the duke begged him to make compromises and save the dynasty from annihilation. The juggernaut of revolutionary change in Russia was now clearly unstoppable; politicians and foreign diplomats had been predicting it for years. Yet Nicholas stubbornly trusted only to his own counsel and that of his wife, a woman determined to protect the Romanovs' absolute sovereignty, their divine right to rule, and with it the inheritance of their precious only son.

Early in 1917, urban economic chaos in Petrograd finally triggered violent industrial strikes, marches and bread riots, bringing mutinous soldiers out on to the streets. The volatile situation erupted into outright revolution at the end of February. Away at the front, Nicholas believed he had no option but to abdicate 'for the good of Russia', the morale of the army and – most pressingly – the safety of his family. He had already been told by his ailing son's doctors that Alexey was unlikely to live to the age of 16, so he took the decision simultaneously to abdicate on behalf of his heir.

Six months of house arrest followed for the Romanov family at the Alexander Palace at Tsarskoe Selo, where they tried to carry on domestic life as best they could. Unburdened of affairs of state, Nicholas appeared to thrive, enjoying the outdoors no matter what the weather, sawing wood, vigorously sweeping snow and breaking ice in the park. He was not deterred by the ominous presence of crowds, who made their way out to Tsarskoe Selo, paying the guards a rouble for the privilege of being able to stand at the perimeter fence and gawp, deriding him with the pejorative names of 'Nikoluchka' and 'Nikolashka'.

With an increasingly tense political situation in St Petersburg and the growing threat of a mob descending on the Alexander Palace, by July 1917 Aleksandr Kerensky, head of the provisional government, was coming under pressure to incarcerate the Tsar and Tsaritsa in the Peter Paul Fortress as ordinary prisoners – or worse, to see them transferred to the custody of the radicalised island naval base at Kronstadt. Diplomatic moves to send the family to England had come to nothing, and Kerensky therefore decided to move them to a place of greater safety, not wishing, he said, to become 'the Marat of the Revolution'. From here the Romanovs could hopefully be evacuated east to Japan or north to Scandinavia. The family were bitterly disappointed not to have been allowed south to the warmth of their much-loved palace at Livadia on the Black Sea, where they would have happily lived out their lives in seclusion as an ordinary family. Instead they found themselves boarding a train for Tyumen in Western Siberia and from there a steamship to what in those unstable times still seemed the politically safe backwater of Tobolsk.

By August 1917, Nicholas, Alexandra and their five children – the Grand Duchesses Olga, Tatiana, Maria and Anastasia and the Tsarevich Alexey – had been installed in the former Governor's House, the grandest accommodation Tobolsk could offer. Here they came perversely to enjoy the simple pleasures of rural life as well as a degree of freedom, whilst still retaining a substantial entourage of 39 courtiers and servants. They had also been allowed to bring many of their most treasured possessions with them from the Alexander Palace: cameras and photograph albums – at least 16 of them, made of Moroccan leather – as well as diaries and letters, and even vintage wines from the Imperial Court Cellars.

But three months into their stay in Tobolsk, a second revolution took place, during which the Bolsheviks overthrew Kerensky's provisional government and seized power. Lenin's new government now determined on a campaign of terror and revenge against 300 years of Romanov rule. Whilst the former Tsar and Tsaritsa languished in the Governor's House, the flamboyant Leon Trotsky planned their dramatic show trial along the lines of the Revolutionary Tribunal that had tried and executed Louis XVI and his wife Marie Antoinette in 1793, with himself, a latter-day Robespierre, as prosecutor.

Meanwhile, the brutalising web of Bolshevism was spreading inexorably beyond the Urals. By April 1918 it had reached Tobolsk, bringing with it a crackdown on the Imperial Family's remaining privileges. Their very presence in the region was exacerbating the tense situation brewing between Bolsheviks in Ekaterinburg and other local factions, who wished to wrest control of the Imperial Family and have a hand in their ultimate fate. In this maelstrom of political tension, very real opportunities to save the Romanovs were dissipated. An ill-assorted cast of aspirants – army officers, monarchists and aristocrats, wealthy merchants, European royals, nuns and clergy – all proved hamstrung by lack of funds and conflicting political agendas, incapable of concerted rescue attempts. Behind embassy doors diplomats and secret service agents strove to come up with viable schemes for the family's forced abduction. Nevertheless, hopes lived on well into the spring of 1918 in a plethora of abortive, fantastical plans both inside and outside Russia, whilst at the Governor's House in Tobolsk the Romanovs waited for a miracle.

Any hopes were dashed in April 1918 when Vasily Yakovlev, an Extraordinary Commissar sent by Moscow in response to all the escape rumours, arrived in Tobolsk, ostensibly to escort the Tsar back to Moscow, where he would be put on trial. But the rapidly changing political situation in the Urals soon prevented this. When the Ekaterinburg Bolsheviks got wind of Yakovlev's mission, they demanded the Tsar be brought to their city. After urgent telegraph consultations with the Kremlin, Yakovlev was instructed to take his prisoners to Ekaterinburg, where he was ordered to hand the Romanovs over.

The Urals in 1918 were far from the romanticised, ersatz Russia set in stone in the Western public imagination by David Lean's 1964 film *Dr Zhivago*. Ekaterinburg was filled with tough, remorseless men. Newly formed radical workers' committees, convinced that attempts would be made to rescue the Tsar, were ready, if given half the chance, to take him out and lynch him. Escalating violence, looting, famine and looming civil war across the country had brought the city to the edge of the abyss. Ten thousand Red Army soldiers and deserters now roamed its streets, and it was bristling too with convicts and exiles on the run from Siberia. There were spies everywhere.

By June, Russia had been engulfed in civil war between Bolsheviks and counter-revolutionary and monarchist forces, led by Aleksandr Kolchak and known as the 'Whites', who had fought their way inland from the Pacific and were pushing into Western Siberia, their ranks bolstered by about 25,000 Czech deserters and prisoners of war from the Austro-Hungarian army. These troops had been on their way east out of Russia by rail to be reunited, via America, with Czech troops on the Western Front, but had mutinied when Russia's German allies demanded they be stopped and disarmed. On 26 May, fighting their way back westwards, the Czechs had taken the major Siberian city of Chelyabinsk. Now they were closing in on Ekaterinburg, a city of crucial industrial and strategic importance. Tension in the Urals was rising. With wild rumours of last-ditch attempts to save the Imperial Family still swirling round, the Ekaterinburg Bolsheviks determined that their valuable prisoners would not be stolen from them. Something had to be done to secure the situation.

Two days before Nicholas and Alexandra's arrival, a house in the centre of Ekaterinburg belonging to a retired engineer named Nikolay Ipatiev had been summarily requisitioned by the local soviet (the Bolshevik-dominated city council) as the Romanovs' new place of detention. Within hours its reassuring bourgeois gentility had been disfigured by the construction of a rude wooden palisade which blocked out the city, turning the Ipatiev House into a prison. From now on it would be referred to by an ominous Bolshevik euphemism as the *Dom osobogo naznacheniya* – 'The House of Special Purpose'. Quite what purpose was implied in the title was never explained, but the local hard men of the Ural Regional Soviet knew full well the house's ultimate, sinister purpose.

Nicholas and his exhausted wife arrived in Ekaterinburg on 30 April, accompanied by their 18-year-old daughter Maria, the Tsar's aide Prince Vasily Dolgorukov, the Imperial family's physician Dr Evgeny Botkin and a severely reduced quota of three servants. The uncertainties of their journey had prompted the Tsar and Tsaritsa to travel only with Maria, the most adaptable of their children. The others – Olga, Tatiana, Anastasia and Alexey – were due to follow later, when the Tsarevich had fully recovered from a severe attack of haemophilia.

Meanwhile, on Saturday 29 June 1918, the six-man presidium of the Ekaterinburg Soviet held an urgent meeting in the opulent surroundings

of the Amerikanskaya Hotel. It had been requisitioned in early June as
the headquarters of Ekaterinburg's newly created branch of the
Chrezvychainaya Komissiya — the Soviet secret police. Better known as
the Cheka, this organisation was soon to become the implacable agent of
state terror. Beyond the city, the faint sound of artillery fire could be
heard. The well-armed and disciplined Czechs were now edging ever
closer along the Trans-Siberian Railway. Ekaterinburg was spiralling into
anarchy and chaos and could hold out for another couple of weeks at
best. With the lines of communication to Moscow becoming
increasingly unreliable, Alexander Beloborodov, the chair of the Ural
Regional Soviet, sent urgent messages to Moscow demanding direct
cable access to Lenin at the Kremlin in the crucial days to come. He and
his group of dedicated Communists were facing a critical moment in
their 'revolutionary path'. The Red Urals were in 'mortal danger' and
there was considerable risk that the former Tsar would fall into the hands
of the Czechs or other counter-revolutionaries and be 'used to their
benefit'.

All through that humid summer afternoon the atmosphere inside room
No. 3, the biggest and best room that the Amerikanskaya had to offer,
crackled with tension. There was only one pressing topic on the agenda.
What was to be done with the Romanovs? The following day, 30 June
1918, Filipp Goloshchekin, a member of the presidium of the Ural
Regional Soviet and the newly appointed regional commissar for war,
headed out of Ekaterinburg on the train to Moscow to confer with Lenin
and his right-hand man Yakov Sverdlov about their fate.

Meanwhile, Ekaterinburg, once the jewel of the Ural Mountains, was
in a state of siege; its infrastructure collapsing, its citizens in the grip of a
mounting reign of terror.

Behind the Palisade

30 APRIL–3 JULY 1918

It took five days of bone-rattling travel by *tarantass* – a crude springless carriage – for the Romanovs to get from Tobolsk to Tyumen. During the journey, Alexandra and Maria huddled together and shivered as they were jolted across rivers and through spring floods and quagmires of mud. Drained and exhausted, Alexandra had been glad of the company of Maria, who had volunteered to come with them as a comfort to her. Nicholas, in contrast, seemed cheerful, glad to be on the move and out in the fresh frosty air.

Faced with the choice of accompanying her husband to Moscow, as she thought, and defending his position, or staying behind to nurse the sick Alexey in Tobolsk, Alexandra had agonised over her decision, torn between the overwhelming emotional pull of her son and her ingrained fears for Nicholas. Eventually she resolved that her first duty was to the Tsar, if only for her malleable husband's own protection.

At Tyumen the royal party transferred to the heavily guarded first-class carriage of Special Train No. 8 VA, commandeered by Vasily Yakovlev. En route Yakovlev continued to give the official line that Nicholas was being sent back to the capital to be put on trial. Privately, the Tsar and the Tsaritsa were convinced that fate would intervene and that this would be but the first stage in the Imperial Family's safe passage out of Russia. After a series of delays, the train arrived at Omsk, the junction of two major lines on the Trans-Siberian Railway, and the couple were suddenly gripped by alarm. Where would they be taken next? Eastwards across Siberia to Vladivostok and out of Russia via Japan? Or west towards Moscow and a public trial? Nothing was said as the train idled for hours in a siding at Lyubinskaya while Yakovlev parlayed over the telegraph with Moscow. Finally a change of plan was agreed. The train moved off, back in the direction of Tyumen. The Tsar and Tsaritsa were to be escorted not to Moscow after all, but to Ekaterinburg, where the Ural Regional Soviet would take custody of them.

At 8.40 a.m. on Tuesday 30 April, the train pulled into the city with its blinds drawn. As it did, Nicholas and Alexandra's anxiety levels rocketed. For here, at last, they encountered the full, ugly force of Russia in revolution. As the Tsaritsa later recalled in her diary, the day might have been 'gloriously warm and sunny', but the welcoming committee had been decidedly frosty. Rumours of the imminent arrival of the hated Tsar and Tsaritsa had spread like wildfire and an angry mob had gathered at the main railway station demanding that they be paraded before them. Fearful of a lynching, the Urals military commissar, Filipp Goloshchekin, who had been waiting to receive the Romanovs, decided to send the train on to the city's freight station No. 2 at Shartash, on the eastern outskirts. The Romanovs' first sight of Ekaterinburg was, after several hours kept sitting in the train, a goods siding at four in the afternoon. Waiting for them on the platform was a group of stony-faced Bolsheviks – Aleksandr Beloborodov, chair of the Ural Regional Soviet, Boris Didkovsky, his deputy, and Sergey Chutskaev, a member of the Ekaterinburg Soviet and the local secret police, the Cheka.

The Tsar and his family were now received into the hands of the Ural Regional Soviet for 'detention under surveillance', along with Dr Evgeny Botkin, their maid Anna Demidova, the valet Terenty Chemodurov and footman Ivan Sednev. With a bureaucratic flourish, Beloborodov signed the official receipt for them, like so much baggage. Aleksandr Avdeev, who with Yakovlev had accompanied the Tsar and Tsaritsa from Tobolsk, was appointed commandant of the Romanovs' new place of confinement. Later that hot summer afternoon the party made the short journey to Voznesensky Prospekt along eerily deserted streets, in closed motor cars, escorted by a truck bristling with armed soldiers. As their car pulled into the courtyard of the Ipatiev House, the former Tsar and his wife looked their last on Russia and the outside world. It was Passion Week and the bells – the beautiful bells that had so beguiled Anton Chekhov – were ringing out across the city. But they could not drown out the sound of the heavy wooden courtyard gates as they slammed shut behind them.

The Tsar and Tsaritsa moved to enter the Ipatiev House, to be greeted at the entrance by Goloshchekin, who had gone on ahead to meet them and now turned to his former monarch and declared: 'Citizen Nicholas Romanov, you may enter.' Impervious to insult, reconciled to his fate, Nicholas did not react, but the slight cut the Tsaritsa to the quick. Though Alexandra would continue, stubbornly, to take exception to Bolshevik disrespect, from now on there would be no more acknowledgement of Romanov status and titles, which, even in Tobolsk, had still been part of the daily protocol observed by staff and guards alike.

The former Tsar of Russia was now an ordinary Soviet citizen like any other, with his own ration card. While he may have looked on their life at Tobolsk as a kind of house arrest, here Nicholas finally found himself in prison, within that vast annexe of the Russian empire that was itself a prison: Siberia.

Via emphatic instructions sent from Moscow by Yakov Sverdlov to the Ural Regional Soviet, it was the clear intention of the Kremlin leadership that the family should now be confined 'in the strictest way'. Seething with class hatred and desire for revenge on 'Nicholas the Bloody', the Ekaterinburg Bolsheviks delighted in withdrawing comforts previously accorded the Imperial Family. If the relative idyll in Tobolsk had prevented them taking their fate seriously, then now, surely, their presence in Ekaterinburg was for Nicholas and Alexandra a stark awakening. On her arrival it prompted the Tsaritsa to inscribe the date and a reverse swastika on the bedroom wall, a last faint gesture that this ancient symbol of faith, love and hope might eventually bring release.

Together with Maria, the Tsar and Tsaritsa spent their first three weeks at the Ipatiev House cooped up together in a single bedroom with only the use of the bathroom and sitting room, where Dr Botkin and the servants Chemodurov and Sednev slept; Anna Demidova occupied a small room in the back. The electricity supply was sporadic, but when she could, Alexandra wrote endless letters to the children in Tobolsk, as Nicholas read aloud from the Gospels. Despite the glorious sunshine, heavy snowfalls had continued well into May and emotional comforts were few until, at 11 a.m. on the unseasonably cold and snowy morning of the 23rd, the remaining four children arrived from the city station. But the 27-strong Tobolsk entourage who had travelled with them were informed that they could go no further. The Ekaterinburg Soviet had no wish to burden itself with the additional expense of their maintenance. They were left sitting on the train at Ekaterinburg station, to be later dispersed, a few to freedom but most to prison (where the Tsar's loyal aide Prince Dolkorukov had already been taken on arrival in April). Only three more servants, the cook Ivan Kharitonov, the kitchen boy Leonid Sednev (the nephew of Ivan Sednev) and the manservant Alexey Trupp, were allowed to follow the Imperial Family into the Ipatiev House, bringing with them Alexey's beloved pet spaniel, Joy, and Tatiana's two dogs, Jimmy and Ortipo.

The arrival of Alexey, Olga, Tatiana and Anastasia from Tobolsk, of which the Tsar and Tsaritsa were forewarned only a few hours before their arrival, greatly lifted the family's flagging spirits. There was no doubt, Nicholas noted in his diary, that the four children had all suffered personally and spiritually when left in Tobolsk on their own. But the closely interdependent family unit was once more reunited and what greater joy could there be than for it to be during Passion Week – the most sacred festival in the Orthodox calendar. That evening they gathered together in front of their treasured icons and said fervent prayers of thanks. But Alexandra had already noted with alarm that her son was worryingly frail and wasted, having lost 14 pounds since his latest attack of haemophilia. That same first evening, all it took was one small slip and twist of the knee getting into bed and Alexey spent the whole of the night in unremitting pain. The Tsaritsa lay nearby, sleepless and watchful, listening to the boy's moans, as she had done for so many long nights now over the last 13 years.

But at least the family had each other again – and God. Their only line of resistance to the new and far more draconian regime imposed on them was to turn in on themselves and draw on their intense religious faith. It would sustain them through the days to come as they entered into a new, strange state of suspended animation. Existing but not living; locked in the deadening familiarity of a narrow, tedious daily ritual which day by day led them ever closer to – what? Release? Escape? Rescue? Whatever their ultimate fate might be, of one thing this strangely insular family were certain. God would take a hand in their fate.

And he was doing so already in that of several of their Romanov relatives now, unbeknown to the Imperial Family, being held in the city. The Tsaritsa's sister Grand Duchess Elizabeth (known as Ella), Grand Duke Sergey, the Tsar's cousin, and Princes Ioann Konstantinovich, Konstantin Konstantinovich and Igor Konstantinovich (three Romanov brothers descended from Konstantin, the second son of Nicholas I), together with Prince Vladimir Pavlovich Paley, had all been brought to Ekaterinburg in May and shut up in the Atamanov lodging house. But at least they had been allowed out to celebrate midnight mass in the cathedral at Easter, a privilege denied the Imperial Family. Here they had stood holding lighted candles of red wax, praying that the transcendent beauty of the Easter liturgy would bring hope and release. Prince Paley, himself a soulful and talented poet, wrote home to his mother of his anguish for his Romanov cousins. He had ventured up to the Ipatiev House in hopes of catching a glimpse of the Imperial Family, but the palisade was too high and the windows at that time were covered with newspaper. Meek, calm, submissive to his fate, he confided to officer's wife Madame Semchevsky his personal anguish for 'our poor Russia'. The country had, for him, become like some once majestic and powerful ship, now being engulfed by the waves and vanishing into the darkness. The great pools of Prince Paley's melancholy eyes spoke volumes for his sense of loss, remembered Semchevskaya, reflected in the lines of a poem he read that evening: 'Our near and dear ones are so terrifyingly far away; our enemies so terrifyingly near . . .' – sentiments no doubt shared by his Romanov relatives a few streets away.

As a place of confinement, the Ipatiev House at No. 49 Voznesensky Prospekt was adequate, if cramped. It had been the original intention of the Ural Regional Soviet to incarcerate Nicholas in the city's prison, but security problems had prevented it. A suitable private house had been opted for instead, the Ipatiev House finally being chosen in preference to the residence of local doctor Kensorin Arkhipov because it was closer to the Cheka headquarters. Though boasting 21 rooms, it was small by the standards of the more spacious and airy Governor's House in Tobolsk. But situated as it was at the top of one of the few gentle hills leading out of Ekaterinburg, it had a fine view of the lake, public gardens and city below, through which the River Iset wound its course. Built between 1875 and 1879 by a mining engineer, Andrey Redikortsev, its present owner, Nikolay Ipatiev, had acquired the house in around 1908 for 6,000 roubles. Boasting as it did a private bathroom and flush toilet, it was considered one of the most modern residences in the city. Ipatiev was a well-respected citizen and intellectual, a member of the Ekaterinburg Duma who had been involved in the construction of the Perm–Kungur–Ekaterinburg section of the Trans-Siberian Railway and who ran his railway engineering business from the house's basement rooms. He had been out of Ekaterinburg taking a rest cure for his weak heart, and friends from Petrograd had been staying in the house, when order no. 2778 had arrived from the Ekaterinburg Soviet on 27 April, giving 48 hours' notice to quit. Ipatiev had hurried back to rescue some personal belongings but largely left the house intact with all its comfortable furnishings, down to the stuffed bear on the upstairs landing.

The house appeared rather low and unimposing from the outside, because it was built into the side of the hill, so that the lower semi-basement was only visible at its full height from the side, along Voznesensky Lane. But it was attractive and reassuringly Russian in style rather than classically elegant. It was built on the site of an old wooden church, pulled down in the eighteenth century when the grand new Voznesensky Cathedral had been built across the road.

Constructed of brick and stone and faced with white stucco, it had carved decorations on the doors and window frames and under the eaves and faced a dusty, unpaved street shaded by linden trees. Opposite was Voznesensky Square with its baroque cathedral and the grandly classical Rastorguev-Kharitonov mansion, but beyond, the poorer log and frame houses of ordinary working-class Ekaterinburgers were a stark reminder of the contrast between wealth and poverty still to be seen all over the city. Near the front door stood a small shrine dedicated to St Nicholas, built where the altar of the old wooden church had been located, but the family could not see this poignant and ironic reminder of the Tsar's patron saint because a palisade blocked it from view.

Having failed to keep the family's presence in the city a secret (it had been announced in the daily *Ural'skiy Rabochiy* on 9 May), the Romanovs' Bolshevik captors had initiated a deliberate policy of isolation and desensitisation from the very beginning. Before the Tsar's arrival the house had been descended on by a gang of 100 workmen who hastily surrounded it with a high palisade of sawn timber and telegraph poles standing a few feet from the front of the house. Originally about 12 feet, the palisade was heightened at the end of May, but worse was to come. On 5 June a second, higher palisade was thrown up in an even larger sweep, enclosing the entire house from the courtyard at the northern end, right across and down into Voznesensky Lane. The front entrance to the house was now dominated by Guard Post No. 1, the first of 10 placed in and around the building, and the exterior of this fortress was patrolled twice hourly – day and night – by a constantly changing roster of guards. All 10 guard posts had connecting bells to both Commandant Avdeev's room and the guardhouse across the street.

With the palisade only 14 feet from their windows, Alexandra's 'lovely world' was now finally shut off from the family. Despite the approach of summer, every window had been sealed tight, and on 15 May the world outside was whitewashed from view when an old man came and painted the windows over, thus ensuring no one could see in or out. Nicholas wrote that it felt 'as if there is a fog outside'. No matter how bright the day, there was a perpetual gloom indoors. As the temperature rose and the rooms became increasingly stuffy, the Tsar made repeated requests to Avdeev for the windows to be reopened. The Bolsheviks were reluctant to accede: the Romanovs already had access to the *fortochka,* a small winter ventilator in the upper section of a window looking on to Voznesensky Prospekt. Repeatedly, early in the morning, the sentries outside had noticed the head of one or other of the daughters peeking out. Warnings were ignored, and finally one morning a sentry had fired when Anastasia's head had appeared, the bullet striking the upper sill and ricocheting into the plaster on the bedroom wall.

Not surprisingly, after this near miss it took weeks of further pleading about the lack of air inside the Ipatiev House until finally the grinding wheels of bureaucracy responded with a formal inspection by the 'Committee for the Examination of the Question of Windows in the House of Special Purpose', after which the second window in from

Voznesensky Lane was unsealed on 23 June. But the guards were ordered to increase their surveillance outside accordingly. The family were strictly forbidden to put their heads out of the window or attempt to signal to people outside – not that they could see them – on pain of being shot. Beyond the window and above the top of the palisade, they could at least detect a small, elusive patch of sky and, rising up from the cupola of Voznesensky Cathedral opposite, a spire topped with the Orthodox cross. If they stood close enough to the window they could still catch the sounds of the city – birdsong and the clatter of the electric tramway. But they could not see the machine-gun emplacement nestling in the cathedral's bell tower that was pointing straight at them. There were two more machine-gun emplacements: one monitored the balcony over-looking the garden at the back of the house, the other the basement window facing the street.

The Special Detachment of about 40 external guards on duty at any one time were drawn from a pool of 100 or so mainly young workers in their twenties, recruited at short notice from local factories. By early June, 35 of these were men from the Sysert metallurgical works located in the Ekaterinburg suburbs, where the workers had been heavily politicised. Before being recruited, the external guard were vetted for membership of the Bolshevik Party and for any fighting experience or handling of weapons. Those who had already fought in Red detachments against the Cossack rebel leader Dutov or the Czechs were given priority; others had served on the Eastern Front. But they were soon complaining about the long hours on duty and an additional 21 men were recruited from the Zlokazov factory, bringing the external guard numbers up to 56, with another 16 men making up the internal guard.

Poorly educated, oppressed by poverty and food shortages, most of the men were attracted to the job by the offer of 400 roubles a month (plus board and lodging in town) while being able to retain their factory jobs. And by signing on they could evade conscription into Trotsky's newly established Red Army. Armed with rifles with fixed bayonets and a few standard-issue Russian Nagant revolvers, they might have seemed a threat, but in reality few had any experience in handling weapons. They all enjoyed frequent visits from wives, families and friends, so much so that requests were made for overnight facilities for them, and the Popov House opposite the side of the house in Voznesensky Lane was requisitioned for the purpose by the Ural Regional Soviet.

These men were overseen by Pavel Medvedev – a civilian Bolshevik from the Sysert works who had already seen action in a Red Army detachment against Dutov – along with three senior guards. At first the external guards lived in the basement, crowded together on camp beds in the storerooms. The additional guards from the Zlokazov works brought in in June were allowed to bed down in the hallway and the small room next to the commandant's quarters on the upper floor of the house where the Romanovs lived. From the courtyard at the northern end of the house, entered through the big double gates, a side door led up a carved wooden staircase to the Romanovs' accommodation on the first floor. The flight of stairs was shut off by a locked doorway. Behind this the Romanovs and their servants were crowded into a suite of five interconnecting rooms, at the far end of which lay the landing, bathroom and toilet and a small kitchen.

Life here for the Imperial Family became noisy, crowded, disruptive, the stuffy summer air fetid with so many living on top of each other. Later the external guards were moved to rooms on the first floor of the Popov House and the internal guard moved down to the basement rooms of the house, but the commandant and his three senior aides had complete access at any time to all rooms occupied by the Imperial Family. The lack of a common landing across the rooms was itself an excellent security feature, making escape from the first floor past the guards impossible, something which might well have influenced the Bolsheviks in their choice of the Ipatiev House.

Nicholas was not one to grumble and, on arrival, had pronounced their accommodation 'pleasant and clean'; as had Maria, who found it 'small but nice'. The Tsar and Tsaritsa had taken the largest, corner bedroom, which had two tall windows facing the street. Two other windows overlooked the narrow lane to the side of the house. With its pale yellow wallpaper and frieze of flowers, the room was congenial enough and contained the usual furniture: two beds, a dressing table, couch, occasional tables and étagère with china knick-knacks, bronze lamp, bookcase, wash basin on a washstand and an armoire for clothes. Alexey, who had shared his sisters' room when he first arrived, moved in here with his parents on 26 June. The only exit from this room was into the Grand Duchesses' bedroom beyond, where Maria had moved in with her sisters.

Reunited in one single room, the Romanov girls happily crammed in together, sleeping on a pile of coats and blankets on the floor until the four portable metal camp beds they had brought into exile arrived from Tobolsk on 27 May. Compared with the communal living and sitting rooms, their room was light and airy, with linoleum on the floor, an Oriental rug and floral wallpaper. The rest of the furniture was sparse – a small table, upright chairs and an incongruously large looking-glass on a stand. What use had the girls for such things now? Their clothes were becoming increasingly worn and threadbare. No more white dresses with satin ribbons like they used to wear every summer in the Crimea. The only significant features on the walls were their family photographs and the miniature icons of saints hung above each of their beds. Setting the room off was a delicate art nouveau chandelier of Venetian glass tulips (which would eventually find its way to England). Beyond the Grand Duchesses' room, towards the back of the house, was a small room where the maid Anna Demidova slept. Originally designated for Alexey, the room had been given to her after his continuing poor health prompted his parents to move him back in with them.

A connecting door to the right of the Grand Duchesses' room led into a large drawing-cum-sitting room, separated into two halves by an archway. In the sitting room the Tsaritsa improvised an altar on Sundays, decorated with her own lace bedspread and the family icons. It was an attractive room with carved, gilded features and unobtrusive wallpaper. Down to the landscapes in gilded frames on the walls and the large potted palm, the furnishings left by Ipatiev included the familiar pieces of the day – a suite of chairs and sofa, another étagère of knick-knacks, a desk and an opulent-looking electrified chandelier of Italian glass. Here the daughters occasionally played the mahogany piano. Botkin and Chemodurov slept at one end of the drawing room, while the servants Trupp, Nagorny, Kharitonov, Sednev and his nephew the kitchen boy Leonid, eventually bedded down in either the kitchen or a small room next to it.

With its parquet floor and large oak doors, the dining room beyond contained a pier glass mirror over the marble mantel and a solid oak sideboard. Reflecting the prosperity of a successful businessman, the furniture was dark and heavy, with ornately carved *fin de siècle* pieces upholstered in leather, but the dark objects soaked up what little light penetrated through the opaque windows. Here the Romanovs sat down to meals together with their servants. It had been the Tsar's express wish that they do so. But the expensive table linen and silver service that they had brought with them from the Alexander Palace lay unopened in an outhouse, and there was not enough cutlery to go round.

The commandant's office was also located upstairs, in Ipatiev's old study, at the northern end of the first floor. With its wooden wainscoting, glass-fronted mahogany bookcase, plush sofa and red wallpaper decorated with golden date palms, it was a genteel room for such unsophisticated, dirty men as the guards. Avdeev, a locksmith by trade and a political commissar at the Zlokazov works who had overseen the dispossession of its owners and their replacement by an 'executive' soviet, made himself comfortable here. He enjoyed his new-found status, issuing memorandums and orders on 'House of Special Purpose' notepaper printed to order. His control over the lives of his illustrious prisoners gave him a sense of power and he liked to show off by allowing his worker friends in to take a look at 'Nikolashka', as he referred to the Tsar. As they came and went in Avdeev's office between shifts, the men of the internal guard would throw their rifles down, skewing the pictures on the walls, soiling the sofa with dirty boots as they lounged around drinking endless glasses of tea from the samovar. They filled the room with cigarette smoke, and slept wherever they could, curled up in every available corner. From the wall, a mounted stag's head stared down as the men listened to the Imperial Family's gramophone records on the confiscated phonograph. In early May they had moved the piano from the dining room in here, and when Avdeev went home off duty, his assistant Moshkin and the night guard would sit around like good *tovarishchi* singing Russian revolutionary songs as well as the 'Marseillaise' and the Marxist 'International' and getting drunk. Avdeev himself was often dead drunk on duty, and sometimes when Beloborodov turned up from the Ural Regional Soviet for an impromptu inspection, the commandant's colleagues had to cover up for him.

Two armed guards were always present on the landing near the lavatory, bathroom and kitchen, but no others were allowed upstairs into the Imperial Family's living area and only the guards on duty upstairs were allowed to use the lavatory. Some could not resist the temptation to scribble political slogans and crude graffiti – relating mainly to the Tsaritsa's relationship with Rasputin – in the hallway and on the lavatory walls. There were 14 more rooms located downstairs in the semi-basement, some given over to Ipatiev's business premises, three of which were used by the external guards on duty during the day. But most of them were storerooms and lay dark and empty.

When they arrived, the family had only been allowed to bring small suitcases, but there was a great deal more luggage to follow from Tobolsk. Case upon case of it arrived at Ekaterinburg station a few days later and nearly sparked a riot from a crowd of onlookers who huddled round to view its contents as it was unloaded with revolutionary shouts of 'Death to the tyrant!' 'Death to the bourgeois!' 'Hang them!' 'Drown them in the lake!' Many of these possessions – everything from fur coats to binoculars, riding crops and – improbably – suitcases full of Alexey's baby clothes – were promptly siphoned off at Ekaterinburg station by local commissars and Bolsheviks. After being thoroughly searched and pilfered again by the guards at the Ipatiev House, what remained had been stored in an outhouse in the interior courtyard.

Nevertheless, when finally allowed to unpack their things after numerous rigorous inspections overseen by Avdeev, the Romanovs had crammed as many precious items as possible into their cramped living space. Essential to them were their prayer books and Bibles, novels and history books for the Tsar, toys and board games for the Tsarevich, sewing, knitting and embroidery materials for the Tsaritsa and her daughters. Surprisingly, they were still allowed to use their bed linen with personalised monograms and Imperial crest, as well as the fine porcelain dinner plates bearing the name 'Nicholas II'. Other valuable tableware and silver from the Alexander Palace had also been packed under Alexandra's strict instructions: faience soup plates, silver sugar tongs, clocks, letter openers and silver pencils, embroidered cushions and delicate crystal vases, all the clutter of their home at the Alexander Palace. Anything to maintain a semblance of the life they had once led.

Other indispensables were the electro-shock machines used to stimulate the Tsarevich's weak leg muscles after long periods of enforced bed rest. Even the Tsar's one indulgence was catered for – bath oil for his daily ablutions before dinner. So great was the Romanov predilection for copious baths that the water supply at the house regularly ran out, provoking much grumbling among the guards, for it had to be carted up the hill in barrels from the city pond and heated up. Strict rationing of this privilege was soon introduced. The Tsaritsa had also brought supplies of her favourite English eau de cologne by Brocard, as well as cold cream and lavender salts. But if one thing dominated the Romanov living quarters, it was the bottles of holy water, jars of ointments and ranks of medicine bottles. These came in every shape and size: aromatic oils, tinctures, drops, medicines and smelling salts – all specially labelled by the Imperial Court pharmacist, Rozmarin. Alexandra had her own personal medicine kit and there was a supply of Cascarine Leprince laxative to ease the Tsar's haemorrhoids. There was morphine too, a precious supply, but not, as one might expect, to control the Tsarevich's agonising attacks of haemophilia; this was a drug his doctor and parents resisted administering, for fear of dependency. The morphine was to dull Alexandra's aches and pains, and sometimes Nicholas's too. This and an array of other cocaine-based liquids and opiates betrayed the increasing physical toll imprisonment was taking on Nicholas and Alexandra, both of whom suffered from crippling headaches and insomnia.

Most precious of all were the family's portable icons, which came in an assortment of sizes, some very simple and rustic, others in diamond-studded silver frames. Among these, by far the most valuable and treasured was the 'Fedorovsky Mother of God' which accompanied the devout Tsaritsa everywhere. Nor had the family been able to travel without the dozens of photograph frames in leather, silver and ormolu that so characterised their obsessive love for each other. But their precious Box Brownie cameras and photographic equipment which, even in Tobolsk, regularly recorded their family life had now been confiscated. Sentiment had prevailed over many of the choices made about what to bring into exile, none more so than in the Tsar's decision to bring with him the 50 volumes of neatly written diaries he had kept since the age of 14, as well as the 653 letters Alexandra had sent him during their 24 years of marriage, the bulk of them during the war years of 1914–17. Only now they both constantly worried about what would happen if all these most personal of documents, packed away in crate number 9 marked A. F. and no. 13 marked N. A., were discovered by the guards at the Ipatiev House.

At Tobolsk, the family had enjoyed regular access to the open compound surrounding the Governor's House. Here they had been able to sun themselves on the greenhouse roof, soaking up the view of the free world beyond. Passers-by would often stop to reverentially acknowledge them. Despite the obvious boredom and monotony – especially felt by young Alexey, whose life was already tragically circum-scribed by illness – the Romanovs had lived a peaceful life for eight months at Tobolsk, enduring the bitter winter in the poorly heated Governor's House without complaint. The simple rural life paradoxically suited this cosily bourgeois family, and for a while it had lulled them into a false sense of security. Indeed Maria had confided to tutor Sidney Gibbes that she could happily live at Tobolsk for ever if only their guards would allow them to 'walk out a little'. Beyond their own self-absorbed world, the family maintained few aspirations or interests. Even at Tsarskoe Selo outside St Petersburg they had lived relatively modestly, preferring the smaller Alexander Palace to the formal rococo splendour of the Catherine Palace next door. Imprisonment at Tobolsk had almost been a positive in their lives, a release into ordinariness and anonymity. There they had both sent and received letters. English, French and Russian newspapers had been provided, while the children enjoyed daily lessons from their German, Swiss and English tutors. Life in Siberia had opened their eyes to a different world, a world free of the hidebound court rituals and official functions that they all hated.

But here in Ekaterinburg, Maria wrote to a friend that 'every day brings unpleasant surprises'. They were not allowed visitors. They could not enjoy the pleasures of working in the kitchen garden as they had done when confined at the Alexander Palace, or even the large exercise yard at Tobolsk, where the Tsar had vigorously sawn wood in winter. The receipt and sending of letters had soon been curtailed and in early June the Tsar no longer received his daily newspapers – the one remaining pleasure left to him. Here they were strictly forbidden to speak any language other than Russian, something which particularly irked the Tsaritsa, who always spoke English with the children. Occasional gifts from relatives had now stopped, chocolate and coffee from the Tsaritsa's sister Ella being the last to arrive. (Unknown to Alexandra, after being held initially in Ekaterinburg, her sister had now been incarcerated along with the Grand Princes at Alapaevsk, 93 miles away.) At the Ipatiev House there would be no more Sunday evening theatricals punctuated by the mischievous laughter of Anastasia, the family entertainer. No excursions to mass at the nearby church were permitted, and a priest had only been allowed in twice since their arrival to conduct services. Yet still the Imperial Family hoped for God's deliverance. In her dreams the Tsaritsa had visions of monarchist knights on horseback riding to their rescue. But Nicholas was more pragmatic, increasingly recognising the impossibility of rescue or flight from this grim Bolshevik stronghold.

Daily life had become a matter of endurance. Beyond devotion to each other and to God there remained one consuming obsession in their daily lives – Alexey's fragile state of health. Since the middle of April, the Tsarevich had been suffering from a recurring haemorrhage in a damaged knee, causing agonising pain that wrecked his sleep and crippled his leg so that he could not walk. Thin, wasting away and with no appetite, the boy no longer had the support of his tutors, the devoted Pierre Gilliard from Switzerland and the sober Cambridge graduate Sidney Gibbes, who had taken it in turns to read and talk with him during his painful attacks. The Tsaritsa and her daughters were exhausted from all-night sessions sitting by Alexey's bed, listening to his moans of pain. The sailor Klementy Nagorny, who for years had protectively shadowed Alexey, sitting with him at nights and carrying him when too weak to walk, had been taken away on the evening of 27 May (along with the Grand Duchesses' servant Ivan Sednev), never to return. By July even the visits of the Tsarevich's physician Dr Vladimir Derevenko, who had been allowed to remain on call in Ekaterinburg and on whom the family relied so heavily, had been curtailed. He continued to come to the house but was refused admittance by Avdeev on the grounds that the Tsarevich was 'well enough' and did not need him. It was more than eight days after his arrival that the weak and sickly Alexey, his injured knee at last taken from its splint, went outside into the garden for the first time, carried by Dr Botkin. But he was never able to walk or play outside again with the others.

By early July the daily ritual of life at the Ipatiev House was rapidly taking on a numbing predictability. The family rose at eight in the morning, washed, dressed and said their prayers together. Tea and black bread were provided by Avdeev at nine, when he made his obligatory roll call to ensure the family were all there. Cocoa was occasionally on offer, but with the Romanovs on rations like all other Soviet citizens, coffee and butter were luxuries beyond their reach; 'they were no longer permitted to live like tsars', Avdeev informed them. At around one in the afternoon a simple lunch of cutlets or soup with meat was delivered to the gates, sent in from a canteen run by the Ekaterinburg Soviet in the Commercial Assembly House, a short distance away on the corner of Glavny Prospket. Supper was delivered to the house around 8 p.m. From mid-June the family's own cook, Kharitonov, had been allowed to prepare some of the family's modest meals on a small oil stove in the upstairs kitchen, where he tried to coax the Tsaritsa's always difficult and now rapidly fading appetite (she was a vegetarian) with the simple, bland dishes of vermicelli she preferred. In mid-June, Dr Derevenko had voiced concerns about the family's poor diet to Commandant Avdeev and, with his consent, had gone to the Novo-Tikhvinsky Convent in the city suburbs to ask the sisters to bring the family eggs, milk, cream and bread on a daily basis from their farm. Other foods were brought as well: meat, sausage, vegetables and tasty Russian pies, but much was siphoned off on arrival by Avdeev for his and the guard's use.

During the morning there was little to do but read, which the Tsar did at length, in an increasingly desperate attempt to counter the physical frustration of his incarceration. He voraciously consumed the collected works of the satirist Mikhail Saltykov-Shchedrin that he had discovered on the bookshelves in the house, followed by Shilder's biography of the Emperor Paul I. During Easter he also daily read out loud from the Gospels and other edifying spiritual works while the women sat endlessly mending their increasingly threadbare clothes, knitting or sewing. True, they had brought plenty of clothes and shoes with them, but most of these were in storage in the outbuilding to which they were persistently denied access, even when Nicholas's boots were clearly falling apart and in need of replacement. In the beginning they had filled up their time writing letters daily to friends, but few reached their destination and even fewer were passed on when they arrived. Now, all there was were endless games of cards – patience and the French game bezique, which was a great family favourite – while Alexey played with his model ship and tin soldiers. Sometimes the women sang sacred songs together, a favourite being the 'Cherubim's Song', the song of the angels from the Orthodox liturgy. Mundane new diversions were created for the girls when the Ural Regional Soviet refused to have the family's large quantities of laundry sent out any more. Even in exile the Romanovs changed their underwear and bed linen with excessive regularity, and the Grand

Duchesses now found themselves learning to be laundresses, helping Demidova the maid. They were also taught by Kharitonov to cook and make bread. With the Tsaritsa and Tsarevich frequently sick or resting, the girls created their own amusements until afternoon tea between four and five. A final modest supper was served at eight, after which the remainder of the evening was filled with further prayers and Bible reading, more games of bezique, more embroidery and sewing until bedtime.

The only break in the monotony of it all was the recreation allowed twice daily in the garden, once in the late morning around eleven, and again in the afternoon before tea. Until mid-May Avdeev had tended to be lax applying the rules, sometimes allowing the Imperial Family as much as 90 minutes when the weather was fine. But this had now been reduced to half an hour morning and afternoon, in order, the family were told, that their life at the Ipatiev House more closely resembled 'a prison regime'. The Romanovs had been under strict instructions not to engage in conversation with their guards, a rule which Nicholas had broken in an effort to establish relationships, particularly after he and Alexandra had recognised one of the guards, a former soldier named Konstantin Ukraintsev, as a beater who had worked for Romanov shooting parties in the Caucasus. But here there was to be none of the camaraderie of Tobolsk, where Nicholas had often gone to the guards' room to smoke and play draughts with his captors. The hapless Ukraintsev was soon dismissed for his sympathetic response to the family, and sent to the Eastern Front.

Grateful for the chance to walk in the sun and breathe the summer air, the three younger Grand Duchesses had also smiled and been friendly with the guards outside, their elder sister keeping herself to herself. The scent of Ekaterinburg's parks and gardens wafted tantalisingly close, and on these brief occasions the sound of laughter could be heard as the sisters chased their dogs Ortipo, Joy and Jimmy round in the hot sunshine or enjoyed the double swing that some of the guards had hung for them in the garden.

But this last remaining luxury was rarely indulged in by Alexandra. Plagued by migraines, heart palpitations and sciatica and intolerant of the heat, she rarely ventured outside. When she did, she donned jacket and hat while her daughters ran around bare-headed. She frequently gave in to her physical frailties, keeping one of her daughters indoors to read aloud as she lay with her head swathed in cold compresses. Her heart palpitations were now so bad that she could hardly walk; at night she was frequently tormented by insomnia. When she did, very occasionally, emerge into the garden, she was too exhausted to do anything but sit in the shade of the porch.

From here she would watch Alexey, when he was not bedridden, sit playing at toy soldiers with the kitchen boy Sednev, who, when Alexey was too frail, would push him around the garden in his mother's wheelchair. Nicholas and the girls meanwhile would take the 40 paces walk that measured the length of the small overgrown garden, going back and forth relentlessly in the sun – as though anxious not to waste a single precious moment of recreation – amidst a few poplars, birches and limes and bushes of yellow acacia and lilac. The man who had once ruled eight and a half million square miles of empire was now master of a single room of his own and a small, scrappy garden. Free of the responsibilities of state, Nicholas seemed unengaged with the unreality of it all, but he sorely missed physical exercise and was bitterly disappointed that his requests to Avdeev to be given something active to do – clearing the garden or chopping wood – had been curtly refused, as had his request to put up a hammock for the children. Dr Botkin's written appeal to the local soviet that the family be allowed two hours' recreation outside daily for the sake of their health fell on deaf ears as well. During June the weather had become increasingly hot and thundery, making life inside their prison even more intolerable. The sealed, airless rooms trapped the smells of cooking and cigarette smoke, human sweat and the lavatory. They also spread germs and that most tenacious of parasites, head lice, forcing Nicholas to trim his beard and the girls to keep their hair short. 'It's unbearable to be locked up like this, and not to be able to go into the garden when we want to, or spend a pleasant evening in the air', wrote Nicholas in his diary, as the humidity and sudden storms of a changeable Urals summer gathered pace.

Had Nicholas been able to see beyond his prison, he would have discovered that, from the day of his arrival in Ekaterinburg, people had been venturing up to the 'Tsar's House', as the Ipatiev House rapidly became known (none of the locals using the official name), in hopes of seeing him – despite the severe warnings not to do so. The guards, rifles in hand, had pushed them away: 'Walk on, Citizens, walk on. There's nothing to see here', they would say, to which came the often argumentative response: 'If there's nothing to see, then why can't we just stand here if we want to?' People tried to get the guards to take in presents and letters for the family and were all turned away, though one or two guards occasionally relented and allowed the curious to take a quick look inside the palisade. Others anxious to see the Imperial Family approached the house from a different direction – congregating at the bottom of Voznesensky Lane, near the Iset Pond. Here, in the centre of town, you could just make out the balcony overlooking the garden at the back of the Ipatiev House. A man in uniform was often seen standing there. Word got round that it was the Tsar. Some thought they had caught a glimpse of him. But the rumours were false; the man on the balcony was only one of the guards. Yet still people came. One of the reasons for the construction of the second, higher palisade had been the discovery that when the Tsar took a turn on the swing in the garden, his booted legs flew up over the palisade and could be seen by the curious outside. That did not stop two young schoolboys, the Telezhnikov brothers, who were caught by the guards outside the Ipatiev House trying to take photographs and hauled off to the offices of the Cheka for a severe warning.

Although the lack of physical exercise was hugely stressful to him personally, Nicholas and his family had by now become long inured to isolation – an isolation that had for many years been largely self-imposed. They had always preferred their own company to anybody else's, including that of most of their Romanov relatives. The life of a prisoner was, as it turned out, nothing new to Nicholas, for he had already observed to Chief Marshal of the Imperial Court Count Benckendorff, during his confinement at the Alexander Palace, that he was hardly less free now than formerly, adding, as he reached for the cigarette that was the ready prop in moments of stress: 'For have I not been a prisoner all my life?'

Whilst he might still be in denial about the true nature of his imprisonment and his ultimate fate, on the morning of 4 July, the former Tsar of Russia would begin, finally, to discover what captivity in the Urals really entailed.

2

'The Dark Gentleman'

THURSDAY 4 JULY 1918

'Today there was a change of commandant', Nicholas noted with surprise in his diary on 4 July. That afternoon the Romanovs had had an unexpected visitor: Aleksandr Beloborodov, chair of the Ural Regional Soviet, had arrived when they were taking their modest lunch. Commandant Avdeev, he announced, had been dismissed and would not be returning. Nor, as they soon discovered, would his vulgar, drunken assistant Moshkin. Whilst they would not miss Moshkin, who had taken pleasure in humiliating them in the evenings after Avdeev had gone home off duty, the Romanovs felt a pang of regret at the loss of the disorderly Avdeev. For all his drinking, his swaggering in front of his subordinates and his occasionally crass behaviour, he had been fundamentally considerate, even kind. He'd made sure they had their own samovar so that the guards didn't take all the hot water for tea; he'd stretched the rules on their time allowed outside in the garden. The Romanovs had grown used to him and at times Nicholas had even found him endearing. The family had sensed his conflicted feelings towards them, and a certain reluctant compassion. They knew what to expect.

The Tsar's response was sympathetic: 'I am sorry for Avdeev, but it was his own fault as he did nothing to keep his men from stealing things out of our trunks in the shed.' Naively, Nicholas thought the shake-up was down to the constant pilfering by the guards from the family's goods in the outhouse that Avdeev had turned a blind eye to, if not colluded in. But there were other, far more sinister reasons for the changeover of which Nicholas could not be aware.

In recent weeks the Ural Regional Soviet had been thrown into a state of increasing paranoia by evidence of monarchist and other groups lurking in Ekaterinburg and plotting, however ineptly, to rescue the family. In addition, reports had been published in Moscow that the Tsar had been murdered, and these had filtered through to the Western press. It had made the Bolshevik government jittery, despite assurances that the reliable local 'troika' of Goloshchekin, Beloborodov and his deputy Didkovsky had made regular inspections of the house in May and June as well as bringing groups of officials to observe the Imperial Family during their recreation periods outside. Doubting the trustworthiness of the Ural Regional Soviet and the levels of security at the Ipatiev House, Lenin had ordered Reinhold Berzin, commander of the Northern Ural and Siberian Front, to travel 300 miles from Perm to make a surprise personal inspection. This had been carried out on 22 June, in the company of district military commissar Filipp Goloshchekin, under the guise of the supposed 'window inspection', when Nicholas had noted the presence in the house of what he thought were 'commissars from Petrograd'.

Berzin's report, which finally reached Moscow on the 28th by a circuitous route, such being the haphazard state of the telegraph lines, had confirmed the rumours about the Tsar's murder as a malicious provocation. But by now the Ural Regional Soviet was becoming aware of other breakdowns in discipline at the house: unruly behaviour and bouts of drunkenness by the night guard, and worse still, a slide towards fraternisation with the Imperial Family that had been strictly forbidden. At Tobolsk the guards had been disarmed by Nicholas's natural, friendly manner and the pattern repeated itself at Ekaterinburg. Some of the guards had even smuggled letters out for the family or brought in books. Others privately admitted to a creeping respect and pity for the Romanovs, persisting in referring respectfully to Nicholas as 'the Tsar' or 'the Emperor'.

In such close contact with the family, day in, day out, the inevitable had happened. The Romanovs and their young captors had developed the classic prisoner–jailer bonds so common in such situations. Some of the guards had found it increasingly difficult to reconcile the gentle, kindly face of Nicholas and his pretty daughters with the one that Bolshevik propaganda had inculcated in them. The three younger girls by now had become open and friendly to the point of flirtatiousness with some of them. They took any and every opportunity of talking and sharing jokes and cups of tea; given the levels of boredom they were enduring, this is not surprising. Their eldest sister Olga, however, did not mix. Now painfully thin and sickly, she had been withdrawing increasingly into a state of melancholy for months. As for the Tsaritsa, she was another matter altogether. Cold, reserved, bitterly proud and defensive of her privacy, she was hostile towards the guards and unrelentingly argumentative about complying with any of the commandant's house rules. She refused point blank to ring the bell that the family were supposed to use every time they wished to leave their rooms to use the bathroom and lavatory on the landing, and was always unsmiling and complaining. The guards found her personality difficult. But she was clearly a sick woman, as was the boy, for whom they had the greatest, overriding sympathy. So thin, so pale and waxen, Alexey seemed to some of them to be already at death's door. In the end, many of the Romanovs' captors, for all their revolutionary talk and Bolshevik persuasions, had succumbed to simple human compassion for what was fundamentally an ordinary, devoted family, blighted by ill health and with no real understanding of their terrible new life in captivity.

Weeks of close confinement and crushing boredom for four hormonal girls aged between 17 and 22, two of them still adolescent and all of them subject to the normal mood swings of menstruating women, must inevitably have brought tensions within those five hot, crowded rooms. Add to that a probably menopausal mother and a terminally ill brother, and the strain must at times have been intolerable. Hagiographers of the Romanovs have always claimed there was never any discord between the family, but this is extremely hard to believe given the circumstances in which they were being held and the often profound fluctuations between hope and despair that any prisoner normally goes through when kept for so long under close surveillance.

Indeed, it may well have been the immaturity and natural sexual curiosity of one of the daughters that helped precipitate the final clampdown. On 27 June, the flirtatious and attractive Maria, whom the guards had found by far the most friendly of the Grand Duchesses, had been discovered, during an inspection of the Ipatiev House by Goloshchekin and Beloborodov, in a compromising situation with guard Ivan Skorokhodov, who had smuggled in a cake for her nineteenth birthday. Skorokhodov was summarily removed to Ekaterinburg jail. Nicholas and Alexandra, as well as Maria's older sisters, were clearly shocked by her behaviour and unsettled by the incident. The resulting introduction of a rigorous new regime at the Ipatiev House and Avdeev's dismissal were no coincidence.

And so, on Thursday 4 July, a new commandant arrived. His name was Yakov Yurovsky, and he brought with him an assistant, an attractive young man called Grigory Nikulin, who in Alexandra's estimation seemed 'decent' in comparison to his vulgar predecessor Moshkin. Little did she know that the bland-looking Nikulin was a ruthless killer who had opted to work for the Cheka rather than go to the Front.

Yurovsky was a tall, well-built man with high cheekbones and a shock of black hair. With his neatly trimmed Van Dyck beard and curled moustache, the 40-year-old looked cultured, almost dapper, and had an air of self-importance to match. He wasn't a drinker like Avdeev. He was highly intelligent, vigilant and motivated. A clampdown was needed and it would be draconian. Yurovsky immediately saw to it that pilfering from the Imperial Family ceased. Such money as the Tsar and Tsaritsa had left had already been confiscated. But after a search of their possessions on arrival, the 16 roubles and 17 kopeks given to Maria by Anastasia for the journey to Ekaterinburg had been taken from her for 'safekeeping by the Ural Regional Soviet's treasurer'. Yurovsky was more meticulous than Avdeev; he now set about making a detailed inventory of all the family's jewellery and valuables. The priceless Imperial regalia had long since been confiscated by the new Soviet state; much of what remained of larger valuable pieces had been stolen, or smuggled out by the Tsaritsa to sympathisers in Tobolsk, in hopes of funding rescue. But the women still had with them many jewels – especially diamonds and pearls. At Tobolsk, during every spare moment, they had been carefully secreting these in their corsets, bodices, hats and buttons, as essential resources to fund their life in exile, should they ever have to leave Russia. Yurovsky knew they had more jewellery than the items he had seen and that they had probably concealed them in their clothes. He knew Moscow wanted to lay hands on it; and sooner or later he would find it. As he itemised the family's valuables, he made few concessions: the Tsarevich was allowed to keep his watch (he would get bored without it, claimed Nicholas), the Tsar his engagement ring which he couldn't get off, and the women only the gold bracelets they wore that fitted so tightly round their wrists that they could not be removed. The rest Yurovsky took away, and locked up in a box, to be returned to them later.

In actual fact, the family had already met Yurovsky twice before when he had visited the Ipatiev House with members of the local soviet. On 26 May he had arrived when Dr Derevenko had come to see Alexey, on which occasion the family had assumed, from his unhurried and dignified manner and his concern about the Tsarevich's health, that he too was a doctor. This afternoon, 4 July, he again asked about the swelling in Alexey's leg. Nicholas was impressed; to his mind, 'the dark gentleman', as he referred to Yurovsky before he discovered his name, appeared solicitous for the family's welfare. Perhaps the new commandant would be more accommodating about the request made that day by Dr Botkin that a priest be sent in to say mass on the coming Sunday.

Neither Nicholas nor Alexandra appear to have inferred anything sinister from this sudden turnaround other than a necessary security measure, nor could they have known the true measure of the man now in control of their lives. Yakov Yurovsky had been born a Jew. His father, a glazier, had been sent into exile to the Jewish settlement at Kainsk in Novosibirsk province in Siberia for theft; there the young

Yurovsky studied at the local Talmudic school. Yurovsky would later observe with bitter cynicism that thanks to the Tsar, he had been born 'in prison'. Some said he was the grandson of a Polish rabbi, but in any event his family appear to have distanced themselves from their Jewish roots after moving to Tomsk, and Yurovsky himself 'converted' to Lutheranism in the early 1900s, perhaps necessary acts to escape religious persecution.

Years of poverty, hunger and deprivation, as one of 10 children, had sown the seeds of profound social resentment and led him to be virulently anti-monarchist. He remembered the smell of growing up in a cramped apartment above the butcher's shop in Tomsk. As a child, he had shared the same naïve belief as others in the Tsar's infallible goodness. 'I thought then one could go to the Tsar and tell him how hard our life was', he remarked. But disillusion rapidly set in as Yurovsky developed a political and social consciousness. Soon the Tsar in whom he trusted was, in his impressionable young imagination, a 'fiend' a 'bloodsucker' and a killer. Yurovsky escaped the stultifying environment of Tomsk as soon as he could, having trained as a watchmaker, but not before serving time in jail around 1898 for an unspecified murder. He settled in Ekaterinburg where he worked in a jeweller's shop, married in 1904 and joined the Bolshevik party in 1905. Soon after that his political activities forced him to leave Russia and he lived for several years in Berlin, where he worked as a watchmaker and also trained as a photographer. Returning to Russia in 1912, Yurovsky and his family (he had three children) lived for a while in Baku in the Caucasus, at that time a hotbed of revolutionary activity under the leadership of a young Joseph Stalin, before returning first to Tomsk and then to Ekaterinburg. Here he set up a photographer's studio with Nikolay Vvedensky at number 42 Pokrovsky Prospekt, next door to the city's noisy market; it is said the premises were also a front for covert meetings of local Bolsheviks. Business boomed for Yurovsky when he started offering the new 'electrophotographs' which could be processed and ready in ten minutes, and he was soon co-opted into taking the official photographs of prisoners in the local jail. He and his family lived in an apartment in the centre, with a dacha at Shartash, on the outskirts of the city. But then war intervened and he was drafted into the Russian army in 1915. Because he had been suffering from rheumatism and tuberculosis, he was allowed to train as a medical orderly, thus avoiding being sent to the Front. When the Revolution came in 1917, he deserted and went home to Ekaterinburg, where he had continued to run his photographic business whilst becoming increasingly involved in local politics.

Yurovsky was by now a totally dedicated Communist and had quickly risen from soldier deputy on the local Ekaterinburg Soviet to executive member of the Ural Regional Soviet. As a member too of the local Ekaterinburg Cheka, he operated as a commissar for justice, exhibiting the absolute self-control and cold cynicism so typical of the professional revolutionary. He kept careful control of his burning hatred for the Imperial Family, on the surface appearing polite, even punctilious. He did not suffer conflicts of feelings or a troubled conscience as had his predecessor Avdeev. Nor did his 23-year-old assistant Nikulin, a cold-blooded killer who had already had a hand in secret shootings of counter-revolutionaries and with whom Yurovsky had a very close father–son relationship. Both were fired by implacable class hatred and had come to the Ipatiev House to settle a long-standing score with the Romanovs on behalf of the Revolution.

On the day of his arrival, Yurovsky instigated 'a complete disinfection' of the guard at the Ipatiev House and with it a tightening of discipline, down to the tidying away of rubbish and an insistence on the daily making up of bunks and maintenance of cleanliness. The men from the Sysert and Zlokazov works were removed from the inside guard to the outside. Overall, the Special Detachment would be increased to 86 men, with Yurovsky announcing that in a few days' time Avdeev's old internal guard was to be replaced with new men of his own choosing.

Four houses and 300 yards away down Voznesensky Prospekt, in sight of the Ipatiev House, the British consul, Thomas Preston, was encountering considerable problems in obtaining any news of the welfare of the Imperial Family. He had caught a glimpse of Grand Duchess Maria when the convoy bringing the Tsar and Tsaritsa from the railway station had passed his door on 30 April, but had not been allowed to see the family at all, despite their close ties with the British Royal Family. (Alexandra's mother was King George V's aunt, and Nicholas and George's Danish mothers were sisters.) Whilst the Red Flag now flew over the city's civic buildings, Preston had kept the British Union Jack conspicuously defiant at his own consulate. But for weeks now he had been experiencing great difficulty in getting telegrams out to his Foreign Office back home. The service was intermittent and those telegrams that did get through were often intercepted by the Bolsheviks.

Preston knew the city well; he had been in the Urals since 1903, as representative of a Leeds-based mining company prospecting there for platinum. He had married a Russian wife and in 1916, thanks to his fluent Russian and detailed local knowledge, had been asked to take on the role of British consul in Ekaterinburg. With the Urals and Western Siberia being completely isolated from the outside world, Preston had rapidly found himself left with 'a kind of enforced carte blanche' to deal with local affairs, often without instruction from the British government. Much more importantly, he had a specific brief to keep a close watch on the Urals platinum industry on behalf of the British War Office. His deputy, a Cornishman named Arthur Thomas, was also a skilled mining engineer, recruited from a British firm, Holman Brothers Limited, that had been mining platinum in the Urals. For either of them to act assertively now in support of the Romanovs, with a new and volatile Bolshevik government in control, was becoming an increasingly dangerous thing to do.

During June, several of the Romanov entourage who had accompanied the children from Tobolsk had remained at Ekaterinburg station. Whilst living in a fourth-class railway carriage awaiting safe passage out of the city, they had taken to daily badgering Preston to do something to help the Imperial Family, as too had Prince Dolgorukov, in pencil-written notes smuggled out from his prison cell. The Tsarevich's two tutors, Sidney Gibbes and Pierre Gilliard, and lady-in-waiting Baroness Sophie von Buxhoeveden (who had been refused permission to join the family at the Ipatiev House) had been particularly insistent, and had even made personal representations to the Ural Regional Soviet. Day in, day out they would make their way to the British consulate and spend long hours discussing with Preston all and any possible ways of saving the Imperial Family. But eventually these three had been put on a train back to Tobolsk.

Nevertheless, other Romanov loyalists, both covertly and overtly, had been congregating in the city, including Princess Helena of Serbia, wife of Prince Ioann Konstantinovich, who was now being held under arrest with the Tsaritsa's sister at Alapaevsk. Helena had had the temerity to go up to the Ipatiev House and demand of the sentries who confronted her with rifles raised that she see the Tsar. Secretly she had hoped also to be able to pass on letters from their relatives that she had smuggled in with her. Her visit was of course refused by Avdeev, who was taken aback by such boldness, but the princess continued to make a nuisance of herself at the Cheka headquarters at the Amerikanskaya Hotel half a mile down the road from the Ipatiev House, on the corner of Pokrovsky Prospekt and Zlatoustovskaya Street. Finally, tiring of her persistent enquiries, the Cheka took her off to the local prison and two weeks later she was put on a train back to Petrograd.

Princess Helena's impetuous behaviour had made Preston's delicate negotiations on behalf of the Romanovs doubly difficult, but nevertheless, under pressure on all sides, day after day the beleaguered British consul would walk up to the soviet offices at the railway station to make enquiries on behalf of the entire consular corps. To do so meant running the gauntlet of men bristling with rifles, pistols and grenades. Ekaterinburg railway station was a far from inviting place to visit, he later recalled: 'the stench was nauseating, the atmosphere charged with the odour of unwashed bodies, dirty boots and the foul-smelling *makhorka* [cheap Russian tobacco] they all smoked'. Outside, the station platforms were crowded with disconsolate, dirty, lice-ridden peasants waiting around with their bundles – hoping for a train, any train, to take them out of the city. Meanwhile, yards away from so much squalor, in the station's first-class restaurant, newly created soviet officials wined and dined and played cards. It was, said Preston, 'one of the first mockeries I saw of the so-called egalitarian society'.

In his office at the station, Preston found Sergey Chutskaev, of the Ural Regional Soviet, a dirty, greasy man in a leather jacket, with baggy *sharovary* (sailor's trousers) tucked into his top boots, lounging in an anteroom strewn with weapons. He told Chutskaev that he and his American and French colleagues had heard rumours that the Imperial Family were being badly treated and that their governments were becoming increasingly concerned for their welfare. As usual, he got the same unconvincing assurances from Chutskaev that the family were all in good health and in no danger. Preston knew he was being fed a lie – he had been getting the same phoney assurances for weeks – but nevertheless he dutifully telegraphed this news on to his government in the hope that some of his communiqués would get through. The Bolsheviks he knew were becoming increasingly hostile to his enquiries, and Chutskaev had threatened him with arrest for his meddlesome behaviour. In fact, he had even told Preston, in a moment of chilling flippancy, that he couldn't make up his mind whether or not to shoot him. No wonder Preston was of the view that the members of the city's new soviet operated like a gang of brigands: 'a more awe-inspiring and cut-throat crowd would be hard to find'.

The increasingly unstable situation in Ekaterinburg was plain to see everywhere; it clearly belied Chutskaev's hollow assertions that the Romanovs were in no danger. From the moment the Bolsheviks, supported by politicised railway workers, had taken control in the Urals and seized the city the previous November, Ekaterinburg had been living under a regime that governed by fear. Prior to the Revolution, the Urals population at large had kept a low profile in Russian political life, and for this reason the most experienced agitators had been sent out from Petrograd to propagandise among the largely negative peasant popu-lation. At the end of May, 500 militant sailor-revolutionaries from Kronstadt had also descended on the city to ensure the new Bolshevik government was 'not being too lenient'. They assaulted and raped women, attacked and murdered members of the local bourgeoisie and raided the local distillery for vodka, distributing it to the mob.

One by one the symbols of the old tsarist system were destroyed. The statue of assassinated Tsar Alexander II that occupied pride of place in the city square was torn down. The homes of the much-despised capitalist bourgeoisie were searched and looted of any valuables, and the houses themselves summarily requisitioned and divided up as accommodation for workers. In late June, those of the well-to-do possessed of more than 10,000 roubles were forcibly sent to dig trenches against the advancing Czechs, 67 citizens being sent to the Front on the 25th. Shops were vandalised, their windows smashed; others were closed down, their goods confiscated and their owners ruined, if they hadn't already been chased out. The hotels one by one shut their doors. The state-run mines and factories and workshops were taken over and nationalised. Civic institutions and businesses lost their educated and skilled workers, many of whom were hounded out as class enemies, thus ensuring, counter-productively, that there was nobody left with the expertise to run them. Everywhere private enterprise was repressed and destroyed, including the flourishing commercial river and rail transport of the region. All the banks and telegraph offices, the post office and printing presses were taken over, the local newspapers replaced with the monopoly of Bolshevik propaganda in the grandly named *News of the Ural Regional Soviet of Workers', Peasants' and Soldiers' Deputies*. Phone lines were cut and the handsets thrown in the river. Societies and clubs were banned and all public meetings, except Communist ones, forbidden. One by one, the city's fine civic buildings fell into neglect, their windows cracked and dirty, their floors unswept and muddied by dirty boots. And now there were sentries with rifles at every doorway.

The once proud Ekaterinburg iron-working industry had already, since the Revolution, been suffering badly from loss of finance; this, coupled with recruitment of its workforce into the army, had led to severe reductions in productivity. Very few, other than key workers, were getting paid anything more than a starvation wage now. Meanwhile the price of basic necessities – flour, bread, potatoes, tea, butter – was rocketing and speculators were making fortunes. Ekaterinburg was a fearful, hungry city. Few felt sustained by Bolshevik promises of a new world order; propaganda did not fill bellies. That summer it was a matter of getting through the daily grind of finding enough to eat. Food queues snaked round the few open shops, for everything was rationed: tickets for bread, tickets for meat, tickets for fish, milk, potatoes – even shoes. The withdrawal of coffee and butter from the Romanov daily diet back in mid–May would seem a minor inconvenience compared to the famine that was now threatening the city's population at large.

But there was no real reason for anyone to go hungry. Out in the villages there were in fact no food shortages, and so, weekly, people trudged there from the city – often as far as 15 miles – to barter whatever they had – old clothes, boots – for flour, bread and potatoes, for the peasants did not trust the new Bolshevik paper money and wouldn't take it. Having secured a few precious supplies, people returned to the city only to be stopped and searched at the entry points and stripped of their purchases. The public square on market day was now a forlorn sight. The dogs and crows and pigeons had deserted it. There was simply nothing left to scavenge.

Yet still people continued to stand in line for hours in the heat, periodically drenched by the rainstorms that regularly swept the Urals in summer. The desperate, the idle and the destitute, as well as bands of deserters from the Front, could be seen on every street corner, listless and broken, drinking and smoking when they could, and spitting the husks of sunflower seeds on the pavements. As the summer heat wore on, there was only one thing you could be sure to get in Ekaterinburg – typhus. With the water supply spasmodic, the disease spread like wildfire in a city of lousy, unwashed bodies, infecting over 40 per cent of the population and overstretching the limited medical resources and overcrowded city hospitals. And then came cholera too.

In Ekaterinburg, as in many other Russian cities, the sharp and unavoidable disparity between Bolshevik rhetoric and Bolshevik practice was now becoming only too painfully clear. Hunger did little but breed political indifference in the population; among the peasantry, the requisitioning by the Bolsheviks of their precious grain and livestock provoked outright hostility, to which the response was brutal. Under the Tsar, people said, there were at least judges who sent you to Siberia. Now you just got taken out and shot without trial. In June, 250 local peasants who had protested the confiscation of their grain and livestock had been thrown into Ekaterinburg's prison no. 2. Night after night, for weeks, they were taken out in twos and threes and shot; only 35 were left alive by the time the Czechs took the city.

People were now being arrested indiscriminately, on the slightest suspicion of counter-revolution. When the prisons were full, hotels and factories were taken over as places of internment. Bolshevik venom was in particular directed at the clergy – 45 members of the Ekaterinburg Orthodox diocese were murdered that summer – shot, drowned, bayoneted, their eyes gouged out, tongues and ears hacked off and their mangled bodies thrown in the river. And it got much worse after news came of the taking of Omsk by the Czech legions on 7 June. The Czechs' rapid advance on Ekaterinburg triggered a terrifying catalogue of executions, with the Bolsheviks vowing that for every Communist killed they would shoot 100 hostages. They began to draw up lists of citizens who would be the first to pay the penalty. At the top of that list were the names of the Romanovs already being held at Ekaterinburg and Alapaevsk. But in reality, the first act in the systematic annihilation of the Romanovs had already taken place, in Perm on the night of 12/13 June, when the Tsar's brother, Grand Duke Mikhail, had been taken from his prison cell and shot in the woods by the Cheka. It is likely that this murder was the Bolsheviks' way of testing the water of public opinion for further Romanov murders to come.

At four in the morning of 29 June, the latest and most chilling act of vicious murder had been perpetrated by the Bolsheviks at Ekaterinburg. Nineteen prominent citizens – priests, doctors, lawyers, merchants, including personal acquaintances of Consul Preston, such as mining engineer Fadeev, Makronosoev, the Russian manager of the English-owned Sysert works, the merchant Stepanov, the grocer Torupechev – were taken to the local sewage dump half a mile outside the city. Here they were lined up and shot in front of a freshly dug grave and then frenziedly bayoneted after they had fallen. One of them miraculously survived to tell the tale. When Preston and the other foreign consuls protested to the Bolsheviks about these killings, they were told they were in revenge for the murder of Bolshevik Commissar Ivan Malyshev, captured and shot by the Czechs at the Kusvinsky works on 23 June. On 30 June the Ekaterinburg edition of *Izvestiya* published the list of names of those killed and an announcement 'From the Ural Provincial Extraordinary Committee for Combating Counter-Terrorism', explaining that this was a response to an act of terror against a representative of the labouring class and that any similar acts would be repressed tenfold.

At home, in the bucolic safety of a cool English summer, Preston's monarch, and the Tsar's first cousin, seemed oblivious to it all, for no doubt the consul's communiqués on the escalating situation in Ekaterinburg had failed to reach the Foreign Office. Back in April, King George had appeared to wash his hands of his troublesome Romanov relatives, though he had subsequently expressed his 'distress' about reports reaching him regarding the family's treatment at Tobolsk. This was about as far as his sympathies stretched, for George had other preoccupations, not the least of which was the war on the Western Front, which was now entering its final stages.

On the afternoon of 4 July, in fact, the British king and his new American allies in the war were making their own small but significant mark in history. In an act of solidarity to mark Independence Day, King George and Queen Mary were among a crowd of 50,000 spectators at a baseball match between the United States navy and army at Chelsea football ground, the first such game to be held on English soil. The British royals, bemused by all the brashness and American razzamatazz, watched the game in a polite state of mystification. Baseball it seemed had none of the dignity of cricket, nor the tremulous tumult of football. What, asked someone in the crowd, would the Kaiser make of such a public display of nationalistic fervour and back-slapping in the midst of war?

Former prime minister of the Russian provisional government Aleksandr Kerensky, in exile in Paris, had been busy that day too, meeting with French Socialists and urging intervention by the Allies as the only thing that now could save Russia from the abyss. Even as he spoke, and the bands at Stamford Bridge played 'The Star-Spangled Banner', a joint intervention force of British and French soldiers backed by a few American marines had been on the move, after landing at Murmansk in northern Russia. Such an act of provocation would make Bolshevik cooperation with any of the Allies over the future of the Romanovs even less likely. It all seemed hopeless. The Imperial Family were too well guarded. Any attempt at rescue would only end in a bloodbath. Consul Preston's view was that the last hope left to the Romanovs was via diplomatic channels.

In Moscow, German ambassador Count Wilhelm von Mirbach, newly appointed in April to build relations with the Bolsheviks and report back on the situation in Russia, was doing precisely that – exercising his diplomatic muscle with his Russian 'allies' and voicing his concerns about rumours that the Romanovs had been harmed during unrest in Ekaterinburg. He had gone to the Kremlin demanding an explanation from foreign minister Georgy Chicherin about rumours in the press that Nicholas had already been assassinated. Even the *Washington Post* had picked up on the story via reports circulating from Copenhagen. The Bolshevik government was embarrassed. Mirbach, who had been at the centre of vigorous German efforts on behalf of the Romanovs all summer, was reassured that there was no truth in the rumour. Maintaining an outward air of inscrutable control over the situation, in order to pacify Mirbach and other foreign ambassadors, the Central Executive Committee of the Communist Party held an urgent meeting. It was attended by Lenin, Sverdlov and Cheka head Feliks Dzerzhinsky, its object to discuss the Romanovs' fate. It wasn't just the ambassadors who were becoming a thorn in their side; challenges had been coming in by telegram from an assortment of revolutionary factions demanding the immediate execution of the Tsar. Lenin and the CEC were now conducting a delicate balancing act whilst they contemplated the best course of action, knowing also that independently of them the Bolsheviks of the Urals Regional Soviet were already having their own discussions on the subject. All the time the Romanovs were alive they were valuable bargaining chips with the Kaiser, and the German injection of millions of gold marks into Bolshevik funds each month would continue. The Treaty of Brest-Litovsk had brought peace with Germany in March and Russia's exit from the war. An ignominious act in the view of Nicholas and Alexandra, for Russia had been forced to cede those territories already occupied by the Germans: the Baltics, Poland, Ukraine (where the Germans had set up a puppet government) and regions in Belorussia and the Caucasus – losing at a stroke one third of its population and many of its most valuable industrial areas, including coal mines. But the treaty had bought the Bolsheviks precious time in which to consolidate their hold on the country. Meanwhile Lenin privately was gambling that a social revolution was imminent in Germany too, and that it would oust the Kaiser from power just like his cousin Nicky, bringing an end to the war and sparking a European socialist upheaval that would keep the Bolsheviks in power. But right now Lenin was facing increasing challenges on all sides: from anarchists, Mensheviks and Constitutionalist and Socialist Revolutionaries opposed to the treaty, who saw it as a sham. He had no doubts about how the Bolshevik government should respond to such threats. On 26 June he had announced: 'We must encourage and promote mass terror against the counter-revolutionists, especially in St Petersburg, to make a decisive example.'

Sensing the weakness of the new Soviet state, the Germans meanwhile were gathering in the south and west of Russia, in anticipation of what seemed to them its imminent demise. For the Germans too had a master plan and their own political gamble at stake: that Russia would collapse and be dismembered, her vast black earth regions in Ukraine to be exploited as an enormous granary by Germany, which would make of the occupied Russian territories virtual German colonies.

With so much at stake in the great power play of international politics, the value to the Bolsheviks of Nicholas was now rapidly receding. It was certainly increasingly unlikely in the current volatile internal situation that he could be brought back to Moscow for Trotsky's great show trial. A trial would, by its very nature, have been a public acknowledgement of Nicholas's innocence till proven guilty, something the Bolsheviks had no wish to invite. It is more likely that talk of a trial was yet another part of deliberate Bolshevik policy to stall Western protests and lend an air of legitimacy to their handling of the Tsar's fate. A few cosmetic preparations for this had been put in motion as a palliative to public opinion, but it is unlikely there was ever any serious intention to go ahead with it. If a trial were now to take place it would have to be in Ekaterinburg. Goloshchekin, in Moscow for consultations with Lenin and Sverdlov, was told to prepare for this eventuality and also, if events overtook them, for the execution of the Tsar, should the situation in the Urals become untenable. Late in the afternoon of 4 July, he received a telegram from his colleague Beloborodov in Ekaterinburg. It confirmed Avdeev's dismissal and the change of regime at the Ipatiev House. Moscow's misgivings that Ekaterinburg had lost control of the situation were 'unfounded'.

Be that as it may, the military situation in the Urals was reaching crisis point. The anti-Bolshevik White forces under Admiral Kolchak had established their own rival provisional government in Omsk in Eastern Siberia and were now fighting their way west with the Czech legion. Well disciplined and well armed, the legions were a serious military challenge to the still badly organised Red Army. They had now also seized the Bolshevik strongholds of Chelyabinsk, Irkutsk and Tomsk. It was clear they were turning the tide against the Bolsheviks in Siberia and were bent on capturing Ekaterinburg, the last major obstacle in their path. But they were not in any hurry. Slowly, slowly the Czechs were approaching the city from the south-west, squeezing it inexorably into submission; and they would strike in their own good time.

Ekaterinburg was now under martial law and the sense of panic was palpable. The Ural Regional Soviet had already suppressed an anti-Soviet rebellion on 12 June when a group of anarchists had attempted to seize the Verkh-Isetsk factory, and the wave of searches and summary arrests was provoking further rallies and protests. Meanwhile ordinary citizens were asking themselves where the Red Army forces to protect the city were. Rumour was rife that the leaders of the local soviet were preparing to decamp by special train before the arrival of the Czechs. People talked nervously on the streets. Hadn't they heard about the trainloads of gold and platinum and precious stones already being evacuated from the Ekaterinburg mint by train to Perm? Of the money being raided from the safes of the city's business magnates, shops and factories? Of the icons and other church treasures being confiscated and shipped out? The government archives had already been taken away to safety. It was a sure sign the city was to be abandoned to its fate.

The Ekaterinburg Bolsheviks did their best to counter the rumours, issuing proclamations assuring the population they would not abandon them and exhorting them: 'All to the front! To the defence of the Red Urals. In defiance of all the bourgeois, we are lighting the universal conflagration! Be ready, workers!' But even at the closely guarded Ipatiev House, the guards were beginning to get nervous. Two possible monarchist plots to rescue the family had already been foiled in June. And then had come threats of an 'anarchist' attack on the house: Avdeev had been warned that the family might need to be evacuated and for days the Romanovs had lived in a state of transit, their bags packed and ready to leave. But the burning question now, with the fall of Ekaterinburg increasingly likely, was would the Czechs, when they got there, attempt to liberate the Tsar? The release of the Imperial Family might have seemed to some a romantic possibility, but the approaching anti-Bolshevik forces had far greater concerns; the Whites certainly had no desire to put Nicholas back on the throne. Privately the Czechs were more concerned with their own stand for Czech nationhood. They had appealed to the US government in Washington on 2 July for support in their campaign, and demands were increasing for the American administration to send in intervention forces to work with British and Japanese troops already landed in the north and the Far East in their great new crusade – the war against Bolshevik class tyranny and despotism. As far as the Allies were concerned, rescuing the Tsar was low on their list of priorities.

As they retired to bed that night, the Tsar and Tsaritsa could have had no inkling of the seething political conflicts going on around them, the perilous way of life now being endured by the citizens of Ekaterinburg, nor the machinations of the Moscow and Ekaterinburg Bolsheviks as to their ultimate fate. Their world now was far too small; all that was left to them was the meticulous daily habit of writing their diaries. But what was there to say about Thursday 4 July 1918? Only the narrow certainties of eleven lives lived within five increasingly claustrophobic rooms: the ritual of meals, rest, books, what the weather was like and the temperature outside. Writing their daily entries was, for Nicholas and Alexandra, a last faint attempt to retain a sense of order and familiarity in a world gone mad, from which they were now totally divorced.

Nevertheless, the ever-circumspect Nicholas recorded the arrival of Yurovsky and his satisfaction with the new commandant's meticulous inspection of the family's jewellery. For Alexandra, that day's events were reduced to a few bald, scribbled sentences. Hers could hardly be called a diary. She no longer dared keep such a record of intimate thoughts and feelings, having destroyed her own extensive ones before leaving the Alexander Palace, along with some of her most precious letters, from her father and from her grandmother, Queen Victoria. But old habits die hard and she still felt compelled to keep some kind of aide-memoire of the day's events. Only now it was one in which physical pain and exhaustion were the constants in an increasingly circumscribed existence.

'Very hot, went early to bed as awfully tired & heart ached more' was how she summarised that day. But there is one thing strangely absent from her diary as well as that of her husband. The one thing each and every member of that close-knit family must have held in their hearts but kept resolutely locked away in their minds. It had for months gnawed away at them but it was too awful to utter. Now, as the weary days of captivity continued, and with them came increasing uncertainty, fear must have been in all their minds. In the first months of house arrest at Tsarskoe Selo Alexandra had talked of how 'each buries the anguish inside'. The family had long since learned stoicism in sickness and adversity; throughout those July days fear was to be the family's constant companion – its presence forever unspoken.

3

The Man with a Cigarette

FRIDAY 5 JULY 1918

On Friday 5 July the editorial offices of London's newspapers were buzzing with the latest news from the Exchange Telegraph in Copenhagen. Tsar Nicholas II – whose assassination had already been falsely reported on several occasions in late June – had, on the good authority of the Swedish Communist newspaper *Politiken*, now definitely been murdered by the Bolsheviks. Word no doubt filtered back to King George, but like most of his royal relatives he was by now in denial about the real dangers his cousins in Russia faced, with so much unsubstantiated rumour and counter-rumour flying around.

Throughout the Western press an assortment of lurid and highly fanciful tales about the Romanov family's life in custody – ranging from the derisive and dismissive to the more compassionate – had been fuelling newspaper stories since the turn of the year. A communiqué from the Pacific on 28 January by an American academic, Professor Edward A. Ross, had reported in all seriousness, after five months' supposed observation of the Bolshevik cause in Russia, that such was the power of the new government's pacifist Socialist message that the Tsar's eldest daughters Tatiana and Olga were said to have espoused the Bolshevik cause and had attended radical meetings in Tobolsk. Another paper countered this claim, alleging that Tatiana was in fact now living in the USA, having fled there from Tobolsk with '$350,000 worth' of the Tsaritsa's jewels, and that she planned to give lectures on Russia and open a school in the United States.

Erstwhile friends, ministers and retainers of the Romanovs, many of them fleeing into exile abroad, all seemed anxious to report their own observations on the Imperial Family. An unnamed former guard at Tobolsk told of the Tsar's 'melancholy' life there – of the outward calm and dignity that crumpled when he thought no one was observing him. At such times the former monarch would walk with bowed head, his face filled with painful dejection. When his children went outside to play he would stand and watch them at a window, his eyes full of tears. In April the *Washington Post* had published the first of a long serialisation that would go on till August – 'The Confessions of the Former Czarina of Russia' – regaling its readers for weeks with the fictionalised and highly salacious 'amazing personal history of Alexandra Fedorovna . . . compiled by Count Paul Vassili, who predicted the fall of the Romanoff Dynasty almost four years ago' and who delighted in telling readers that Alexandra was a product of the 'hereditary madness' of the House of Hesse-Darmstadt. Twenty-two members of the family had been confined to lunatic asylums over the last 100 years. Count Paul, it turns out, was none other than the prolific émigrée adventuress Princess Catherine Radziwill, a woman who had turned Romanov-baiting into a personal cottage industry.

Despite the repeated denials from Moscow of this scandal-mongering by the 'capitalist press', rumours in the West about the Tsar's execution or even escape from Russia persisted. The patent unreliability of witnesses who spread the rumours – first of execution, then of escape – clearly played into the Bolsheviks' hands, as part of a general softening-up process of public opinion to the idea of the Romanovs' eventual deaths. As early as January the *Washington Post* had reported that Nicholas and the children had escaped from Tobolsk, abandoning the now hopelessly insane Alexandra to a mental asylum in the city. Again, in late June the papers were full of stories from Russia that Nicholas had been shot during a vehement dispute with his guards on a special train taking him to Moscow. The former Tsar, reported Russia correspondent Herman Bernstein to *Washington Post* readers, was soon to face trial for despotism and violation of the people's rights, followed by public execution to appease the starving and exhausted Russian masses. There was rumour too that the Tsarevich had died not long after his removal from Tobolsk. And now the latest rumour was that Nicholas along with his wife Alexandra and one of their children, the Grand Duchess Tatiana, had been murdered, this latest piece of fantasy coming from a priest at Tsarskoe Selo, who had already sung prayers for the dead to a weeping congregation. One New York paper even went so far as to bring out a premature obituary, which reflected the general lack of sympathy for the Tsar in the West, where a war still raged, now in its fourth devastating year, and he had already been virtually forgotten. The Tsar's assassination, it claimed, had 'long seemed a matter of course'. Nicholas had been 'virtually a helpless figurehead born into outworn institutions with the shaping of which he had nothing to do and for the reform of which he was totally incapable'. Russia's former ruler, it would seem, was already an irrelevance.

In Ekaterinburg, of course, the Tsar and his family were still very much alive. Indeed their lives could not have been more uneventful. The Romanovs had 'spent the day as usual', as the Tsaritsa noted in an unusually short entry in her diary, recording that the only event had been the now daily inspection of their valuables by Yurovsky. A jolly good thing as far as Nicholas was concerned; it meant that Yurovsky and his subordinate Nikulin had begun to understand what kind of people had been 'surrounding and protecting' the family whilst simultaneously stealing from them. In the ever narrowing routine of his daily life, Nicholas found a welcome displacement activity in worry about his few remaining possessions.

He had now turned 50, having noted in his diary with an air of tired surprise the arrival of his half-century on 19 May. It had never been an auspicious day, for he had been born on the feast day of St Job, the silent, patient sufferer. 'Let the day perish wherein I was born' was the lament that echoed through this biblical tale of sorrow, and many Russians, with their propensity for reading signs and symbols into everything, saw this as ominous. Not the least among them was Nicholas himself. Sooner or later, as he accepted, God would put him to the test, and like Job he would be called upon to endure calamities without reproach, trusting only to Divine Providence. Conforming to Job's biblical archetype of unquestioning self-sacrifice, Nicholas had seemed, without any resistance to fate, to grow into the same qualities as obedient son, pious tsar and dutiful husband. Such profound mysticism was, from the beginning, the hallmark of his sense of himself as tsar, of his relationship with his people, and of his duty – to them, to his country, and to God. He grew up in the sincere belief that he could redeem the sins of Russia through his own humiliation and suffering, on his personal road to Golgotha. A greater power was controlling his destiny and resistance was futile. It was this knowledge that had enabled him so easily to give up the throne and to endure the monotony of his life in captivity. Soon there would be an end to it all, as he so often told himself, *kak Gospodu ugodno budet* – according to God's will.

The physical and spiritual weariness that overwhelmed him now at the age of 50 had finally divested the Tsar of his one great quality. For virtually everyone who ever met Nicholas Alexandrovich Romanov said that he had the finest, kindest, most velvety blue eyes they had ever seen. It was an inheritance from his mother's Danish side of the family. But behind those gently smiling, sensitive eyes, which every now and then drooped as he spoke, as though to block out the intimate gaze of others, lay a whole hidden world – a lifetime's thoughts and anxieties forever deeply repressed. For all his obvious, superficial charm and modesty, there was no guessing at the true nature of the Tsar's reticent personality. It was perhaps only his wife who ever saw what lay beyond – an inner, profoundly melancholic loneliness. But even she found it hard at times to overcome her husband's pathological reticence. And beautiful though they were, Nicholas's eyes also had a strange, blank impassiveness about them. They reflected nothing back of the inner man, and now they were greatly changed. Even at Tsarskoe Selo the previous year, as a famous photograph of Nicholas in captivity had testified, the bags underneath them were very pronounced, the shadows darker too. Those who saw the Tsar before he was taken away to Tobolsk said that his eyes seemed sunken. The soft, clear light remarked on by so many so often had now departed, leaving the whites tinged with yellow.

Nicholas's spiritual and mental decline had begun with Russia's ill-judged and catastrophic war against Japan in 1904, a year that would be his *annus horribilis*, for it also marked the terrible discovery that his new-born and much longed-for son and heir had the incurable condition of haemophilia. The strain of knowing that Alexey could at any time have a fatal attack, coupled with the 1905 revolution and the war years after 1914, had worn him out. When the moment came, he had been glad to abdicate. Shortly before, he had suffered a painful coronary occlusion whilst standing during a service in church, the first sign of the stress that was wearing his body down. But then, ironically, during the nine months at Tobolsk, when he had worked hard outdoors chopping wood and clearing snow with an indefatigable energy that everyone marvelled at, Nicholas had briefly become healthier and fitter than in a long time.

But that was all gone now and with it any hopes of a quiet life in exile. His face bore the indelible signs of fatigue and listlessness, broken only by his enduringly sad, wistful smile. Nicholas now had a large bald patch; his hair was receding and going grey at the temples. His distinctive reddish-brown beard was going grey too. His teeth were rotten and long neglected and must have caused him pain, their decay, combined with his heavy smoking, bringing severe halitosis too. Nicholas looked prematurely aged, with hollow cheeks, his face weathered and wrinkled, coarsened to a dark reddish brown from so much exposure to the sun. His clothes too were worn and patched. He might no longer be tsar or head of the army but he persisted in wearing his *gimnasterka* – a khaki soldier's shirt and officer's belt fastened by a buckle round his waist. But his boots were worn and down at heel. After two months of close confinement at Ekaterinburg he was spent – both physically and mentally.

For months now he had calmly and knowingly been on the edge of the abyss. But he never complained, even in his diary. His own fate and that of his family was in the hands of God. Several observers have remarked that Nicholas at this time demonstrated a puzzling lack of interest in what was going on around him. Commissar Yakovlev had noted during the journey from Tobolsk that there were only three things that preoccupied the Tsar: 'his family, the weather, and food'. The rest of the world – power, politics, affairs of state – was past history and excised from his brain.

Such necessary and onerous preoccupations had, for Nicholas, been imposed as an accident of birth, and in that lay his tragedy. He had never wanted to be tsar and had been in a state of perpetual denial at the prospect until the moment the role was thrust upon him. As a boy he had had a conventional, authoritarian upbringing at home with tutors, growing up in awe of his great bear of a father, Alexander III, and his charming but controlling mother, Maria Fedorovna. Alexander was disappointed in Nicholas's smallness of stature – he was only 5′ 7″ and had narrow shoulders and short, stocky legs. He derided his son's weakness, his feminine laugh and handwriting, referring to him as a *devchonka* – 'a bit of a girl' – capable of nothing other than 'infantile judgements' with regard to affairs of state and not one to be entrusted with them.

Nicholas met his father's criticisms, and both parents' patent disappointment in him as heir to the throne, with what would become his familiar passiveness and diffidence. His natural timidity grew in the face of Alexander's charisma and his mother's smothering indulgence. Knuckling down to his studies of mathematics, history, geography and chemistry, he displayed a natural flair for languages, becoming fluent in English, French and German. He certainly was not without intellectual gifts and the ability to read – fast – and absorb facts and issues very quickly, but he lacked any natural curiosity about most of the subjects he was obliged to tackle. His youthful diary demonstrates limited powers of self-expression and empathy and a chilling lack of interest in anything other than the most bourgeois, personal and domestic trifles. Political or cultural observations are almost entirely absent. But his photographic memory for names, faces, facts, dates was something that put him in good stead for the mountains of official documents with which he would have to deal as tsar, and it enabled him to read and digest endless volumes of the classic works of Russian fiction and history, including his favourite historians Karamzin and Solovev. For years, the Imperial Librarian had provided the Tsar monthly with 20 of the best books from all countries, military history being a particular favourite.

Nevertheless, educated as he was in seclusion without the luxury of the free exchange and exploration of ideas with others, Nicholas's world view remained narrow and unchallenged. Worse, he lacked any real friends of his own. His thoughts and opinions about issues in which he remained untutored were not solicited or broadened, leaving him often surprisingly ingenuous. A selection of professors and generals were later recruited to teach him the complexities of military science, political economy and international law. But amidst the circle of servile bureaucrats, army men and aristocrats who made up his entourage, none were capable of teaching him the true qualities of statesmanship. Nicholas's natural intelligence was dissipated in the dull and stultifying curriculum imposed upon him, and in response he was a dull and dutiful student. One man among them, however, exerted a considerable influence in shaping the young Tsarevich's mind: the coldly ascetic Konstantin Pobedonostsev, Procurator of the Holy Synod and an arch-conservative, anti-Semite and adherent of autocratic monarchy. Pobedonostsev 'put the final seal on an already closed mind', convincing Nicholas that parliamentary institutions were corrupt and decadent and instilling in him an unshakeable belief in the high ideal of his role as *batyushka-tsar* and God's chosen protector of an Orthodox-observant nation. Nicholas was, as his brother-in-law Aleksandr observed, a man 'vividly of the old system', who trusted ever after to his vision of a plain, honest, God-bearing people (as Dostoevsky saw them) loyal to their tsar – even when all the signs were there that he had long since lost their respect.

Nicholas's life at home in the great gloomy 900-room palace at Gatchina was spartan, like that of a military cadet, despite his vast retinue of servants. He became a creature of simple habits: he slept on a camp bed with a single hard pillow and a very thin mattress in a room with few home comforts, taking cold baths daily, eating the plainest of Russian food and allowing himself only a single glass of Madeira at dinner. He remained ever after a man of simple habits and simple tastes, modest in his style of dress (he always wore the belted tunic and tall boots of a soldier, and only donned civilian clothes on visits abroad) and utterly unworldly with regard to the value of things; after his marriage, his and Alexandra's lifestyle at Tsarskoe Selo was simple to the point of parsimony, and he never carried money. Lots of fresh air was de rigueur and he quickly turned it to his advantage, making it an outlet for his repressed emotions. Exercise became an absolute fundamental in his daily life, with Nicholas enjoying the country pursuits of hunting, shooting, fishing, swimming, playing tennis, rowing and, most particularly, long, vigorous walks.

But within the confines of his narrow, proscribed existence as heir to the throne, nothing had given him greater pleasure than joining the Preobrazhensky Guards when he was 19. Now, at last, he was released from the dreariness of studies and initiated into the macho world of fine uniforms, military exercises and the officers' club. Like any young initiate, Nicholas had thrown himself into army life with gusto. He stayed up late drinking, dining and playing billiards. He joined fellow officers on visits to the gypsies. Night after night he could be seen living up to the classic royal playboy image – going to balls, the theatre and opera. And soon he entered into a discreet affair, after falling for the Imperial Ballet's prima ballerina, Mathilde Kschessinska. His love of the army and all its associated pageantry never left him, and even in 1916 he would privately confide that his most agreeable duty was going to the Front and being among soldiers; it also provided welcome opportunities for avoidance, even in 1917: 'My brain feels rested here – no ministers and no fidgety questions to think over.'

When the time came, Nicholas, as heir to the throne, dutifully set off on the necessary rites–of–passage world tour, a 10–month journey to India and the Far East in 1890. On a stopover in Japan he was attacked with a sabre by a mentally disturbed man and wounded in the head, as a result of which he suffered for the rest of his life from severe headaches. But his preparation for the onerous duties of state, daily dealings with ministers and ambassadors, speech-making, and the complexities of official policy had barely begun when his father died prematurely, of kidney disease, in 1894. Nicholas found himself tsar at the age of 26 – too young and guileless, ill prepared by a father who had constantly stalled about giving him responsibilities. His sister Olga was very clear on the matter: it was all their father's fault – 'He would not even have Nicky sit in the Council of State until 1893.' A year later the bewildered Tsarevich found himself at the head of what had seemed to him till then one vast ancestral family estate of which he was now the unexpected, benign landowner. He was terrified at the responsibilities to come. He did not yet know his people and they certainly did not know him. 'What is going to happen to Russia?' he asked his uncle Grand Duke Alexander. 'I am not ready to be a tsar. I cannot rule the Empire. I have no idea of even how to talk to the ministers.'

There was only one way in which Nicholas could cope with the huge and unending burden of official papers, many of them tedious and utterly trivial, that rapidly piled on to his desk. He adopted a rigorous routine to which he strictly adhered. Everything about his daily life was tidy, systematic, down to the rows of neatly ranked pens and pencils on his desk, the pedantic orderliness with which he carefully stuck thousands of photographs in his albums, the laborious way in which he composed letters. He was extremely hardworking and thorough in an unimaginative way, perversely refusing the help of a private secretary let alone a secretariat, and often sitting up late over a vast range of documents that would have taxed the mental energy of several men. His coping strategy for the onerous responsibilities before him came from an extraordinary self-control – developed from a very early age with the help of his English tutor Charles Heath as a deliberate counter to an inborn hot temper. Whilst such calmness was repeatedly misinterpreted as indifference, if not a total absence of feeling, Nicholas's personal rigour ensured an exceptional tolerance of the tedium of official work and endless audiences and state functions. But diligence could not make up for the absence of monarchical *gravitas*, or for the fact that whenever he found himself in a difficult or confrontational situation he was incapable of dealing harshly with people face to face. Such were the contradictions in a man who sought the opinions of others and courteously listened as they expressed them, but who was then incapable of making independent judgements. In the end he frequently resorted to accepting the advice of the last person he spoke to. He rarely acted on anyone else's advice other than his wife's, but when things went wrong he blamed his political misfortunes on his ministers, and rather than come into conflict with them simply dismissed them out of hand.

Avoidance became Nicholas II's métier when faced with a stronger will than his own. And that included his wife. Alexandra was unendingly frustrated by her husband's pathological timidity, his lack of moral courage. From the beginning she had recognised this fatal weakness and she spent her entire married life attempting to instil in her meek husband the magisterial demeanour of the great Russian tsars – Ivan the Terrible, Peter the Great – who had gone before him. Traditionally Russians had long since seemed to respond best to 'a touch of madness or magic in their rulers', and Nicholas had neither. Marriage to the sickly and highly strung Alexandra, and with it capitulation to her baleful influence, dulled his natural gregariousness and he gradually ceased to engage with people in his normal way. Nevertheless, he remained confident that he had his own personal window on to what was best for the Russian people, refusing to face up to the many social and political problems confronting the country.

No doubt the seeds of Nicholas's mistrustfulness of change, and with it a lifetime's dread of assassination, had been sown when in 1881, at the age of 13, he had watched his horribly mutilated grandfather Alexander II die, the day they carried him into the Winter Palace after a bomb attack on his carriage on St Petersburg's Ekaterininsky Canal. Nicholas's own father's reactionary response to the assassination and the threat of terrorism had been to govern Russia with a hard and retrogressive hand. He passed his autocratic policies on to his son and with them a profound suspicion of any form of constitutional government. Fearful of innovation and change, Nicholas shrank back, clinging to his Oriental fatalism and to the steadying rock of 'Papa's policy'. He had no wish to break the oath made at his coronation to maintain and transfer to his long-awaited heir the autocratic system he had inherited from his father. And so he resisted the guidance of strong-minded politicians such as his prime minister Petr Stolypin and finance minister Sergey Witte. When men such as they attempted to take the initiative and suggest reform, he dug his heels in, seeing their action as a usurpation of his power. He could not bear to lose control. He preferred instead the reassuring mediocrity of those who did not challenge him and who told him what he wanted to hear. In his social contacts Nicholas eschewed the company of modernisers and industrialists, court society and representatives of contemporary culture in a backward-looking preference for the rituals and etiquette of what seemed to him the safe old order. The Russian masses were incapable of dealing with any other form of government, of that he and Alexandra were certain, and none was more vocal than she in expressing it: 'We are not a constitutional country and dare not be; our people are not educated for it.'

But after the 1905 revolution and the horrific debacle of the massacre of nearly 200 marchers by Cossacks on Bloody Sunday, the faith of the common people in their benign *batyushka* had been seriously undermined and a rapid alienation of tsar and people had set in, irrevocably damaged by the Rasputin scandal. A rising tide of insurrection in St Petersburg forced the Tsar reluctantly into a 'constitutional experiment', announced in a manifesto of 17 October 1905. It was the beginning of the end of the old autocratic regime that Nicholas had cherished. The inauguration of the Duma did nothing to quell growing unrest in the country and the resurgence of a revolutionary movement that Alexander III had so rigorously suppressed. Repressive measures introduced in the wake of a string of terrorist murders, including that of Grand Duke Sergey in 1905 and Stolypin in 1911, now earned the Tsar the epithet of 'Nicholas the Bloody'. Noble, high-minded, conscientious, courteous, selfless, chivalrous towards women – in every possible way the Tsar had once been viewed as a true gentleman. But now there was blood on his hands and the testimonies to his fine personal qualities as a private individual that had poured from the pens of courtiers, friends, priests, diplomats and ministers alike could no longer counter the new propagandist images portraying the Tsar as the repository of all the despotism and brutality of a corrupt and antediluvian system. Between 1906 and 1910, 3,741 people were executed for political crimes and thousands more sent into forced labour, exile and prison. The wave of revolution continued to rise until

1914; then the war came and with it an almost overnight reunion of tsar and people in one cause – defence of the motherland. But this lasted barely a year before a massive loss of faith in Nicholas's wartime leadership brought further troubles and prophecies of the imminent collapse of the monarchy.

If Nicholas had abdicated in 1905, as many in retrospect have felt he should have done, he and his family might well have lived out their lives in quiet provincial retirement somewhere abroad. But instead of confronting the turbulent issues that Russia faced, Nicholas and Alexandra retreated to their palace at Tsarskoe Selo, to where they felt safe and unthreatened. Nothing, however, could stem the tide of gossip about the true nature of the Tsarevich's haemophiliac condition and the increasing hostility towards Alexandra after she invested all her hopes for Alexey's survival in the hands of Grigory Rasputin. Gossip and rumour, crude propagandist cartoons in the papers of the most salacious kind, all stoked the fires of disenchantment with their monarch among the population at large. And with it, the Imperial couple increasingly became subject to nameless fears. They saw plotting and betrayal at every turn and withdrew increasingly into the selfish protectiveness of family life. It gave them a false sense of security, and like the court of the Sleeping Beauty they slumbered on at Tsarskoe Selo, in wilful ignorance of what lay outside, beyond the palace gates.

When Nicholas finally abdicated, on 15 March 1917, he took it with complete equanimity, as part of God's greater plan for him. As he confided to Anna Vyrubova, the Tsaritsa's closest friend, if a scapegoat were needed to save Russia, then God's will be done, he meant to be that scapegoat. One thing became clear: even at such a moment of crisis, no one was allowed to cross into the forbidden territory of the Tsar's inner thoughts. To the end Nicholas remained inscrutable, enigmatic, a riddle to those around him. That day, while his mother sat sobbing and his entourage contained their own distress, he signed the abdication document and then, as the train taking him back to Petrograd pulled out, stood calmly staring out of the window of his carriage, lighting one cigarette after another. Within a couple of months of giving up his throne, his empire, his power, Nicholas was confiding to his diary the pleasures of now being able to spend more time with his 'sweet family' than in 'more normal years'. Rowing, walking, sawing wood, digging the garden, riding bicycles with his daughters around the park at Tsarskoe Selo – such for him was true happiness. The only thing he missed about his former life was contact with his dear mama. 'But I am indifferent to everything else', he wrote.

He had not always been so detached. Throughout his reign, the signs had been there of a constant inner battle in the Tsar to suppress his apprehensions and indifference when in the company of others: the deliberate slowing down of his speech, punctuated by pauses for thought, his unhurried movements, a scrunching of his toes in his boots or a shrugging of his shoulders – all signalled moments of insecurity or self-consciousness, as too did a nervous cough and the constant self-comforting stroking of his moustache and beard with the back of his right hand. His eyes, whilst warm and kind, never lighted for long on the person he was talking to but constantly flickered distractedly out into the distance. But of all the props Nicholas increasingly relied on to ease the anxieties and tensions of his burden as tsar, none was more important than cigarettes, which he chain-smoked, often using a pipe-shaped meerschaum cigarette holder. His smoking had become even heavier after the outbreak of the First World War. Cigarettes provided a literal smokescreen behind which Nicholas concealed his anxieties or lack of will to discuss issues or confront problems. He constantly lit one, stubbed it out half finished and lit another. Which was all very well all the time he was able to indulge his craving for nicotine with his usual Benson & Hedges bearing the imperial crest, or the delicious Turkish cigarettes sent to him by the Sultan just before hostilities with the Turks broke out in 1914. Even in Tobolsk a loyal member of his army staff, Major General Vladimir Voiekov, had managed to send the Tsar cigarettes. But by the time he arrived in Ekaterinburg, the fine cigarettes would probably long since have been exhausted and Nicholas was reduced to relying on his captors to give him cheap *papirosy*, with their cardboard tubes filled with the stinking *makhorka* tobacco so beloved of ordinary Russians. Nicholas hated the stuff and perhaps chose, as part of his road to Calvary, to suffer the agonies of nicotine withdrawal until occasionally the nuns from the Novo-Tikhvinsky Convent were able to bring him tobacco with the daily supplies of milk and eggs.

For it was in captivity that his great powers of self-control and restraint – till then seen as negative characteristics in a monarch – ironically became his strengths during the increasingly uncertain days of July. They impressed even the guards at the Ipatiev House, one of whom observed that the Tsar's self-mastery was almost 'supernatural'. The quiet inner force of the man was not like that of other mortals; it belied his appearance and the outward manner he had of an ordinary little colonel of the guards. Other more intriguing rumours had reached the ears of British ambassador Sir George Buchanan in Petrograd, from both Prince Felix Yusupov and also Grand Duke Nikolay: that Nicholas's almost childlike indifference to the loss of his throne had been the result of his smoking narcotics – probably a blend of henbane and hashish –

administered by a Tibetan doctor, P. A. Badmaev, recommended by Rasputin to counter stress and insomnia. Some courtiers in the know about this claimed that the habit had 'seriously affected his mental powers' and had produced in the Tsar 'a state of callousness and complete insensibility to anything that befell him'. This seems unlikely, but the drug may well have had a sufficiently anaesthetic effect for Nicholas to endure the abdication crisis with such uncanny calm. Now, however, there were no palliatives left. They might take away his cigarettes, but in the end Nicholas had one last refuge, the most powerful narcotic of all – prayer.

As for his diary, he had nothing useful left to say in it, despite writing it being a lifelong habit. His thoughts and feelings were becoming increasingly internalised as the 'intolerable boredom' of having no physical work became an ever greater strain. Over the years his wife's catalogue of ailments had become, as he had admitted to his cousin Konstantin, tiresome and depressing; it had taken all his superhuman tolerance and tact to remain loving and supportive but it was wearing him down and forcing him further in on himself. Commandant Avdeev at the Ipatiev House was of the opinion that Nicholas 'feared his wife more than the devil himself'. The Tsaritsa openly berated him in English in front of people, both inside the house and outdoors, taking him to task for being friendly and talkative with the guards whilst she persisted with her ingrained autocratic manner. But it was all water off a duck's back; Nicholas had for so long now learned how to inhabit his own profound loneliness and had developed such a blankness of mind that during these final July days he was merely riding the tide towards his inexorable fate. For the Orthodox faithful, such calmness is perceived as a mark of the Tsar's Christlike resignation and meekness; for the more cynical Bolsheviks it seemed a kind of 'idiotic indifference' that ran counter to his natural intelligence. Such behaviour was incomprehensible in the ruthless logic of his captors. Each day now inside the Ipatiev House came and went for Nicholas in a state of self-induced mental anaesthesia; hiding his thoughts behind the books he read and re-read all morning and pacing relentlessly up and down the garden twice a day. Alone with his daughters on the frequent occasions that Alexandra did not go out into the garden, he was able to occasionally relax, to laugh with them and sit on the swing. But the nights were now increasingly welcome, 'the best part of the day', a time briefly to forget, as he himself had observed in Tobolsk in January.

Something different was now in the air at the Ipatiev House; even Nicholas had, since June, noticed a change in the guards and their reluctance to talk when the family were outside. He had taken this as an affront, uncomprehending of the true significance of this distancing. But that Friday, as Nicholas worried about the safety of his possessions, the net around the Romanovs, and the threat to his very existence, was tightening.

For in Moscow, Lenin was now facing a major crisis, with armed insurrection brewing among the Bolsheviks' political rivals the Left Socialist Revolutionaries (several of whose leaders had taken important roles in the provisional government and who had broken away from the party in December 1917). At the 5th All-Russian Congress of Soviets which had opened the previous day as a showcase for Lenin's new Bolshevik government at a Bolshoy Theatre packed with 1,164 delegates, there had been a violent quarrel between the Bolsheviks and the Left SRs (as they were known) about the peace treaty with Germany. Workers and soviet deputies had crowded the gangways and stood on their seats amidst the chandeliers, plush and gilding of the Bolshoy's opulent Imperial interior, gesticulating at the Grand Duke's box occupied by Ambassador Mirbach and other representatives of the German government and hurling abusive shouts of 'Down with the Germans' and 'Down with Mirbach'. This fine building, that had once echoed to the voice of the great bass singer Chaliapin singing *Boris Godunov* and where the newly nationalised Imperial Ballet provided a final dying vestige of Imperial culture, now resounded with angry shouts of condemnation of the Bolsheviks for their perceived sell-out of Russia to the Germans at Brest-Litovsk.

The most vociferous critic that afternoon was the 32-year-old Left SR Mariya Spiridonova, now back in Russia after 11 years of exile in one of the harshest prisons in Siberia for murdering a brutal tsarist official. Small, sober-faced, dressed in black with a stiff puritanical white collar, she was the archetypal fanatical female revolutionary, her big grey eyes full of anger behind her pince-nez as she took to the stage. From here she virulently condemned Lenin and the new regime for using the 'toiling peasantry' to their own ends and allowing the martyred Ukraine to be occupied and despoiled by the Germans. It made her 'burn with shame' that the Bolsheviks, with whom she had fought 'behind the same barricade', had now betrayed the Revolution. The auditorium was quickly in uproar; Chairman Sverdlov's attempts at tinkling the bell on his table to call the meeting to order failed dismally.

Holed up in the backwater of Vologda – a railway junction halfway between Moscow and the northern port of Murmansk, where the foreign diplomatic corps had been evacuated to safety from Petrograd after the Revolution – US ambassador to Russia Richard Francis seized news of the conflict at the Congress of Soviets as a welcome justification for his continuing arguments to President Wilson for American intervention in a Russia that he felt was about to collapse in turmoil. Germany he sensed was ready to step in for the kill, and this must be prevented at all costs.

That morning, the calendar on the wall in Nicholas and Alexandra's bedroom had been changed, with its usual regularity. The 'amazing' aroma of Ekaterinburg's summer gardens was one of the few lingering pleasures left to the Tsar during his now increasingly brief periods of recreation, an evocative memory perhaps of hot summers at his palace in Livadia in the Crimea. The smell of blossom, the summer sun overhead and the warmth on his face, exercise in the outdoors: these were the things he most valued, next to his family. Everything else had long since been exorcised from his shuttered mind. But now even the consolations of the weather were not enough. After Friday 5 July, time in the Ipatiev House stood still. The calendar would not be changed again.

4

The Woman in a Wheelchair

SATURDAY 6 JULY 1918

If Queen Victoria had had her way, her granddaughter Princess Alix Victoria Helena Louise Beatrice of Hesse and by Rhine would one day have been Queen of England and Empress of India. Alix (as she was known in the family, rather than by her official name, Alexandra) was not a particularly eminent candidate, coming as she did from a relatively minor German principality. Nevertheless, the Queen, in her insatiable drive to keep control of the dynastic marriages of her vast extended family, earmarked her as a suitable bride for one or other of her two grandsons, Eddy or George, the next two in line to the British throne after their father the Prince of Wales.

But the wilful Alix would have none of it. Much to the Queen's disgust, she turned down the proposal of Edward, Duke of Clarence, who seemed genuinely infatuated with her. Acknowledging her grand-daughter's strength of character – not without much surprise and a little offence – the Queen observed that 'she refuses the greatest position there is'. George, the next in line, never even made it into the frame, for Alix by then had fallen for the handsome young Russian Tsarevich Nicholas. The unimaginative George settled instead for a rather poor second best after Eddy died unexpectedly in 1892. He married his dead brother's fiancée, Princess May of Teck, yet another minor German princess.

And now, today, Saturday 6 July, King George and Queen Mary (her official name) were celebrating 25 years of what had turned out to be a surprisingly successful marriage. That morning, after a carriage procession from Buckingham Palace to St Paul's Cathedral and a service of thanks-giving, the royal couple had gone on to London's Guildhall for their silver wedding celebrations, where they had been the recipients of a 'humble address' by parliament expressing warm appreciation of their Majesties' 'unfailing devotion to duty in this time of stress'. During his reign, George and his wife had, said the *Times*, 'strengthened the bonds of affection binding them to the people'. At the King's insistence, gifts of silver to celebrate the occasion would be donated to the Red Cross for the war effort.

George and Mary were now at the height of their popularity as wartime figureheads. Such, too, ought to have been the role of their royal cousins, Nicholas and Alexandra. Still a year short of her own twenty-fifth wedding anniversary, how Alexandra must have wished her own bonds of affection with the Russian people could have been appreciated rather than so sorely misunderstood all these years. She was consumed by bitterness and anger at the ruination into which Russia was now being led. It was a wicked war and her cousin Kaiser Wilhelm was responsible. It was, she was sure, God's punishment for the country's sins, and she prayed fervently for his mercy and Russia's redemption. She was tormented too by the invective that had been so unjustly hurled at herself and the Tsar – her husband's sufferings she viewed as nothing less than Christlike, and such 'black ingratitude' at his self-sacrifice broke her heart. Her attitude to Russia was that of an indulgent but wise parent of a sick child, and she doggedly refused to abandon her loyalty to her adoptive country, in the naïve hope that one day it would recover its health – and its senses. God would save Russia, of that she remained certain. Discipline, order, faith – these were what was needed to put the country back on track; for they were, after all, the tenets to which she had long adhered in her own life.

For months now the Tsaritsa had been living increasingly in the past and 'in the hope of better days'. The earthly things of her former life had slipped away and the present had become a matter of endurance and giving thanks for each day as it came. But she felt so bitterly misunderstood. All she and Nicholas had ever wanted to do was to 'live tranquilly, like an ordinary family, outside politics, struggle and intrigues'. Ironically, in captivity after the abdication, they had achieved precisely that. Alexandra had spent her time knitting socks, sewing and patching the family's clothes and linen. But her eyesight was troubling her, as too were her many other long-term physical ailments. Her mental collapse in 1904 on discovering that her only son had the incurable disease of haemophilia – unknowingly passed down to Alix and on to him by Queen Victoria – had surrendered her finally and irrevocably to her accumulating neuroses. Thirteen years of living in false hope of Alexey's miraculous recovery had utterly destroyed her. Her body was a wreck: five pregnancies in quick succession – all of them producing large babies and difficult births – plus a miscarriage and a phantom pregnancy would be enough to debilitate many women. But add to it heart pain and shortness of breath brought on by nervous anxiety, sciatica so bad that she often could hardly walk, facial neuralgia, cyanosis (blue lips), acute earache, swollen legs and severe headaches and it meant that she had for years spent hours if not days in bed, reclining on a couch, or sitting in a wheelchair.

The Tsaritsa was now hopelessly addicted to a whole range of narcotics and sedatives, prescribed by Dr Botkin to control her various neuroses, her chronic headaches and insomnia. She had long since admitted that she was holding out physically thanks only to Veronal (a barbiturate-based proprietary drug), so much so that she was 'saturated with it'. She also took morphine and cocaine for menstrual pain and a whole range of other complaints, and occasionally smoked French cigarettes – all in an attempt to dull her anxieties. But the compensations were few and the side effects only added to her overwhelming sense of physical exhaustion.

At a time when Freud's methodology was in its infancy, Alexandra demonstrated all the classic psychosomatic symptoms of the recently described condition of 'hystero-neurasthenia'. Its inexorable progress, through increasing levels of irritability, restlessness, fatigue, a lack of pleasure in ordinary things, a fear of impending calamity and a marked preoccupation with her mental and physical condition, had begun in Alexandra's youth with a succession of family bereavements and had escalated ever after. A detailed report on his wife's mental and physical condition had been presented to the Tsar in 1910 by a German specialist, Dr Fischer. What the eminent doctor had to say was, however, deemed too close for comfort and he had not been invited back to the palace again. Instead the biddable Dr Botkin had been appointed and told the Tsaritsa what she wanted to hear, she having come to the unshakeable conclusion that she had a serious heart condition. The discomforting truths of the 1910 report may well explain the Tsar's saintlike tolerance of his wife's increasing sickliness and paranoid behaviour over the last few years. Seeing her so physically and mentally vulnerable, he was desperate to protect her. But by then he himself was, as he admitted to his mother, 'completely run down mentally by worrying over her health'.

Unlike her husband, who clung to the few paltry pleasures and diversions allowed them in the garden at the Ipatiev House, Alexandra spent most of her time indoors, lying on her bed or the couch, lost in sober thoughts of Christian resignation and the afterlife. An unrelenting diet of biblical and scriptural texts read to her by one or other of her daughters filled the blank pages of her days. For she always kept one of the girls with her when the others were allowed their daily recreation, no matter how fine the weather. She was achingly tired and had aged terribly since the abdication. Her hair was grey and she was painfully thin. There was a perpetual look of strain and anguish in her eyes. Yet even though broken in health, she remained an indomitable woman, convinced that her necessary suffering and that of her family was but one trial on the path to Christian self-perfection.

Alexandra Fedorovna seemed to have been born into sorrow, to look upon life as a battle of endurance, and yet that had not always been the way. For with her dimpled cheeks and her happy disposition she had been called 'Sunny' when she was a little girl. Her joylessness, for all the consuming marital love and devotion she received from Nicholas and their children, did not endear her to the Russian people. It was hard to fathom for those who did not know her, but the seeds of a melancholy temperament had been sown in early childhood. She had suffered the loss of her adored little brother Frittie, a haemophiliac, in 1873. Then, in a double tragedy in 1878 when she was only six, her five-year-old sister May and her 35-year-old mother Princess Alice of Hesse had both succumbed and died when the whole family went down with diphtheria. With their deaths the sunshine departed from Alix's life for ever.

Queen Victoria's eldest daughter Vicky, the widowed Empress Frederick of Germany, did not much care for her niece. To Vicky's mind, the death of her mother had meant Alix had been spoiled and indulged as compensation, and had grown up with a streak of obstinacy and an excessively high opinion of herself. Alexandra was burdened by the enduring sin of pride, her austere manner accentuated by her tallness and her straight-backed deportment (the result of a spinal condition which limited the flexibility of her upper vertebral column; early newsreel footage reveals this awkwardness of manner in her strange stiff nodding, from the neck up, at crowds during public ceremonials). She became withdrawn and difficult, reticent about showing affection and suspicious of strangers, fearful of giving love to someone who might be taken from her. Further traumatised by the premature death of her father when she was 18, Alix retreated to the protective wing of her grandmother Queen Victoria in a state of nervous collapse. She spent long periods in England – at the royal homes at Windsor, Balmoral and Osborne – and English soon became her natural language. The manners and morals of the strong-minded British Queen left their indelible mark on her, everything from Victoria's extraordinary tolerance of copious draughts of freezing cold air through open windows all the year round, to her morbid obsession with death and her perpetual state of mourning for her dead husband Albert. Such unhealthy preoccupations rubbed off on the impressionable young Alix, who was encouraged to pay regular visits to the crypt where her own dead mother and siblings lay.

From Victoria, Alix also inherited an indomitable will and stubbornness, as well as her idiosyncratic brand of Victorian prudery and reserve. Duty to family and to the state (in which her grandmother was a devout believer) was ingrained in her – French ambassador Maurice Paléologue called it a 'militant austerity' of conscience – as well as her grandmother's idiosyncratically unsophisticated bourgeois tastes. Alix grew up disliking modernity in all its forms, wedded instead to the limited, homely tastes of the conventional hausfrau. Everything she did was dictated by an attention to thrift and industriousness in that most English of ways – hence her later insistence that her own daughters never sat idle and always had something to sew. When she gave presents, they were not the usual ostentatious objects expected of an empress, but personal hand-sewn, painted or knitted items. Such un-Russian behaviour, down to Alexandra's insistence on showing her maids how to black-lead the grates in the royal apartments, later made her the butt of jokes among the sophisticates at the St Petersburg court. Privately, however, she also had that most contradictory of her grandmother's traits: an intense, impulsive sensuality and need for physical passion that ran absolutely counter to her prudish, censorious exterior. Tragically she did not, however, inherit the one abiding grace of her grandmother that might have saved the Romanov dynasty from collapse – a scrupulous observance of consti-tutional monarchy.

It took five years of waiting and superhuman persistence on the part of the Tsarevich Nicholas to wear down Alix's resistance to conversion to Russian Orthodoxy from Lutheranism in order for their marriage to take place. He had first been captivated by her when she was 12 and he 16 at the wedding of her sister Ella to Grand Duke Sergey of Russia in 1884. Puppy love turned to consuming passion on his part when he saw Alix again, now a radiant beauty, in 1889. Nicholas set his heart on marrying her. His parents had their own ideas about a suitable bride, preferring Princess Hélène of Orleans, daughter of the Comte de Paris, the pretender to the French throne. But he resisted; it was the one time the Tsarevich stubbornly and uncharacteristically refused to accede to parental wishes. When Alexandra declined the marriage proposal of Edward, Duke of Clarence, in May 1890, Nicholas renewed his addresses, despite Alix's tearful protestations about the impossibility of giving up her faith.

One of Queen Victoria's ladies-in-waiting, Lady Edith Lytton, wrote that what finally won Alix's heart was probably Nicholas's reappearance at a family wedding in Coburg in 1894, without his wispy adolescent moustache but with a full and manly beard. Alix finally melted in the face of the handsome Tsarevich's persistent attentions, and after many hours spent in fervent prayer she made her peace with God and her conscience and finally agreed to convert to Orthodoxy. Queen Victoria declared herself to be 'thunderstruck' by such a turnaround in her devout and pious granddaughter. At the end of October 1894, as her poor 'gentle little simple Alicky' set off for Russia, the Queen worried terribly about her fragile granddaughter marrying into such a dark and unstable monarchy and a society with 'such a want of principle'. Her blood ran cold at the thought of Alix being sacrificed to 'those dreadful Russians'. Certainly Alix's arrival was not auspicious, for it came in time for a sombre reunion with her fiancé at his father's deathbed. Within three weeks she found herself a 'Funeral Bride' and Empress of Russia, under the new name of Alexandra Fedorovna. It was a gloomy start to her marriage, as had been that of her mother, Princess Alice, who had also married in front of a muted congregation drowned in black, only six months after devotedly nursing her father Prince Albert during his fatal illness.

Nicholas the Silent Sufferer and Alix the Funeral Bride were thus united under clouds of gloom and much superstitious prediction about what fate had in store for them. And so they clung to each other, with an incredible tenacity and all-inclusive passion that demonstrated the deep inner needs each found fulfilled in the other. The intensity of Alix's love as 'Wifey' to Nicholas's 'Huzy' was smothering, oppressive, over-heated; but Nicholas seemed to thrive on it, like a hothouse plant under glass. They knew each other 'through and through', Alexandra asserted, and only ever needed to be together, with their children, 'utterly cut off in every way'. Fine aspirations for any modest, devoted suburban couple; only they were not ordinary, private individuals but Emperor and Empress of Russia, and they had a duty to their public.

Queen Victoria's affection for Alexandra and Nicholas grew after the couple visited her at Balmoral in 1896 with their first child, Olga. They were, she thought, 'quite unspoilt and unchanged and as dear and simple as ever'. And within the very close circle of family and the handful of friends that knew them, indeed they were. Alexandra was after all very beautiful, with delicate features, lovely reddish-gold hair and fine blue eyes. But much like her mother Princess Alice, she had a severe kind of beauty, accentuated by the sharp nose, that lent an austerity and coldness. The thin, taut lips rarely mellowed into a smile in public; indeed they had a perpetually mournful expression that suggested a lingering sense of life's disappointments rather than its pleasures. Such seriousness of manner spilled over into a remorseless religiosity – another inheritance from Princess Alice. Alexandra had surprised everyone with the speed and messianic fervour with which she had embraced not just the Russian faith, but Russianness itself. With her sister Grand Duchess Ella, who had also converted on her marriage into the Romanov family, she shared the same levels of 'charitable exaltation' that intensified as the years went by.

She had no hesitation in pronouncing herself entirely 'Russian' in sentiments and displaying all the loyalty of a native-born patriot. Indeed, Orthodoxy became a consuming passion and a solace, the motor that drove Alexandra spiritually and emotionally. It also, indirectly, became her undoing.

Sadly for Alexandra, the perception of her at court and among the Russian people at large started off on a bad footing and never recovered lost ground. For she failed dismally to take on board that most important piece of advice given her by her grandmother: that it was her first duty in her adoptive country to win the love and respect of the people. Crippled by reserve, lonely and isolated, with her husband's time taken up by affairs of state, Alexandra proved incapable of doing so. She lacked Nicholas's great gifts: his charm, his engaging manner and his self-control. She seemed vain and self-willed, forever closed off and undemonstrative. From the day of her arrival she was viewed as a foreigner – as the *nemka*, 'the German woman'. Her prudery and serious-ness counted against her, as did her lack of taste in clothes, her poor dancing skills and her religious piety. Her response to the hostility she encountered was to retreat even further. She was reticent if not brusque with strangers, she spoke in a whisper, avoided coming down for meals, was picky and disdainful about food when she did, and frequently retired from them 'indisposed'. She did everything she could to avoid being put on display in public ceremonials. Knowing she could not hold her own against what she saw as the decadent sophisticates of St Petersburg or the 'spider's net' of the Moscow social set, in whose presence her whole face, neck and chest flushed crimson with nerves, Alexandra sought friends and companions among the upper middle classes and moneyed bourgeoisie. To friends such as these – her ladies-in-waiting Lili Dehn and Anna Vyrubova, who knew the extent of her many and distressing physical ailments kept secret from the public at large – the Tsaritsa was sweet, long-suffering, gracious and kind. They became her obedient, admiring poodles. Alexandra effortlessly dominated them, their lowlier social status ensuring an unquestioning devotion to her as a superior spiritual and moral being. But, being the clever woman she was, she often found the toadying attentions of the intellectually challenged, immature Anna Vyrubova irritating. She frequently reviled Vyrubova in letters to Nicholas and was jealous of her doting affection for him, yet she never failed to exploit her as a captive audience for her interminable religious homilies, making of Vyrubova her almost constant companion during the war years when Nicholas was away at the Front.

To the public beyond the palace gates, therefore, Alexandra remained an enigma. They saw so little of her that her almost permanent absence from view proved a fertile breeding ground for rumour, malevolent gossip and ultimately hatred. Alexandra failed to learn the one big lesson of her grandmother's reign after Victoria had retreated from public view in 1861 with the death of Albert. Twenty years of reclusive life, refusing all public appearances, had brought upon the once popular and unassailable British monarchy the full brunt of public criticism and had aroused a great deal of republican dissent. A monarch could not afford to be invisible. In Alexandra's frequent absences Nicholas worked the Romanov publicity machine hard with his five lovely children, but in the end it was not enough. Although the Imperial Family were frequently photographed and *cartes de visite* of them were widely available, in dozens and dozens of family photographs Alexandra is either absent or, if seen at all, sits solemnly in profile or looking away from the camera. Others show her reclining in her favourite environment – her mauve boudoir. This was her world: surrounded by varying shades of the colour of mourning, the walls smothered with hundreds of icons from floor to ceiling, and with the suffocating smell of lilac, lilies of the valley and violets sent daily from the French Riviera. Rarely upright and active, let alone vigorous, the Tsaritsa, for her husband and her children, became the woman in a wheelchair. She seemed to be always sickly, indisposed, struggling with her many demons, real and imagined; when she ventured outside, she hid herself under a parasol, always absorbed in her own thoughts, conscious of the watchfulness of others. True, she did her best to suffer her ailments stoically, and always revived in spirits when relaxing on board the royal yacht the *Shtandart* or at the family's summer palace in Livadia, but the shades of Alexandra's sick room followed the young family wherever it went and blighted all their lives.

In Alexandra, Nicholas undoubtedly found a surrogate for his own lack of will and forcefulness, as well as a consuming maternal protectiveness he had never had from his own mother. Behind the scenes, his impressionability and his malleable personality were rapidly moulded by Alexandra's powerful and assertive character. In public she might have appeared awkward and self-conscious, but in private she was vocal, emotional and highly strung. With her domineering, masculine mind she articulated her personal opinions in long and hectoring letters to her husband in which she exhorted him to be everything he inherently was not – firm, decisive, intractable and at all times asserting the dignity of his position. Convinced of her own infallibility, Alexandra would brook no criticism from even the most well-meaning and concerned of friends and relatives. Blindly obstinate in her determination to hang on to power, she relentlessly belaboured the hapless Nicholas with her paranoid suspicions about 'rotten' ministers and her reactionary opinions on domestic policy. That she truly believed she was right there is no doubt; so much so that she worked herself up into a frenzy in her attempts to inject her own willpower into her husband's flaccid spirit: 'I am fighting for your reign and Baby's future', she would repeatedly remind him. In order to defend that inheritance she reeled off endless admonitions: 'a Sovereign needs to show his will more often' . . . 'let others feel you know what you wish' . . . 'If you could only be severe my love' . . . 'They must learn to tremble before you' . . . 'be more autocratic' . . . 'show everybody that you are master' . . . 'let them feel your fist at times'. Alexandra would not let go; when Nicholas's command of the army finally took him away from her in late August 1915, in scribbled page after page, several letters a day, she bombarded him with her increasingly hysterical ramblings.

Even at her most cloyingly devoted, kissing Nicholas's cushion and wishing she could hold him tightly in her arms and mop his fevered brow, in the next breath she would be unrelentingly manipulative, exhorting him, 'Forgive me, but I don't like the choice of Minister of War.' Nor did she like anybody who uttered a word of criticism against their 'friend' Rasputin. The Holy Man's critics were all misguided bigots. She knew best – for the country and for her husband: 'sweetheart needs pushing always and to be reminded that he is emperor'. This included being turned against his devoted uncle Grand Duke Nikolay, of whose popularity as a military leader Alexandra was consumingly jealous. Sound reason to oust him came, in her view, when the Duke openly expressed his grave anxieties about Rasputin's malign influence over her. In response, Alexandra, like a female Iago, proceeded to sow the seeds of doubt and suspicion in her husband's mind, as she did about anyone of whom she disapproved, wheedling and insinuating until Nicholas capitulated and removed his uncle from his command of the Eastern Front.

But Nicholas did not always succumb to his wife's perpetual moral blackmail or her stated longing to 'poke [her] nose into everything'. 'Silly old Wifey' might have thought she wore the trousers, but at other times 'sweetheart' refused to be pushed. He turned a deaf ear, as he did to all advice to which he did not wish to respond, lit another cigarette and moved on to the next dispatch on his desk. For all his devotion to his controlling wife, there were times when the Tsar relished the opportunity of escaping to the all-male world of military HQ at Mogilev, where he could distance himself from the relentless diet of Alexandra's overweening sentiment and tedious shrewishness. The Tsar was a 'saint and an angel' in the opinion of his German brother-in-law Ernst, but he did not know how to deal with his wife – and that was his problem.

As she grew older, somewhere deep inside Alexandra there developed an earnest and sincere impulse to set herself free, to control her irritability and temper and open-heartedly warm to others, to comfort them and win their affection. But such were her high standards of what was right, moral and proper and her implacable opposition to anyone who disagreed with her that she found few people around her attractive. It was only those who were weak and suffering passively – the sick and the wounded – who, were by default unchallenging and grateful for her ministrations, in whom she could find a channel for her undoubted virtues. During the war, Alexandra's practical skills came to the fore. Despite her physical limitations, she threw herself into charity work, taking on responsibility for organising St Petersburg's hospital system, a project encompassing 85 hospitals; she set up new ones as well as rehabilitation centres for the wounded, and involved herself in women's nursing training and the supply of medicines and linen. Mindful too of the need for spiritual comfort in the field, she also concerned herself with the distribution of thousands of Bibles and psalters to the troops. In so doing she demonstrated the same deep levels of compassion for the sick and wounded that her own mother had shown before her during the Franco-Prussian War of 1870–1. Nursing provided an absorbing outlet, if not a positive therapy; it consoled Alexandra's 'aching heart'. For in it she could subsume all her frustrations and suspicious meanderings by doing something practical. From their infancy she had devotedly nursed all her children when sick and had shown the same loving vigilance at Nicholas's bedside through a serious bout of typhoid in 1900. Early in 1917 she exhausted herself nursing the children at Tsarskoe Selo when one by one they were laid low with measles. Dressed in her Red Cross uniform, dignified and courageous, whilst living in a state of continual anxiety about the safety of the children and the Tsar, who was away at the Front, Alexandra wore herself to total physical collapse in attending them as well as Anna Vyrubova, who also caught the disease. She did so again at Tobolsk during the winter of 1917–18 when all of the children except Anastasia went down with German measles. It was and remains her great redeeming quality. Count Benckendorff, who had found much of the Tsaritsa's behaviour irrational and impossible to deal with till then, was forced grudgingly to concede: 'She is great, great . . . But I had always said that she was one of those people who rise to sublime heights in the midst of misfortune.'

Somewhere between the two polarised perceptions of Alexandra – the virago and the saint – lay the real woman. But her true qualities and the depth to which she embraced her country's suffering during the war years remained hidden from the world at large. The criticism and hostility were relentless, and became increasingly vitriolic by 1916, so much so that various members of the Romanov family and the aristocracy discussed the possibility of removing her from power and putting her in a convent; even assassination was suggested. When ultimately she did lose power she did not relinquish it with her husband's effortless grace. She balked at the loss of authority, at the withdrawal of titles and acknowledgement of status. She fought tooth and nail against the daily little humiliations of being a *former* tsaritsa. But as time and her collapsing health wore on, Alexandra's profound Christian acceptance of her fate dulled her sense of outrage, and by the beginning of 1918 she had become increasingly reconciled to, if not preoccupied about the life to come. Her preparation for her own fate had begun back in January, in a prayer written on a postcard she sent from Tobolsk:

> O Lord, send us patience
> During these dark, tumultuous days
> To stand the people's persecution
> And the tortures of our executioners.

She took it all very seriously, with a strange kind of exhausted calm, assuring friends by letter that she and her family were 'readying ourselves in our thoughts for admission to the Kingdom of Heaven'.

As Nicholas and Alexandra in Ekaterinburg wearily reconciled themselves to their fate − whatever that might be − in Moscow, Count Mirbach was closely monitoring the breakdown in order and the tenuousness of Bolshevik rule. Russia, he was convinced, was 'headed for a still greater catastrophe than the one inflicted on her by the [Bolshevik] coup' of October 1917. 'We are unquestionably standing by the bedside of a dangerously ill man, who might show apparent improvement from time to time, but who is lost in the long run', he remarked. Even the coldly confident Lenin had been forced to admit to Mirbach that he was surrounded on all sides by enemies and that it was only their lack of organisation that prevented them from being a serious threat to his government. Mirbach advised the German government to consider switching support to rival political groupings in support of the restoration of a monarchy under the Tsar's younger brother Mikhail. Such however had been the success of Bolshevik deception that nobody yet knew that Mikhail had already been murdered. The cause of the Tsar himself was now hopeless, as the indifferent reaction in Russia and abroad to his frequently misreported death had shown. If the Germans chose now to throw in their lot with opposition groups, they would have to renegotiate the terms of the unpopular treaty of Brest-Litovsk and make territorial concessions. The alternative was to bolster the Bolshevik regime with large injections of money – three million marks a month by Mirbach's estimates – in order to keep them in power. It would not have taken much during the chaos in June, should Germany have so chosen, to move in and seize Petrograd and Moscow and set up a puppet government, but in the end the Kaiser had vetoed the idea.

Meanwhile, the Left Socialist Revolutionaries had raised the levels of invective against the Bolsheviks' German allies to fever pitch at the 5th Congress of Soviets. The atmosphere at the Bolshoi on 6 July had been heated, the weather outside sultry. The Left SRs, who made up about one third of the delegates, had once again been trying desperately to stir up protests against the government during debates over Russia's future domestic and foreign policy. Led by Mariya Spiridonova, they had been extremely vocal in their condemnation of Russia's humiliating reduction to Germany's vassal under the Treaty of Brest-Litovsk and denounced Lenin's government for having betrayed the Revolution to German militarism.

On the afternoon of the 6th, in an attempt to provoke the Germans into breaking the treaty or the Russians into breaking off diplomatic relations with them, the Socialist Revolutionaries struck in a plot masterminded by Spiridonova. Two of their members, Yakov Blyumkin and Nikolay Andreev, with the faked credentials of Cheka agents and secretly armed with revolvers and grenades, went to the German Embassy and asked to see Ambassador Mirbach. When Mirbach appeared, they pulled revolvers from their briefcases and in a shambolic assassination scene, after their gunshots failed to kill him, threw a grenade at him as he tried to run from the room. He died of his wounds shortly afterwards. By evening, around 1,000 Left SRs and their supporters were out on the streets in a spontaneous mass demonstration – one could hardly call it an insurrection – at a time when most of the crack Latvian Rifle Brigade guarding the Moscow garrison was on a day's leave. Had they so wished, the Left SRs could have stormed the Kremlin and taken control of the government. But these were not organised revolutionaries, and though they had ground support from the peasantry thanks to their strong agricultural policy, they lacked the structure of the Bolsheviks. They were, rather, a band of dedicated and fanatical idealists and revolutionary romantics who wished to stir the Russian masses into further action – its precise nature and objectives unclear – against Bolshevik despotism and German imperialism.

Beyond Moscow, a group of disaffected Socialist Revolutionary officers led by a former adventurer, Boris Savinkov, had organised themselves loosely into a 'Union for the Defence of the Motherland and Freedom' and sparked further insurrection in defence of the suffering nation. The Council of People's Commissars had brought ruin to Russia, they proclaimed, 'Instead of bread and peace it has brought famine and war.' Unrest broke out in a number of central Russian cities, the most serious being in Yaroslavl, 150 miles north-east of Moscow on the Volga, as well as in Murom and Samara. The local militia and Bolshevik commissars in Yaroslavl had been taken unawares by a group of army officers aided by local workers and peasants, as they were at Murom, but the success of the insurgents was short-lived. Bolshevik reinforcements soon regained Murom and Samara, and Savinkov's men were only able to hold out for two weeks in Yaroslavl before the Bolsheviks retook the city and initiated mass arrests. Three hundred and fifty 'former officers, counter-revolutionists, and White Guards' were singled out and shot in reprisal.

During the confused few hours that followed the assassination of Mirbach, in which the Left SRs dissipated their political chances, the Latvian Rifles were summoned and regrouped. Early in the morning of 7 July, they launched a counterattack against Left SR strongholds that resulted in four days of street fighting before the Bolsheviks finally crushed them. In its official statement, Lenin's government blamed the assassination of Mirbach on 'agents of Russian-Anglo-French Imperialism' and other counter-revolutionists. The Germans for their part were now demanding the right to send a battalion of infantry to Moscow to protect their embassy and their foreign nationals in Russia. Inside the Kremlin, Lenin and his colleagues resorted to frantic damage limitation, fearing German reprisals and possibly even an invasion. They also initiated a swift and brutal response to the Left SR rising. Within days, Left SRs in regional soviets all over Russia were removed from their positions; 13 of the ringleaders of the uprising in Moscow were shot without trial. Spiridonova was arrested and sent to jail. The Bolshevik government, as Lenin later admitted in a telegram to Stalin, 'had been within a hair's breadth of war'. Having mercilessly put down this opposition, Lenin resolved to tighten central political control. From now on the CEC would 'carry the burden of the Revolution alone', which meant closing ranks and imposing Communist control over all govern-ment institutions, especially the army. They now turned their attention to the threat from the Whites and the Czechs in Siberia, and to resolving how to deal once and for all with their various Romanov captives.

For now a new threat from outside was about to further exacerbate the precarious political situation in Russia. That afternoon, 5,390 miles away, at the White House in Washington, President Woodrow Wilson had finally capitulated under pressure from his British and French allies to demonstrate concrete support for the Czech legions in Russia as well as send a relief mission to the Russian people. An Allied War Council in Versailles on 2 July had called for US intervention to extend to rebuilding the failing Eastern Front and bringing the Russians back into the war against 'the Hun'. But this was a political step too far for the democratic idealist Wilson, who was reluctant to intervene in this way. Back in March he had agreed to a small, symbolic American presence at Murmansk to help protect the billion-dollar investment of American guns and equipment along the Trans-Siberian Railway sent to assist Russia in its fight against Germany. But now, with Russia out of the war on the Eastern Front, and in light of the Bolshevik government's continuing trade-off with the Germans and the unexpected military success of the Czech legions as they pressed westward, Wilson reluctantly rubber-stamped the sending of 5,000 US troops to Archangel in the north of Russia and 8,000 to Vladivostok in the Far East. He liked to think that his action was largely in support of the Czechs' romantic struggle for nationhood, but he later amended his view, hoping that the legions could become the spearhead of a powerful force for political regeneration in Russia and the inception of a new, democratic government there. American troops now on their way to Siberia would offer peaceful economic aid in support of the Russian people's right to determination in the face of the Bolshevik dictatorship. News of the advance parties that had landed in Murmansk in May and June and of a possible Allied invasion in July had had some influence in the recent Left SR revolt. In response, fearful of a major Allied intervention in Russia, the Bolsheviks now intensified their campaign of terror by means of the Cheka.

Several showers during the course of 6 July had brought a welcome coolness to the stuffy rooms on the first floor of the Ipatiev House in Ekaterinburg. The punctilious Yurovsky had that day returned a watch in a leather case belonging to Nicholas that had been found in one of the service rooms downstairs, purloined by one of the guards. A silver spoon with the Imperial crest, found in the garden where it no doubt had been hidden after being stolen, was also dutifully returned. That day's crushing boredom for the Romanovs had seen the minor diversion of two women sent by the local soviet to wash the floors of their living quarters. Nicholas was now racing through volume seven of the complete works of Mikhail Saltykov-Shchedrin; Alexandra was allowed the now rare luxury of a bath. All was in order. Life was as uneventful as ever.

But Yakov Yurovsky had other plans. For all his apparent deference to the welfare of the Romanovs, he had made an important decision. That day he replaced the old Colt machine gun at guard post no. 9 in the attic with a much faster and more efficient Maxim gun, a weapon perfected by the British during the Second Boer War that could fire 500 rounds a minute. A necessary security measure no doubt, in view of the approach of the Czechs and the still circulating rumours of rescue attempts, but a mark also of a hardening of Bolshevik resolve to keep control of a situation from which there would be no possible hope of a Romanov escape.

5

Girls in White Dresses

SUNDAY 7 JULY 1918

The Romanov family awoke to a bright, sunny day on Sunday 7 July. Indeed, such was the fineness of the weather, the air so 'nice' and 'not too hot', that for the first time in a fortnight Alexandra ventured out into the garden with everyone else. It was the one highlight of an uneventful day, but a significant one for the four Romanov sisters. The sight of their sick mother outside enjoying the sunshine for once, instead of being closeted indoors with a headache or some other ailment, must have brought joy to their hearts. For so long now Alexandra's sufferings – real and imaginary – had coloured their every waking moment. Indeed, they had never really known their mother well. 'O, if you knew, how hard Mama's illness is for us to bear', Tatiana had said plaintively in a letter to Rasputin 10 years earlier. It had been so ever since they were very young, but increasingly since the birth of their brother and the many crises in his fragile health. The painful uncertainty of being around so much unrelenting maternal suffering had taken a huge emotional toll on the young, affectionate Romanov daughters. But they were highly resourceful and had fallen back on their own strengths and profound sisterly affection. They had created their own coping mechanisms by uniting in a fierce loyalty to each other and a determination always to share the burden of attendance on their mother and sickly brother.

One after another, Olga, Tatiana, Maria and Anastasia hovered attentively over Alexandra, constantly at her beck and call, forever fearful of offending her or upsetting her fragile equilibrium. But, as growing girls, they also longed for her energy, her time, for real emotional engagement with them. Mama loved them very much; they knew that, of course. But if only she could be well and whole like other mothers – that was all they ever wanted. Yet there were many days when she did not join them at breakfast . . . or at lunch . . . or dinner. Afternoon tea was sacrosanct: the Tsaritsa liked to share it in private with her husband,

and the girls only attended if she specifically invited them. During Alexandra's frequent bouts of illness and the Tsar's inevitable pre-occupations with matters of state, they were left a great deal to their own devices, Alexandra sharing the view of many Victorian parents that her children should find their own amusements.

Such were Alexandra's absences from their view, even within the family, that the girls had often been reduced to writing plaintive little notes expressing their love, apologising for being naughty, enquiring after Mama's welfare – notes that were full of unspoken longing. There was always the hope that perhaps tomorrow they would see her not in bed but in her sitting room and that her head would not be aching. Suffering was Mama's cross, and it had to be borne without question or complaint. This was a fact that Alexandra constantly impressed upon the girls; but it meant that they too had to bear Mama's cross, their young minds filled with her morbid fatalism about endurance, duty and Christian submission.

For a brief while the Romanov sisters had had a governess, but such were Alexandra's very strict views on parenting that she had abandoned the idea, preferring instead to oversee their care and education herself with the assistance of Russian and English nursemaids and a team of tutors led by Pierre Gilliard, their French teacher. Like both their parents before them, the girls adhered to a strict schedule of study combined with physical exercise, all closely monitored and approved by Alexandra, who was insistent on imposing her own moral and religious values at all times. The girls learned to be good needlewomen, had a drawing master, a religious instructor and a teacher of mathematics. Russian language and literature were also included in their curriculum, as well as English lessons with tutor Sidney Gibbes. As a patrician Victorian parent, Alexandra did not believe in pampering her daughters: they slept on simple camp beds as their father had before them, and were taught to keep their things tidy and never sit idly but always have something to knit, sew or embroider. They were allowed limited amounts of pocket money monthly and wore each other's hand-me-downs. Their rooms contained only the most simple of furnishings, the one indulgence being the family photographs they pinned up on the walls and the many icons hung above their beds. They were trained to be indifferent to the cold; their rooms were well ventilated and they took cold baths in the morning. Warm ones followed in the evening, perfumed with the only luxury allowed them – fragrances made by Coty of Paris. Rose for Olga, jasmine for Tatiana, lilac – one of several favourites – for Maria and violet for Anastasia. As for jewellery, Alexandra presented to each daughter, on her birthday, a single pearl and a single diamond, so that by the time they reached 16 they had sufficient for one simple, plain necklace of each.

Apart from occasional trips into St Petersburg with their adored Aunt Olga on Sundays during the years 1906–14, when they had tea and enjoyed games and dancing at her house and met other young people, the girls were given very few opportunities to make friends. Their mother was of the view that most of those at court were a pernicious influence on their innocent young minds and were to be shunned; the girls therefore were only occasionally allowed to play with the children of members of the Imperial entourage. Even among their own close relatives, however, they had no real friends. But they longed for them, for the secret confidences and shared giggles that adolescent girls grow up with, as much as they did for the loving embrace and warmth of a mother who all too often was physically incapacitated or engrossed with their sickly brother. With very little protest, the Romanov sisters grew used to their isolation and the relative austerity of their lives, becoming extremely self-sufficient, turning to each other, their china dolls, their pet dogs and their treasured Box Brownie cameras. They photographed each other incessantly and shared everything. They seemed totally bonded, despite the inevitable occasional tiffs and petty rivalries for the attention of their parents, so contented in their narrow world. They were lively girls, full of energy, curious about life, always wanting to run in different directions. Yet somehow they ended up living in a bubble, which they accepted without complaint, as Count Mosolov, head of the Imperial Chancellery, observed: 'I don't honestly think that it ever entered the Grand Duchesses' heads that life could be other than it was.'

Such isolation inevitably left them all to a degree innocent for their years and thus more emotionally vulnerable. It meant that when they did have to go out into society they sometimes seemed gawky and ingenuous and tended to talk to each other like girls far younger than their years. Such was the sublimation of self within this collective of four that when the sisters sent letters to favourite tutors or relatives they often did so jointly, signing themselves 'OTMA' – the first letter of each of their names – a sign of their unity and also, perhaps, of a passive acceptance of their collective anonymity. Even in the elegant and uncontroversial way in which they posed together in publicity photographs, their identity as a group rather than individuals was reinforced once their brother was born and became the centre of attention. Their diaries too largely recorded collective activities. With the onset of puberty, there inevitably were times when the girls resisted their mother's control over their every waking thought and deed. 'They rarely understand my point of view on things, even the most trifling ones', noted Alexandra with exasperation.

'They always consider themselves right and when I tell them how I was educated and how one should be educated they cannot understand' – in other words, they were growing up and finding their own way as young women. If the Revolution had not intervened, perhaps they might at last have begun to assert their individual personalities more. But now, as prisoners in the house at Ekaterinburg, the sisters were forced in on themselves even more, in close and constant proximity to their mother's terrible physical decline and her increasingly obsessive religiosity.

But there had of course been happier days when they had seen her smile – halcyon, cloudless summer days during that final idyllic period before the Great War of 1914–18 changed the world for ever. As a family they had enjoyed many happy summers between 1904 and 1913, living out the fairy-tale life of the rich and privileged: long, hot summer holidays often in the company of their various royal cousins, as part of an extended European royal dynasty soon to be torn apart by war and revolution. Summers on the Imperial yacht sailing the fjords off the coast of Finland, or at their lovely white marble Italianate palace in Livadia were always the best of times for the Romanov sisters. In the Crimea, they lived in a virtual paradise, enjoying the subtropical climate of the Imperial estate, surrounded by pine forests, mountains and densely covered valleys, and with craggy cliffs descending to a perfect blue sea, the air thick with the scent of bougainvillea, roses and honeysuckle. Olga, the eldest, had no doubts on the matter: 'In St Petersburg we work, but at Livadia we live.' Livadia breathed life into all the family; no wonder it had been their chosen place of exile after the Revolution, a wish never to be fulfilled. For the girls, life at Livadia or on the royal yacht was such a joy: to savour the pleasures of picnics, mushroom-gathering, walks, sea-bathing, tennis parties, roller-skating, games of boules and dancing on the deck of the *Shtandart* with the yacht's lively and entertaining junior officers – it was all so magical compared to their stultifying existence at the Alexander Palace.

When they were in the Crimea, visits to their Romanov cousins at their Aunt Xenia's estate nearby at Ai-Todor also brought great pleasure. On such holidays the four young sisters were much photographed, dressed alike, as so often they were, in soft white cambrics, Brussels lace and muslins, their hair tied back in blue bows, or wearing distinctive large-brimmed summer hats decorated with lace frills or flowers. The photo opportunities were not missed for promoting these seemingly perfect, innocent young girls as archetypes of Russian feminine beauty, the modest and charming offspring of parents who lived by the pious values of Christian family life. In their simplicity, always smiling and vibrant, the Romanov sisters and their handsome young brother projected an Imperial fantasy world where the sun always shone and at the heart of which the four girls were forever young and incorruptible – the fairy companions in white to the Tsarevich's eternal Peter Pan.

At the time of the Romanov tercentenary in 1913, when the Romanov children were first publicly paraded to an adoring Russian public, the virtues of the Tsar's daughters had been much extolled – again collectively, in commemorative books such as Georgy Elchaninov's popular hagiography of the Tsar – as having been 'trained to be good and careful housewives', who took a pleasure in doing kindnesses to others and were equipped with the social graces of painting, piano playing and photography. But who were they as real people, as individuals?

The closeness in years between Olga, Tatiana, Maria and Anastasia belied a marked difference in character which the public image glossed over. There were only six years between them but it was a sufficient time span to mean that the girls naturally gravitated into two pairs, becoming known in the family as 'the big pair' and 'the little pair' and sharing bedrooms accordingly. The separation into two age groups became further accentuated once, having reached the age of 16, the older two (between whom there was only 18 months) started putting their hair up in neat ripples of marcel waves, whilst the younger girls, their hair still loosely beribboned, remained gawky and plump.

The Tsar and Tsaritsa had been delighted with Olga when she was born on 15 November 1895 – even though in the Romanov family for generations the first-born had usually been a boy. There was plenty of time yet for a son and heir. A huge, fat, bonny baby, Olga turned into rather a plain, serious little girl. But then, at 15, she suddenly became pretty. She was not a beauty like her younger sisters Tatiana and Maria, but was somehow very feminine and vulnerable. With her round face, turned-up nose ('my humble snub', as she called it), high cheekbones, light chestnut hair and blue eyes, Olga Nikolaevna Romanova was the epitome of Slavic beauty. She was never conscious of her charming looks and did not pay much attention to her appearance. From the start she was someone for whom the inner life was paramount, and it showed in her face. True, on the outside she had a gentle, timid charm and softness all her own – like that of her father, whom she most resembled. But of all the sisters she was the most serious and thoughtful – a melancholic dreamer who loved poetry and music. Unlike her father, however, she never learned to control her outbursts of sometimes violent temper and could be impetuous and capricious. Her fierce intelligence meant that sometimes she would be too outspoken in what she said, and her remarks could be wounding. Being the eldest, she was expected to set an example to the others, and as time went on she occasionally clashed with her mother and would go off into moody sulks when reprimanded. Alexandra had problems controlling her behaviour, exhorting her to 'try to be an example of what a good little obedient girlie ought to be' for her younger sisters. But Olga found it hard to toe the line and as she grew older sought to assert her independence, tending to separate off into her own inner world. There was always, from a young age, a deep, sometimes lost expression on her face, and as the years went on it became ever more marked in the photographs taken of her.

One might say that her high domed forehead was an indicator of her cleverness and natural wit. Of all the sisters she was the most shrewd and intellectually mature. She was quick to learn – an accomplished pianist, good at languages, an avid reader. And she was utterly devoted to her father. There was nothing Olga loved better than to go for long walks with him whenever the opportunity arose, often clutching him tightly by the arm; she also frequently accompanied him to church, sitting close to him. There is no doubt that she, of all the Romanov children, was the one most aware of the cruelty and injustice in the world outside. After she reached the age of 20, when she was allowed access to her considerable fortune (bequeathed to his grandchildren by Alexander III), she regularly made donations to the poor and sick. She seemed deeply troubled by the plight of Russia after the outbreak of war and then revolution in 1917. She was highly sensitive to her father's position; she read the papers regularly and could not understand why the feeling in the country had so turned against him. In 1915, with her mother and sister Tatiana, she took up nursing training and worked with the wounded. But Olga could not handle the stress and anguish of it all, nor the sight of her mother wearing herself to exhaustion, and was forced to take lighter duties. Her health declined during the war years; she became thin and pale, suffering from anaemia and bouts of depression. She was clearly worried about the family's tenuous future after they were sent to Tobolsk; on leaving the Governor's House she told Baroness von Buxhoeveden that they were lucky to be still alive and reunited with their parents once more. Now, at Ekaterinburg, even the guards noticed how sad and tired she looked for most of the time and how, during exercise periods in the garden, she kept herself apart, her melancholy gaze fixed on the distance.

By any normal royal standards of the day, Olga should have long since been married off. But in matters emotional and sexual she was still an innocent at 22. Her mother had tortured herself pondering the future: 'Oh if only our children could be as happy in their married life', she wrote to Nicholas. The couple were acutely aware of how fortunate they were to have had a love match, and it is hard to believe that Alexandra

(*Above left*) The young married couple: Alexandra, poised and unsmiling, as always in official portraits; Nicholas in civvies, circa 1895

(*Above right*) Girls in white dresses: the Romanov sisters in a photograph mass-produced for public consumption in 1915. From back left, Maria, Anastasia and Olga; Tatiana is seated

The Imperial Family shortly after the birth of Alexey, 1904: Tatiana, her mother's favourite, leans against Alexandra, Olga clutches her adored father's arm, Maria is front left, and Anastasia right

The man with the cigarette: Nicholas II doing what he liked best, relaxing on his yacht, the *Shtandart*

The woman in a wheelchair: Alexandra, crippled by sciatica, at the Alexander Palace at Tsarskoe Selo, spring 1917

A 1916 photograph that captures Alexandra's obsessive, domineering influence over her husband

'The handsome twins': cousins Nicholas II and George, Prince of Wales at Cowes in 1909 with Edward (later briefly Edward VIII) left, and the Tsarevich Alexey – the eternally appealing boy in the sailor suit

Alexey at Army HQ in 1916, with his cat and spaniel Joy. The dog survived the massacre at Ekaterinburg and ended its days at Windsor

Alexandra, centre, with Olga, left, and Tatiana, right, and some of the Russian wounded in their care during the First World War. Maria and Anastasia, far left and far right, were still too young to nurse

Members of the Czech Legion standing by the obelisk outside Ekaterinburg that marked the border between Europe and Asia

Dr Evgeny Botkin, who loyally followed the Romanovs into exile

The Ipatiev House, with the palisade erected just before the Tsar and Tsaritsa's arrival on 30 April

Nikolay Ipatiev's study, taken over as the Commandant's office by Avdeev, and later Yurovsky. The guards dossed down here between shifts

The gloomy dining room where the Romanovs shared frugal meals with their remaining servants

Ekaterinburg in the 1900s. The northern end of the Ipatiev House is in the front left-hand corner, with the river Iset snaking around the city

A 1900s view showing the bell tower of the Voznesensky Cathedral, from which a machine gun was trained on the Romanovs' rooms

would have been prepared to sacrifice her daughters to dynastic or political expediency, as her grandmother Queen Victoria had done. Writing in 1915, Alexandra intimated her anxieties for her eldest child: 'I look at our big Olga, my heart fills with emotion and wondering as to what is in store for her – what her lot will be.' Rumours of suitable dynastic alliances with the Greek, Serbian and Romanian royal houses had begun circulating once Olga had reached the age of 16 in 1911, on which occasion she had enjoyed her coming-out ball – the only real ball ever organised specially for the two eldest girls. In 1912 there had been talk of her marrying her father's cousin Dimitry, but Alexandra had vetoed the idea after she heard tales of his unacceptable private life. For a few months at the end of 1913 Olga had had a crush on Pavel Voronov, a junior officer on the *Shtandart*. But of course there was never any future in a relationship with a commoner, and that December Pavel became engaged to a lady-in-waiting. Finally, in the autumn of 1913, she was introduced to Crown Prince Karol of Romania, when the Imperial yacht made a royal visit to Constanta. Olga did not warm to him and refused point blank any suggestion of marriage. She would never leave Russia or convert from Orthodoxy: 'I am a Russian and I wish to remain Russian', she said most emphatically, and nothing would change her mind. Karol, as it turned out, preferred the prettier Tatiana, but failed to impress her with his coarse and tactless behaviour. Finding a suitable husband of sufficiently high status for Olga within Russia, let alone for three more daughters (who may well have shared their sister's feelings), would have been even more problematic once the Russian Grand Dukes had all been discounted. Meanwhile Olga continued to fall for the most obvious candidates with whom she came into contact during the war years – the wounded soldiers in her care.

There is no doubt that a high-calibre union would eventually have been the lot of the second Romanov daughter, Tatiana, born on 11 June 1897. She was a picture-book beauty and perfect bride material for the dynastic matchmakers of Europe. Taller even than her mother, willowy and with a tiny waist, she was the most elegant and 'aristocratic' looking of the four sisters and exuded a sense of her status from head to toe. People often remarked that she behaved 'like the daughter of an emperor'. Confident in her beauty, with a fixed, almost challenging expression in her eyes, Tatiana could look effortlessly imperious. Her profile was exquisite; with her pale, almost marble skin, lovely dark chestnut hair and a slightly mystical, Asiatic look about her wide, tipped-up dark grey eyes, she was naturally photogenic. She loved clothes and carried them with grace and elegance, as well as a slightly coquettish air. But she was very much her mother's daughter: reserved, inscrutable, less open and spontaneous than her sisters and less inclined to smile. The guards at the Ipatiev House had sometimes found her 'stuck up'; she would often throw disapproving looks at them when confronted with their uncouth behaviour, though when she smiled her disarming smile in order to ask a favour of some kind, it was a quite different matter.

By nature Tatiana was a romantic idealist and a dreamer, but she never let this get in the way of her very practical talents and her sense of balance, which meant she was very focused and at times opinionated about what she wanted. Although younger than Olga she was the more forceful of the two, and her elder sister frequently deferred to her judgement. For Tatiana's fragile features and figure belied a physical strength and energy that she constantly applied around the home and in organisational skills. She had natural gifts as a housekeeper and decision-maker, as well as being good at handicrafts. Her mother came to rely on her heavily as friend, nurse and adviser, ready to take responsibility for her younger siblings when she was sick or indisposed. Yurovsky found her by far 'the most mature' of the four girls and their natural leader, who often came to his office requesting one thing or another on behalf of the family. She was always ready to do what was asked of her and would persevere to get it right, so much so that her sisters nicknamed her 'the governor' for her purposefulness.

It was crystal clear to everyone that Tatiana was her mother's favourite daughter, and slavishly devoted to her, even though she had a knack too for winning her father's favour when needed. Despite this, there is, in her childhood letters to her mother, written begging forgiveness of 'deary' (such an oddly grown-up term for a child to use to a parent) for some minor misdemeanour or other, an air of heightened anxiety. She lived in fear of her mother's disapproval and was desperate for her love and time, and so learned to pander to Alexandra's moods and demands. She willingly became the 'conduit of all her mother's decisions' and therefore more readily than all the others inculcated Alexandra's superstition and religiosity and was quick to mouth her platitudes.

Poor little Maria. Everyone inwardly groaned when she was born on 27 June 1899, including her grandmother, the Dowager Empress, regretting 'the 3rd girl for the country'. The Dowager knew, as did the royal couple themselves only too well, that 'an heir would be more welcome than a daughter'. But Mashka, as she was affectionately called in the family, soon won everybody's hearts. She was enchantingly pretty in a very rounded Russian way, with a glowing peaches-and-cream complexion, a full mouth, and lustrous thick light-brown hair. Beneath the finely shaped sable eyebrows shone out the biggest, most luminous grey-blue eyes. Everyone remarked on them and it earned them the nickname of 'Maria's saucers'. She was not particularly bright at her studies but had a wonderful gift for painting in watercolours. She had a tendency to be clumsy and earned herself another playful family nickname – 'fat little bow wow' (*le bon gros tutu*). Modest, placid and biddable, Maria allowed her younger sister Anastasia, to whom she was devoted, to rule her. Of all the sisters she was the most natural earth mother, having the voluptuous broad-boned figure to match and possessed of a truly loving heart. No doubt she would have been one of the first of the sisters to marry and would have made a fine mother, for she loved little children and had an instinctive way with them. She exuded good health and energy and seemed easily contented with very little, having had no complaints about the family's quiet life at Tobolsk. Indeed she had told the commandant there, Vasily Pankratov, that the family now was healthier and more physically active and useful than during all its years at court.

Because of her natural nurturing skills, Maria was the one who most often remained indoors with her ailing mother when the others went outside – 'my legs', as the Tsaritsa so often called her. She had been the obvious choice to accompany Alexandra as carer when she and Nicholas travelled on ahead to Ekaterinburg, and she was equally patient and attentive with her brother. Maria was a stoic; she had tremendous reserves of energy and was strong enough to carry Alexey when needed. But there were times, when younger, when she had suffered bouts of insecurity and anxiety as the third daughter and had felt unloved. Perhaps it had been her mother's increasing preoccupation with her own ills and Alexey's that had prompted her more and more to seek conversation and company among the guards who surrounded the family – first at Tsarskoe Selo, and later at Tobolsk and Ekaterinburg. Gauche and naïve, she was an innocent abroad in the company of men. Sometimes her flirtatious, skittish behaviour provoked unwarranted innuendo from the guards in their responses; sexual curiosity was a dangerous thing in girls such as the Romanovs who had been so little prepared for the real world outside. And it bubbled under the surface the more they grew and experienced the normal hormonal changes of adolescence and the longer they had no other male company than the guards surrounding them. The men of the Special Detachment at the Ipatiev House clearly liked Maria best of all the family: she had a natural openness and a lovely smile. Even Yurovsky later remarked that her 'sincere, modest character' had impressed them all. And she truly enjoyed being with ordinary people, talking to them about their lives, their homes and children; she even showed the guards her photograph albums. Her open flirtation with the guards brought consequences of which the details are very sketchy, but it is clear that in the final weeks at Ekaterinburg her mother and eldest sister froze her out

for her behaviour. From the outset Alexandra had strongly disapproved
of Maria's fraternisation with the Ipatiev House guards and constantly
whispered sharp admonitions to her, but at the age of 19 Maria, by now
aware of her own sexuality and attractiveness, was only behaving as most
girls of her age would have done, lacking as she did her youngest sister's
boyish disinterest in men.

The day that the long-suffering Alexandra struggled to give birth, on
18 June 1901, to yet another large baby – and yet another girl – Nicholas
lit a cigarette and took off on a long walk around the park at Tsarskoe
Selo. 'My Lord! What a disappointment!' his sister Xenia wrote in her
diary. Master of self-concealment that he was, Nicholas managed not to
show his true feelings and grew to love his impish, wayward fourth
daughter as much as all the others.

It was clear from very early on that Anastasia would be the wild child
of the family. Although the youngest daughter, she compensated for this
by being by far the most forceful and outward-going. She was far less
subservient to parental control or sisterly anonymity, inhabiting her own
self-created world of imaginary friends, monsters and comical characters.
Such was Anastasia's irrepressible curiosity and vivacity that her Aunt
Olga, the Tsar's sister, called her *schwipsig* (a German affectionate
expression meaning 'merry little one'). And it stuck, the name being as
quirky as the girl herself: awkward, obstreperous, noisy, unconventional.
Her love of life was so infectious that it forever redeemed her endless acts
of naughtiness, though there were times when she could be rough and
spiteful during games with other children – a fact complained about by
some of her Romanov cousins.

Perhaps of all the sisters Anastasia would have been destined for a less
conventional life: she always took risks and looked on everything as an
adventure. An out-and-out tomboy, she was vigorously active, ignoring
the warnings to take care of her weak back and climbing trees with the
best of the boys. She had inherited the cornflower-blue eyes of the
Romanovs, just like her father. Shorter than her sisters, she lacked their
natural grace and became lumpy and awkward after the onset of puberty.
The family found another nickname for her: *kubyshka* ('dumpling'); even
at the Ipatiev House, despite the rationing, she was often described as
being chubby. Indeed everything about Anastasia was ungracious and
unconventional, down to her deportment, which lacked the elegance of
a Russian Grand Duchess and is evident in group photographs with her
far more dignified sisters. But some could see the beautiful girl she would
one day become once the puppy fat was gone.

Anastasia's mercurial nature meant she was constantly restless; she
wanted to grasp life by the throat and hated sitting at her studies. Her

thoughts were so chaotic and undisciplined that she found it impossible to concentrate, even when writing a letter – those to her father are full of quirky humorous expressions and private jokes shared between them, reflecting an unconventional personality. 'I just grasp at whatever enters my noddle', as she wrote in May 1918.

Anastasia might have been a poor student, but she did not lack natural intelligence, and Sidney Gibbes, who found her too unpredictable and a nightmare to teach, was nevertheless impressed by her self-possession and her bright and happy disposition. A tease and a brilliant mimic, Anastasia employed her natural intelligence in the observation of others: she watched and absorbed the physical idiosyncrasies and speech mannerisms of those around her, keeping everyone amused with her comical voices and grimaces through the long freezing winter in the draughty Governor's House at Tobolsk, performing in amateur theatricals and doing circus tricks with Tatiana's dog Jimmy. She was absolutely fearless and refused to be cowed by misfortune and the restrictions of imprisonment. Even at Ekaterinburg she remained irrepressible: she would poke her tongue out at Yurovsky behind his back and entertain the guards with her pratfalls and practical jokes. Perhaps her subversive humour was a defence mechanism, a cover for her own inner unease and apprehension. Perhaps it was a mark of something deeper, more altruistic. Her Aunt Olga always said that Anastasia had a heart of gold, and in her own free-spirited way she worked hard to dissipate the fears and anxieties of those around her. Whilst her eldest sister Olga had long since capitulated and retreated within herself, bold, brave Anastasia remained always on the offensive. Of all the sisters, Yurovsky noticed that she seemed the one best adjusted to their confinement.

During all their years largely closeted from the world at the Alexander Palace, the Romanov sisters had been trapped in a kind of time warp, but the war years and an increasing responsibility for their mother, as well as their sick brother, after Nicholas had left for the Front in August 1915, had brought with them a sudden and cruel awakening into the real world. Now, one of the girls always slept with their mother in her room – Mama was not strong, they could not leave her alone. And then at Mama's instigation 'the big pair', Olga and Tatiana, had undertaken nurses' training, whilst 'the little pair' had been recruited into charitable work and visiting hospitals for the wounded. The war and then the Revolution had finally, to differing degrees, made women of them – courageous, dignified and mutually supportive in the face of adversity. Their uncle, Grand Duke Alexander, had seen Olga and Tatiana that last winter of 1916–17 in their Red Cross uniforms and their nurses' wimples, looking so plain and serious, their faces drawn.

And now, at the Ipatiev House, the four girls were being forced increasingly to contemplate their own suffering and the family's uncertain future. They worked hard at concealing their apprehensions from each other and at lifting everyone's flagging spirits. Their clothes were worn, their famously long glossy hair grown back barely to chin length – their heads had all been shaved in the spring of 1917 when they had been recovering from measles – and they were now far from being the idealised girls in white dresses of the Imperial publicity machine. Olga in particular seemed so much older and troubled, 'like the sad young heroine of a Turgenev novel with the eyes of a gazelle'. Baroness von Buxhoeveden, who had travelled with her as far as Ekaterinburg in mid-May, had noted even then how the 'lovely, bright girl of 22' had become 'a faded and sad middle-aged woman'. Yet even so, some of the guards were moved by the sisters. Aleksandr Strekotin thought 'there was something very special about them', even in their old and tattered clothes, something 'especially sweet'. He thought that they would not have looked better 'even if they had been covered in gold and diamonds'.

That last Christmas at Tobolsk in 1917 the girls had put on a brave face for their parents' sake, but seven months later, in Ekaterinburg, they were still incarcerated, with no sight at all of the outside world and hopes fading of ever seeing their beloved Livadia again. Olga seems to have welcomed with quiet calm what she, in her profound religious faith, believed – that passive acceptance was the only answer. It was what their parents had taught all of them – to turn the other cheek – which perhaps explains why the sisters remained quiet and uncomplaining, watching out for their mother and brother and constantly buoying each other up through the monotony and sometimes despair of their lives with false bonhomie and mutual protectiveness. In the absence of any physical ability to escape their situation, love was the last and only defence the family had. And it did not take much: only a moment of sympathy or commiseration from the guards, one of them later said, for the girls to recover their equilibrium and smile.

But how many times must those four sisters – aged 22, 21, 19 and 17 – have sat and stared at the whited-out windows, wishing they could see the world beyond once more. They had sat for hours on the window ledges at Tobolsk watching people pass by, smiling and waving. But now the Russia they all loved so passionately was out of sight, a distant blank, and their future with it. That evening, 7 July 1918, as a violent storm broke outside and washed the dust of summer from the city's streets and shook the already yellowing leaves from the trees in the Ipatiev House garden, all the Romanov daughters could do was sit and listen to the rain and wonder, perhaps, as Chekhov's three sisters did when faced with an uncertain future in a provincial backwater, 'Why do we live? Why do we suffer? If only we knew . . . if only.'

In his untidy, smoke-filled office across the hallway, the new commandant of the Ipatiev House, Yakov Yurovsky, knew only too well what the future held for the four Romanov sisters. He had now completed arrangements to replace the friendly but increasingly untrustworthy internal guard of workers from the local factories with men of his own choosing – hand-picked from the Ekaterinburg Cheka. From now on, the younger three girls, Tatiana, Maria and Anastasia would even be denied the casual conversations and flirtations that had alleviated the agonising boredom of their lives. A wall of silence was about to descend and the screw to be turned ever tighter on their isolation.

6

The Boy in the Sailor Suit

MONDAY 8 JULY 1918

W hen the Romanovs emerged to use the bathroom and lavatory on the morning of 8 July, they found themselves confronted by a group of strangers. 'Inside the house new Latvians are standing guard', Nicholas noted in his diary. The cool of the showery early morning was matched by a new and chilly atmosphere inside. These shadowy new figures would from now on be overseeing the family's life at the Ipatiev House, along with the three remaining senior internal guards from Avdeev's original detachment from the Sysert works – Anatoly Yakimov, Konstantin Dobrynin and Ivan Starkov. These three, however, were now designated to guard the hallway area and no longer had the run of the Romanov's rooms. That was now the province only of Yurovsky's men.

Yurovsky had requested the new guards be chosen by the local Cheka from the volunteer battalions at the Verkh–Isetsk factory; he had to have men who were dedicated Bolsheviks and who could be relied on to do whatever was asked of them. The new guards therefore had been hired on the understanding that they would be prepared, if necessary, to execute the Tsar, about which they were sworn to secrecy. Nothing at this stage was said about killing the rest of the family. In order to prevent a repetition of the fraternisation that had occurred under Avdeev, Yurovsky had ensured a further emotional distance between the guards and their charges by choosing mainly foreigners, hence Nicholas describing them as 'Letts' – a term commonly used in Russia to define someone of European, non-Russian origin. The only Russians among them were Viktor Netrebin, an 18-year-old from the Verkh–Isetsk factory who had already fought against the Whites under Dutov, and the brothers Mikhail and Alexey Kabanov, the latter a former soldier in the Imperial Guards.

Adolf Lepa, the leader of the new guards, was Lithuanian; a man called Jan Tsel'ms (or Tsal'ms; in English sources often transliterated misleadingly as Soames), who was, according to Yurovsky, probably Latvian, had been recruited from a Latvian communist rifle detachment that had arrived in Ekaterinburg at the end of June. The remaining foreigner, Andras Verhas, was, like Yurovsky's household servant Rudolf Lacher, an Austro-Hungarian prisoner of war. Verhas and Lacher, like many of their kind, had been forcibly conscripted into the Bolshevik war effort and sent to work in the munitions factories of the Urals; Lacher had been sent from the Verkh-Isetsk factory to the Ipatiev House during Avdeev's tenure, to assist in various household duties, such as keeping the samovars filled, and had stayed on.

Yurovsky was intent on keeping his new special guards close at hand and under his thumb. He treated them as equals and often spoke to them in German. He moved Avdeev's old internal guard members, except for Lacher, out of their quarters in the basement of the Ipatiev House and into the Popov House across the street, and the new men took over their billet, eating their meals upstairs in the commandant's room. Yet, extraordinarily, one afternoon soon afterwards, when out exercising in the garden, Olga recognised one of the new guards – Alexey Kabanov. Had he not been in one of her father's Guards regiments? Kabanov grudgingly conceded it was so but he did not tell her he was now assigned to man the new Maxim machine gun in the attic.

The arrival of the new guards would have fascinated the ever-curious Alexey, a boy whose inability to run from room to room like other children was compensated for by a capacity to watch and take in everything going on around him in great detail.

The whole focus and dynamic of the Romanov family had shifted dramatically when, at 1.15 p.m. on Friday 30 July 1904, Nicholas and Alexandra's fifth child had been born. At last the family had been 'visited by the grace of God', Nicholas wrote in his diary. He had answered his and his wife's years of fervent prayers and had sent a son as comfort 'in time of sore trials', Russia then being in the midst of a disastrous war with Japan.

In St Petersburg, a 301-gun salute sent the news of the birth of an heir to the throne thundering across the city as the Tsar, his mother and his daughters headed for church and a great Te Deum of thanks. Across Russia, church bells rang out all day long celebrating the news. Eleven days later the baby was taken in a gilded state coach drawn by six plumed white horses to his christening at the palace of Peterhof, his escort a phalanx of Chevaliers-Gardes in white and a detachment of scarlet-coated Cossacks. Lying on a cushion of cloth of silver like some sacred offering, Alexey was ceremoniously carried into the church by the Mistress of the Robes, Princess Maria Golitsyn. The Imperial Court had assembled in all their finery – the men in full dress uniforms and medals, the women in traditional Russian *kokoshka* headdresses and long gowns of silver and gold brocade encrusted with jewels – for a four-hour ceremony presided over by Metropolitan Anthony of St Petersburg. As an act of gratitude Nicholas had abolished corporal punishment in the army and navy. Far away in Manchuria, where Russia was fighting the Japanese, the entire Russian army was named as the baby's godfather. The little Tsarevich was given the name Alexey – after Alexey Mikhailovich, the meek and mild tsar who had reigned in the seventeenth century – as a mark of Romanov hopes for reconciliation between tsar and state. But others shook their heads and saw the name as foreboding; it was an unlucky name. According to a seventeenth-century prophecy, the Romanov dynasty would end with an Alexey as heir.

The Tsaritsa had no doubts that she had redeemed herself in the eyes of her husband, her God and her adoptive nation by finally producing a son and heir. Her many prayers to the early nineteenth-century mystic St Serafim of Sarov for a miracle had borne fruit; her years of religious devotion and self-castigation, of pain and sorrow at being vilified by the court – all that was behind her. Now the nation would love her at last. Her son Alexey came into the Romanov family's lives as a ray of hope, a 'Sunbeam' as she called him. He was her 'Baby', and forever after, even when he was an adolescent, that would be the pet name she would call him by.

But then, on 8 September, only six weeks after Alexey's birth, the Romanov family's world imploded and Alexandra's delirious joy turned to implacable grief. Her baby started bleeding from the navel. It was the first unmistakable sign of the deadly condition of haemophilia – passed down unwittingly in the female line from Alexandra's grandmother Queen Victoria to the royal houses of Germany, Spain and Russia. Privately, Nicholas and Alexandra were advised of the truth, but there would be no public pronouncements, not ever. Although the Imperial physicians understood something of the nature of haemophilia, science had yet to explain the realities of the defective gene that transmitted the condition, or its physiology, and it was 1936 before a clotting agent was developed to control the bouts of bleeding. The Tsarevich's life-threatening condition would therefore be a closely guarded secret, even within the extended Romanov family. A pall of gloom descended over the royal couple and courtiers became afraid to smile in their presence, conducting themselves as though in a house where someone had died. Nicholas and Alexandra thereafter were forced to carry their grief over their son's condition hidden inside them, for nothing could be said that might undermine his eventual ascent to the throne or indicate that he was in any way physically unfit to rule. But this also meant that all their hopes of regaining the nation's sympathy and affection through the public promotion of their beautiful son after the debacle of the war with Japan and the political damage of the 1905 Revolution had to be sacrificed. The Tsarevich was too frail to parade in public and sooner or later people would have noticed that something serious was wrong with him.

It was, for Alexandra, yet another terrible cross to bear; there might briefly have been the suggestion that she try for another son, but she was worn out with childbirth and the strain of another pregnancy might well have killed her. Perversely the slings and arrows life threw at her – even this terrible burden of grief over her only son – gave her something to live for. It was all part of the necessary road towards· self-perfection through suffering, and ultimate redemption. And so she enveloped Alexey in a suffocating cocoon of love and the family withdrew to the protective bubble of their palace at Tsarskoe Selo. At Alexandra's behest, the walls of the Imperial nursery and even baby Alexey's cradle were festooned with icons and religious images; day by day her increasingly sickly fanaticism about her son's health grew.

But how could such an enchanting, elfish child be so sick? For those who did not know the truth, Alexey seemed the epitome of the beautiful baby, with a great tumble of golden-brown curls as a toddler that turned auburn as he grew up. Like his father, he had the most expressive eyes, blue-grey, set in a finely chiselled narrow face, and they grew even bigger and more plaintive when overtaken by pain and suffering.

From the moment he was able to crawl and then walk, the Tsarevich's life was highly circumscribed. Although small cuts could be controlled by tight bandaging and the application of pressure, such was the life-threatening nature of Alexey's condition that any minor knock to his joints could set in train copious internal bleeding because of the absence in his blood of the essential clotting factor to control it. This was further undermined by a genetic weakness of the veins and arteries that made them rupture easily. Under the surface of the skin the blood would accumulate in the joints, causing inflammation of the vascular membrane surrounding them and creating large swellings that turned the skin purple. The swellings would press on the nerves and cause shooting pains so excruciating that Alexey would not be able to sleep for days on end. Each attack also brought with it irreversible degradation of the tissues and cartilage around the joint, causing lameness for weeks after; his left leg was particularly badly affected. This meant that he would never be able to ride a bicycle, climb trees, play tennis with his sisters and father, or indulge in any of the normal boyish rough games. He might be able to sit on a pony and be led around, but he would never be able to gallop off at will, and even the simplest of activities like climbing in and out of a rowing boat had to be carefully monitored in case he slipped and banged himself. It meant that such playmates as he had had to be closely vetted and watched in order to ensure their games were not too rough. Even though Klementy Nagorny, from the Imperial Navy, and Andrey Derevenko, a boatman on the royal yacht the *Shtandart*, were assigned as Alexey's full-time *dyadki* ('uncles') when he was five, Alexandra found it hard to trust her son's safety to anyone. She constantly watched over him. One young princess remembered being invited to the palace and how she was forbidden to play any games where Alexey might fall. Sometimes the Tsar would lift one or other of them on to his back for a 'horse-ride' round the room, but the Tsaritsa would always be there, hovering protectively in the doorway, watching, waiting, anticipating disaster.

Such constant cosseting by Alexandra and the fussing round him of four loving sisters, all of whom allowed him to get away with naughtiness that would never be countenanced in a normal child, inevitably combined to create a little boy who was insufferably spoilt. Alexey was suffocated by so much female affection; he had a naturally boisterous nature that he found hard to contain. So instead acquired a taste for infantile pranks, such as head-butting people and crawling under tables and pulling off the shoes of lady courtiers. He derided his sailor attendant Derevenko as 'fatty' and was frequently bad-mannered and disruptive at table, licking his plate and rolling bread into pellets and throwing it at people. His childish and wilful behaviour was the despair of his tutors at times, and even his exasperated father dubbed him 'Alexey the Terrible', though with the tongue-in-cheek pride of a doting parent, confiding in his quaintly affected English to a British officer one day, 'Lor, he does love ragging.'

Alexandra tried half-heartedly to suppress her son's capriciousness, but it was only to his father's authority that Alexey ever capitulated. For while he had clearly inherited his mother's streak of imperiousness and was aware of his regal importance thanks to her constant reminders, he had a natural charm and empathy like his father that often shone through. He was a bright, inquisitive child with a quirky originality of thought that was never exploited, for his studies were frequently interrupted by attacks of haemophilia and his natural intelligence, when he did get down to his books, was dissipated by a lack of concentration. In one respect, however, he did outstrip his sisters; thanks to Pierre Gilliard's diligent tuition Alexey learned to speak much better French than the girls and prided himself on being able to write notes to his father in that language. But like his sister Anastasia, whom he adored, he did not enjoy being sedentary and was always restless, preferring to be out of doors, playing games with his pet animals – a King Charles spaniel called Joy to which he was devoted, an elderly donkey called Vanka and a cat called Zubrovka; he also had a very good ear for music and was a gifted balalaika player.

Meanwhile, for Alexandra, her son's fragile health had become a daily crusade, a battle for the Tsarevich's survival and with it that of the dynasty. It changed her irrevocably, opening the door wide to the pernicious influences of every faith-healer, soothsayer, clairvoyant, charlatan, and miracle-worker who came offering a cure. Not the least among them was the 'holy man' Rasputin, whose appearance in 1905 and the Tsaritsa's subsequent dependence on him set the doomed dynasty on its final one-way path to vilification and eventual annihilation. Trapped in a perpetual state of denial that her son was doomed to die young, Alexandra became hostage to endless self-torment for having been the unwitting conduit of his condition. Her escalating desperation, bordering on hysteria, to find a miracle 'cure' meant she was perfectly primed to embrace Rasputin's powers as a *bozhii chelovek* – a man of God and healer. When Alexey had attacks of bleeding, Rasputin demonstrated an uncanny ability to calm, if not mentally 'tranquillise' him through the medium of hypnotism or autosuggestion of some kind, thus slowing down the bleeding by lowering the stress that raises blood pressure. No one could explain Rasputin's power except the Tsaritsa; she put it all down to God's intervention, and thus she would defend the man she called 'Our Friend' as her son's last hope to the bitter end, no matter what odium it brought on her and the monarchy. She refused to listen to tales of Rasputin's lasciviousness, drunkenness and womanising, or accusations about his meddling in political matters, at the risk of alienating her last few friends and closest relatives. As for the Tsar, he capitulated to his wife's neurotic dependency on the man and kept his reservations about Rasputin to himself: 'Better one Rasputin than ten fits of hysterics a day' had been his weary comment.

The Tsarevich's haemophilia inevitably also transformed the lives of his four adoring sisters, pushing them irrevocably into the background in their mother's heart, for Alexey now consumed her every waking concern. It fell to the Romanov girls to take on the role of carers and watchers – over both their brother and their increasingly sick mother. There were many times when both would be laid up in bed – Alexandra with one of her vast array of complaints; Alexey with bouts of haemorrhage and swelling to the joints. Physical suffering was now a constant in the Romanov household, and with it came the unending apprehension of what might happen to Alexey when he next had an attack. For when they came, there was little anyone could do for the suffering boy other than administer ice packs to counter the pain and his raging temperature, and sit and talk and amuse him in any way they could in order to distract him, his parents having vetoed the used of morphine. To compensate, Alexandra would sit for long hours by Alexey's bedside, stroking his head and kissing him, tormented by the child's pitiful groans as his body contorted in spasms of pain. For the boy, his mother became the constant light in his moments of darkness, just as he was the 'Sunbeam' who had brought light into hers.

Through it all Alexey suffered his debilitating condition with extraordinary stoicism and never dwelled self-pityingly on it. He developed a precocious wisdom and dignity uncanny for his age, and this, combined with his transparent sympathy when confronted with the suffering of others, redeemed his often monstrously spoilt behaviour. But there were times when the face of the child seemed too old for its years, too exposed already to too much suffering. Yet for all that, Alexey's simple, childlike acceptance of his own mortality remained uncoloured by his mother's prevailingly morbid obsession with sickness and death. Whilst Alexandra could never face up to the possibility of her son's death, Alexey himself lived his life fully aware that it could at any time be snatched from him. But it did not stop him from wanting to take risks and be like other boys. At times, such was his restlessness at being so restricted that he seemed almost deliberately to challenge his body by taking physical risks, sliding down stairs on silver salvers, climbing on tables, jumping in and out of baths and boats, tumbling in the snow when he knew he shouldn't. At other times, when sick, he became thoughtful and contemplative and would lie outdoors on a couch, watching the birds and staring up at the sky, commenting that he 'liked to think and wonder' and enjoy the sun in case his health should one day prevent it. One day, when he became Tsar, he was determined that 'nobody would be poor or unfortunate'. He wanted everybody to be happy, as he himself inherently was.

The obverse of the doom and gloom around the palace when Alexey was sick was the transformative power of his good health when he did enjoy it, and he was often fortunate enough to do so for months at a time. When the Tsarevich was well, as Pierre Gilliard observed, everything and everybody at Tsarskoe Selo 'seemed bathed in sunshine'. Alexey would take centre stage as the adorable, happy boy in a sailor suit – innocent, vibrant and lovable, Russia's great hope for the future.

But the realists in the Imperial entourage, such as the Tsar's physician Dr Evgeny Botkin, were doubtful that the boy would ever live to become Tsar. They did their best for him, administering regular massage and electrotherapy during the prolonged enforced periods of rest that followed attacks, which left his leg muscles weak and atrophied. But sooner or later they anticipated his premature death. In October 1912 in Bialoveza in Poland, Alexey cheated it by a whisper. Showing off in front of his attendant Derevenko one day by jumping into a sunken bath, he stumbled and hit his groin. The ensuing swelling seemed to go down, but two weeks later when out with his mother for a carriage ride at the family's hunting lodge at Spala, the jolts of the road caused him to cry out with pain in his back and stomach. A haemorrhage in his upper left thigh had spread, with blood from the injury seeping into his abdomen, the pressure of the swelling on the nerves of his leg causing agonising pain. Huddled on his side with his left leg drawn tightly up against his body, Alexey shrieked as the spasms came and went, his cries reverberating along the dark, damp corridors of the wooden hunting lodge. His temperature rocketed to 40 degrees; as the days wore on, he became too exhausted even to cry but simply moaned and kept repeating 'O Lord have mercy upon me'. Thinking their son was dying, Nicholas and Alexandra capitulated to Alexey's pitiful pleas for help and finally allowed the administering of morphine. With Alexey hovering between life and death, on 8 October the first of several official communiqués was released to the public about his perilous condition. Prayers were said across Russia and a flood of letters, telegrams and icons arrived praying for Alexey's recovery.

For 11 days Alexandra refused to leave her son's bedside, rarely taking time to rest or eat and only occasionally allowing the Tsar to replace her. Privately, Nicholas wept for his son, his only way of dealing with the situation being to internalise his grief and carry on hunting. For four days Alexey drifted in and out of delirium; at one lucid moment entreating his mother in a whisper, 'when I am dead build me a little monument of stones in the wood'. A priest administered the last rites and the whole of the Imperial entourage at Spala held their breath. As a last desperate act Alexandra begged Anna Vyrubova to send a telegram to Rasputin in Siberia. The message came back that the doctors should not attempt to intervene; 'the little one will not die'. Within an hour the crisis was over and the haemorrhaging stopped. The combined medical specialists of Russia were baffled: they could find no explanation for this spontaneous recovery. So severe had been the attack that Alexey, now painfully thin and pale, was kept in bed for a month. He was not able to walk again properly for a year and had to have a metal brace fitted to his leg to prevent him becoming permanently lame. For Alexandra, Spala was final vindication of her faith in Rasputin, the absolute, incontrovertible proof she needed to silence his critics. She would not tolerate a word said against him thereafter – by anybody, including her own sister, Ella, whose words of warning about Rasputin's destructive influence prompted Alexandra to turn her back on her for ever.

Alexey's slow recovery after the attack at Spala meant that during the crucial Romanov publicity campaign for the tercentenary in 1913 he had to be carried in public ceremonials, prompting people to ask themselves whether the future of Russia was to be in the hands of 'a cripple'. Rumours went about that the Tsarevich was seriously ill with tuberculosis, but the lid was kept tightly shut on the true cause of his disability. Something changed in Alexey after 1912; he became more subdued, less childish in his behaviour and more considerate of others. He seemed finally to have grasped the seriousness of his condition. In October 1915 Alexandra allowed him to join his father at Army HQ at Mogilev. Alexey was delighted: he was glad to get away from all the women fussing round him at Tsarskoe Selo and the monotony of his closely monitored life there. The outbreak of war had at last allowed Alexandra's 'Sunbeam' – her 'Baby' – to leave off the childish sailor suit and put on a soldier's greatcoat. He wanted so desperately to be a man. Given the rank of an ordinary private (he was promoted to corporal the following June) and a made-to-measure army uniform and miniature rifle to match, Alexey loved the life at Mogilev with his father. They slept together on camp beds in the same simple room; Alexey accompanied Nicholas when he reviewed the troops and visited the wounded, and took great pleasure in talking with his father's entourage of officers. The all-male environment matured him, even if his education suffered; his male tutors came with him but despaired at how far behind Alexey was falling with his studies. But the idyll at Mogilev did not last long. A fit of sneezing in December brought on a nosebleed and another attack of haemophilia. Alexey was rushed back to Tsarskoe Selo and the healing powers of Rasputin.

After the Revolution and their journey into exile, for seven months at Tobolsk Alexey had been well again. But then in a typical act of daredevil defiance of the illness that had haunted his life, he had provoked another serious attack by hurtling down a staircase in the Governor's House on his sled, falling and injuring his groin. Before his mother departed for Ekaterinburg, forced to leave the sick Alexey in the care of his sisters, he told her in one of his moments of pain: 'I would like to die, Mama; I'm not afraid of death, but I'm so afraid of what they might do to us here.' When finally he was able to travel with the others to join his parents in mid-May, he was still extremely frail. His carer Nagorny had carried him from the train at Ekaterinburg station that day, so pale and delicate, his collar bones sticking out and his thin hand clutched tight round Nagorny's thick bronzed neck. Those who saw him arrive were moved by the protective loyalty of Nagorny and had little doubt about the look of mortal resignation in the Tsarevich's huge sad eyes. He had the look of a martyr to suffering, and one not long for this world either. It was a sight that shocked the hardest of hearts, not least the guards at the Ipatiev House. Alexey's spectral, jaundiced appearance reminded his mother of Spala, and she was filled with dread.

Approaching his fourteenth birthday, Alexey had spent a lifetime being watched by a retinue of family and carers, and now he was doubly watched in an even closer place of confinement at the Ipatiev House. It was hard for him, very hard and he seemed to have a sense of foreboding that he and his family were doomed. For the first three weeks after his arrival he was in a lot of pain with a swollen knee, and Dr Derevenko was allowed in to put on a plaster of Paris splint. Later, as the leg recovered, Dr Botkin applied electrotherapy to his wasted leg muscles with the Fohn apparatus they had brought with them. His only playmate now was the young kitchen boy Leonid Sednev, his carer Nagorny having been taken away in May. Nicholas, or sometimes Maria or Dr Botkin, carried Alexey downstairs on the rare occasions he went out into the garden, but he could rarely walk let alone run in the sunshine. If he went out at all, he mainly sat with his mother under the balcony. Lately, however, both invalids increasingly remained in their bedroom, taking their frugal meals there together.

Alexey coped with his intense boredom by playing childish games with his tin soldiers and paper boats and filling his pockets with the random detritus boys like to collect: coins, nails, stones and buttons, bits of string and scraps of paper. There were also games of draughts, bezique and chess with his parents in the evenings. There still were occasional flashes of the naughty boy: one day he caused a stir by letting off some fireworks that Avdeev had given him in the garden with Leonid Sednev – much to Yurovsky's fury. Avdeev had allowed him to play bows and arrows too, sometimes even firing them out of the upstairs window and nearly hitting passers-by. But that all changed with the arrival of Yurovsky. He would allow the boy no such indulgences.

Slowly, the condition of Alexey's leg began to improve as a result of being so closely confined, but he was still dreadfully weak and the visits of Dr Derevenko became increasingly infrequent; on 8 July Alexandra noted in her diary that yet again the doctor had not been permitted to come in response to their frequent requests to see him. The absence of Dr Derevenko was one of many subtle changes to life in the Ipatiev House under Yurovsky. Neither Nicholas nor Alexandra seemed to read any significance into it. In his diary that day Nicholas observed that 'our life has not changed one bit with Yu.[rovsky]' – except for the continuing morning checks on their valuables and further tightening of the security of their possessions in the storehouse outside. Alexandra recorded that 'nothing particular happened'; even the guard duty book noted that 8 July was 'without change'. But there *were* changes afoot, deliberate and sinister ones. That day Yurovsky, as well as bringing in his own new, internal guards, had added two more guard posts at the Ipatiev House – no. 11 in the garden at the back and no. 12 in the dormer window at the top of the house. For most of the day men had been at the house 'fixing' the electricity – as both the Tsar and Tsaritsa noted, thinking perhaps it was for their benefit, since the supply had been intermittent. In fact the purpose had been to install a new and more reliable warning system of bells between guard posts to replace the existing defective one.

Yurovsky was in fact turning the Ipatiev House into an impregnable fortress as the unstable situation in Russia at large escalated. The threat of the recent Left SR insurrection, which had spread to some of the regions, had brought the Bolshevik government to the brink of collapse. Instructions had been sent to regional soviets to clamp down on all possible counter-revolutionary activity. In response Aleksandr Beloborodov and Grigory Safarov of the Ural Regional Soviet had posted a proclamation to the Ekaterinburg population exhorting them: 'Increase your vigilance, mercilessly eradicate insurrection against Soviet power no matter from where it emanates.' Meanwhile, all that day the Ekaterinburg Cheka had been busy rounding up any possible suspects who might be involved in an attempted Romanov rescue.

Beyond Ekaterinburg, to the immediate south and south-east, a combined force of four Czech detachments of about 10,000 men, with artillery and two aeroplanes as support, was closing in on the city from its base at Chelyabinsk. Further Czech forces were now stretched out along the Trans-Siberian Railway from Samara in the west to Irkutsk on Lake Baikal in the east, with another large contingent of about 14,000 out at Vladivostok. As men from Czech armoured trains routed the Bolsheviks from town after town along the railway line, they were hailed as deliverers to the sound of church bells. The Czechs now held the longest front in the war – 3,000 miles across Siberia. From this consolidated military position they were bolstered by news of the resolution made in Versailles by the Allies to shorten the war, attempting to reconstitute the Russian Front against the Germans by sending in an intervention force in support of the Czechs. Informed of this, the Czech commanders decided to press on with their march westwards to the Volga, in the vanguard of the Allied intervention.

Meanwhile, the central Czech forces under the overall command of White general Sergey Voitsekhovsky were now assigned to take Ekaterinburg and were approaching from their base at Chelyabinsk along the densely forested railway line to the south. Soon they would be at the

Sysert works outside the city. The vice was tightening around Ekaterinburg; every man with a gun and who knew how to shoot it was leaving for the Front, piling on to every available train at Ekaterinburg station. With 300 valuable men now assigned to the roster of guards at the Ipatiev House, revolutionary necessity and the defence of the October Revolution increasingly demanded they be released for military duty.

Knowing the game would soon be up, and intent on looking after his own, Beloborodov asked a colleague, Gabriel Myasnikov of the Perm Cheka, who was now busy evacuating the government reserves of gold and platinum out via Perm, to escort his wife and three children to safety by rail (a week later they drowned when a crowded ferry they had boarded to cross the River Vytchegda capsized). Ekaterinburg now was effectively unprotected, except for a rabble of Red Army soldiers and Cheka men from the Verkh-Isetsk factory, under the command of Petr Ermakov, a Bolshevik commissar. The moment for evacuating the Tsar and his family north to safety or back to Moscow for a trial, which had been feasible all the time the Czechs were approaching from the south, had passed. It is doubtful that it had ever been a realistic Bolshevik intention, but rather a ploy to keep everyone guessing about what the leadership's plans for the Imperial Family really were. Sooner or later, Yurovsky knew, he would have to take a stand on the 'question of liquidating the Romanovs'. Which was why his colleague Filipp Goloshchekin was in Moscow right now, consulting with Lenin and Sverdlov.

7

The Good Doctor

TUESDAY 9 JULY 1918

Dr Evgeny Sergeevich Botkin was feeling his age – and his own mortality. He was 63, and like everybody in the Ipatiev House he was becoming increasingly tired and disconsolate. His kidney problem had flared up at the end of June, laying him low for days. The pain had been so bad that Tatiana had given him an injection of the family's precious supply of morphine. He had had to stay in bed for several days and had not been able to venture out into the garden again till only two days ago. Time in the Ipatiev House was dragging terribly, and the pain in his back nagged at him; he had tried to distract himself from gloomy thoughts by reading the satirist Mikhail Saltykov-Shchedrin – the same set of his collected works that the Tsar had also been enjoying – but he couldn't concentrate. His mind had constantly been wandering and he was increasingly haunted by gloomy thoughts and visions of his children, especially of his dead son Yuri, killed on the Eastern Front during the war.

And so, after the arrival of Yurovsky at the house and sensing the tightening of the screws, Botkin had now judged that the time had finally come to put pen to paper. Some time in early July the doctor had begun, intermittently, to write a letter – his last letter, a letter he knew would never be sent and never received. It was a testament of sorts – a statement of resignation and also expectation of what was to come. Addressed to his brother Sasha (Alexander), with whom he had studied at medical school, it began starkly with all the pragmatism of the medical man

I am making a final attempt at writing a real letter – from *here* at least – although that proviso to my mind is utterly superfluous. I don't think I was fated to write again from anywhere – my voluntary confinement here is not so much limited by time as it is limited by my earthly existence. In essence, I am already dead, dead for my children, for my friends, for my work . . .

Facing reality with such clear-eyed calm typified the doctor in him. Botkin knew that he could not share his musings with those around him, so he quietly acceded to the general atmosphere of denial, or rather exhausted acceptance, that now pervaded the upstairs rooms of the Ipatiev House and kept his real thoughts to himself.

Botkin was an old-school medical man and prided himself on being so: upright, hard-working, incorruptible, a man who always put duty before self. Tall and stout, he had a neat beard, gold-rimmed spectacles with thick pebble lenses, and even in confinement dressed formally in a stiff shirt and tie; Nicholas's valet Chemodurov noted before he left the house sick on 24 May that the doctor even slept with his tie on. It all gave him an air of solidity, dependability. Medicine ran in the family; his own father, Dr Sergey Botkin, had been a highly respected scientist and medical pioneer before being appointed court physician, serving both Alexander II and Alexander III. Three of Sergey's sons in a family of 13 children had followed him into the medical profession. Evgeny had studied in St Petersburg and in Germany before becoming a lecturer at the Army-Medical Academy. He had served during the Russo-Japanese War in 1904, overseeing Red Cross care of the wounded on a hospital train. Decorated for his efforts, he was invited to the Russian court by Alexandra, who had been greatly impressed by his war service, as a physician-in-ordinary in 1905. In 1908 he was appointed Honorary Physician of the Imperial Court. But the honour was an onerous one, for the stresses and strains of the Tsaritsa and Tsarevich's various medical crises meant he was often on call for long and exhausting periods of time, and this in addition to continuing his teaching and his private practice. It made great demands on Botkin, not least the battle with the Tsaritsa's own very stubborn views on what *she* thought was wrong with her – which was often at odds with the pronouncements of the medical men. He was forced to capitulate time and again rather than provoke a hysterical response in his patient by telling the truth. He therefore obligingly doled out the Veronal and other opiates that were the Tsaritsa's lifeline, kept his distance from Rasputin and passed no opinion on him, and remained silently loyal, never indulging in gossip about the Imperial Family. Although he accompanied the Tsar sometimes to Army HQ at Mogilev, Botkin spent most of his time at Tsarskoe Selo attending the Tsaritsa and her children. As a result, his own family saw very little of him. His marriage broke down; his wife had an affair and in 1911 they were divorced.

Having once undertaken to serve, Dr Botkin was unswervingly devoted to his monarch and the principles he upheld, and increasingly shared the same conservative attitudes on politics, religion and morals as the Tsar and Tsaritsa. He also, during the final years, had grown to share their religious fatalism. When the Tsar abdicated and the Imperial Family were confined to the Alexander Palace, Botkin had no hesitation in asking Kerensky's government to allow him to join them. A few days later he accompanied the Imperial Family into exile at Tobolsk. It had not been a difficult decision: his sense of duty demanded it, as Botkin told Count Tatishchev at Tobolsk: 'I have come here knowing quite well that I shall not escape with my life. All I ask is to be permitted to die with my Emperor.' Even his jailer Yurovsky, for whom Botkin with his endless requests on behalf of the family became a thorn in the side, remarked that the doctor was a 'true friend to the family'.

Which is why the doctor had not hesitated again – when he was asked to make the final sacrifice of leaving behind at Tobolsk his son Gleb and daughter Tatyana, who had followed him into exile – to accompany the Tsar and Tsaritsa to Ekaterinburg. At the Ipatiev House he became an essential intermediary between the Romanovs and the commandant, sent to negotiate over any day-to-day matters, and sometimes more serious ones. At every opportunity he defended the family's physical and spiritual welfare, asking Avdeev to allow them more time out of doors for recreation, appealing for a priest to be allowed to come and conduct services and repeatedly requesting visits from Dr Derevenko. Derevenko had been appointed in 1912 after Alexey's near fatal attack of haemophilia; he had followed the Imperial Family to Ekaterinburg but had been excluded from the Ipatiev House, remaining in lodgings in the city. Avdeev had allowed him in fairly regularly, but the family had now not seen him for five days and Yurovsky was becoming irritated by Botkin's persistent requests and his continuing insistence that the Tsarevich needed to be in a hospital as his own supply of medicines and bandages was running out. Such had been Botkin's intense frustration that back in May he had written a very strong letter to the Ural Regional Soviet Executive Committee describing Alexey's very poor state of health, and asking that Pierre Gilliard and Sidney Gibbes be allowed into the house to share the load of keeping him amused and distracted from the 'indescribable pain' that he endured, day and night, so that he, Botkin, and the family, who were all drained from sitting up with him, could get some rest. Botkin was only too aware of the psychological importance of Derevenko and his tutors for the Tsarevich, as well as for his mother. Gibbes and Gilliard were, he asserted, 'irreplaceable', and he begged the URS to allow them to continue in their selfless service to the Tsarevich. The request was denied, Avdeev explaining that Alexey already had enough grown-ups, including his sisters, to attend him.

As he sat writing his last letter, Botkin's mind turned back to his and

Sasha's graduation year – 1889. As a young, idealistic medical student he had had no religious concerns and had been decidedly liberal in his thinking, looking on religion from a detached, aesthetic point of view. One did not need religious faith in order to work as a doctor, or so they all thought then. But the death of his firstborn son, Sergey, had changed all that, and his subsequent years of medical experience had taught him to be increasingly concerned for the patient's 'soul' – their mental well-being. It was why, he said now in his letter to Sasha, he had unhesitatingly 'orphaned' his own children in order to carry out his physician's duty 'to the end, as Abraham did not hesitate at God's demand to sacrifice his only son'. At Tobolsk, buoyed by the fine weather and the presence with him in the merchant Kornilov's house of his children (he was not resident in the Governor's House), he had expended all his remaining energies in offering medical assistance to anyone in the town who needed his help. Conditions in the house were very cramped, but between 3 and 5 p.m. every day he had held a surgery for local residents. As word got out, peasants began arriving from outlying villages as far as 50 miles away seeking his medical help – distance being meaningless to Siberians. Botkin had been greatly moved by their simple, unswerving trust in him and their gratitude for the way in which he treated them, not just as equals, but as sick people who had every right to his care and attention as a doctor. They tried to pay him but he never took their money. When Botkin could, he went out and visited those peasants too sick to travel; when he refused their money, they tried to pay his driver.

The same kind of unquestioning loyalty to the Imperial Family had also been demonstrated by the servants and kitchen boy who had voluntarily gone with the family to Ekaterinburg and now, in July, were still with them. It was as though by travelling with the family they felt they could in some way protect them from harm. Four of the original seven now remained: the Lithuanian Catholic Alexey Trupp – a 61-year-old ex-army officer who was the Tsaritsa's footman; the Tsaritsa's 40-year-old parlour maid Anna Demidova; the 48-year-old cook Ivan Kharitonov and the little kitchen boy Leonid Sednev – a nephew of Ivan Sednev, the Grand Duchesses' valet. Leonid was two years younger than Alexey, and the Tsarevich had grown to greatly rely on him as a playmate. Demidova, a tall blonde whom the family called Nyuta and the guards with playful obsequiousness 'Freylina', was dutiful but rather timid and probably the most overworked, with all the bed linen and family laundry to deal with. But there was no ceremony to the very simple meals prepared from Soviet rations in the tiny, stuffy kitchen by Kharitonov – who had left behind a wife and daughter in Tobolsk – and eaten communally at the dining room table; and the family hardly needed a footman such as Trupp to serve them.

When the Romanovs had arrived at Ekaterinburg the Bolsheviks had ordered that the servants from now on address them not by their titles but by their names and patronymics, something the servants had found difficult to adjust to. The Tsaritsa had complained bitterly and often about the reduction in their retinue, but one wonders quite how any more servants could have been accommodated in such an already over-crowded space – five rooms compared to the 18 the Imperial entourage had occupied at the house in Tobolsk – or what they could have occupied themselves with all day. Alexandra remained in denial about her reduced status, constantly complaining, and asking repeatedly for the return of Nagorny to help Dr Botkin watch over Alexey at night when he was sick and carry him from room to room.

Not knowing what had happened to Sednev, Nagorny, Dolgorukov and Chemodurov, who had all now been taken from them, as well as Tatishchev who had been arrested on 23 May after arriving in Ekaterinburg with the rest of the children, worried the family, for they had no way of knowing whether they had been sent away to safety or had suffered some terrible fate. They were fobbed off with lies by Avdeev, and Yurovsky after him, but lack of information about what was going on in the world outside and how long they were to remain in Ekaterinburg was beginning to wear everybody down. Bouts of boredom were interrupted by moments of irritation and periods of acute stress; meanwhile, Alexey and Alexandra's health continued to decline. Today the Tsaritsa's eyes were hurting so much that she couldn't read for more than five minutes at a time. Her teeth were troubling her too, and she noted in her diary that she had taken arsenic – often used in dentistry as a painkiller. Olga stayed in with her all day when the others went out to the garden. Otherwise, it was the same routine: Alexandra sitting playing patience with Alexey and Dr Botkin, or 'tatting' – making knotted lace – whilst the servants hovered aimlessly, their roles largely redundant but their familiar presence reassuring.

For Nicholas, the physical constraints had become increasingly intoler-able since he had been forbidden even to exchange pleasantries with the guards. The arrival of Yurovsky had curtailed what free association there had been to help lighten the monotony, but for the sake of his family, of whom he was fiercely protective, Nicholas had kept his frustration bottled up. When the distraction of cards and reading failed him, he would pace incessantly back and forth across the sitting room humming military tunes and army songs, anything to keep the black dog of despair at bay. After which he would often sit listlessly in a chair, leafing through the book in the collection at the Ipatiev House that most interested him: a copy of *The House of the Romanovs* published to celebrate the tercentenary in 1913. Fond memories of happier days and illustrious ancestors.

Meanwhile, in London, another European monarch, Albert, the beleaguered King of the Belgians, and his wife were continuing their visit for the royal silver wedding, during which they had been garnering further support for the 'long-drawn sufferings of the high-souled people of Belgium', who since the German invasion in August 1914 were still living under the 'heel of the enemy'. King Albert, a popular, democratic monarch, seemed a paean of incorruptibility. He had refused to sacrifice the honour of his country for the price that Germany offered, insisting that 'Belgium is a nation, not a road', had kept Belgium neutral throughout the war despite the invasion of German troops, and had stalled for time to allow Allied preparations for the crucial assault against Germany at the Marne that was now taking place. He had earned British respect as a man who had remained 'unbowed by the misfortunes of his kingship'. The obvious comparisons with Nicholas of Russia, who to outside observers had buckled and abdicated all too easily, abandoning his country to German domination, were unspoken but palpable. The 'indomitable' King of Belgium was soldiering on whilst Nicholas was now languishing, a forgotten man, out of sight, out of mind.

Early in the morning of 9 July, while it was still dark, the small Red Army garrison under the command of Ensign Ardatov charged with protecting Ekaterinburg had realised the time had come to abandon their posts. They could hear the distant boom of artillery approaching from the south, and decided to flee, defecting to the Czechs. Later that morning, across the road from the Ipatiev House, an angry mob gathered in the square outside the Voznesensky Cathedral, fearful for the security of their homes, their lives and the city itself. All over Ekaterinburg, hidden eyes were watching and assessing the crumbling political situation. Czech agents had already arrived undercover and were warning foreign consulates to ensure that they haul up their flags so that the Czech relief forces, when they came, would avoid hitting them with artillery fire. Other spies lurked in the city. One, from France, was holed up at the British consulate down the road from the Ipatiev House on Voznesensky Prospekt, sent to check on the rumours that the Tsar and some if not all of the family had already been killed. He managed to get a telegraph out confirming that the 'rumours about the Romanovs are false'. Thomas Preston knew there had been British agents in the city too, observing the goings-on at the Ipatiev House; but such had been the situation for months. These shadowy figures – spies, monarchists, would-be rescuers – all came and went, but nothing changed for the Romanovs.

It took men of an entirely different calibre, of icy calculating calm and implacable political intent, to plan not a Romanov rescue, but the annihilation of a dynasty. And the person who now had this most firmly in mind was Lenin's close associate Yakov Sverdlov. He was small and lean, with dark, exotic Jewish looks, a huge mop of black hair, flashing eyes and a neat goatee beard. He liked to dress in a long leather coat, the favoured dress code of the Cheka, often sporting a floppy Bohemian black cravat. He might have seemed rather fey, but he had a thunderous voice, and behind the pince-nez there lurked a fierce and calculating intelligence and a photographic memory. He carried a huge amount of information in his head about the names and faces of core party activists and collaborators, as he built up a network of party officials across Russia. Whilst Lenin might have been the mastermind and theoretician of the Revolution, and Trotsky its outstanding orator, in Yakov Sverdlov it had found a brilliant organiser who oversaw the apparatus of government.

Practical organisational skills were Lenin's one great failing, and Sverdlov was quick to capitalise on this deficiency. He was 'like a diamond', as fellow commissar Anatoly Lunacharsky described him, that had been 'chosen for its absolute hardness to be the axis of some delicate, perpetually revolving piece of mechanism'. Sverdlov shared the same crystalline political nature as his good friend Lenin – a ruthlessly rational and unsentimental line of thought. They had not met till 1917 but had immediately established a very close rapport. According to Sverdlov's widow, 'It took only a word or two for them to understand each other'; her husband instantly grasped and accepted without question Lenin's every idea and every instruction because, she insisted, 'they had identical views'. Like all good revolutionaries, Sverdlov was not showy and had the ability of the chameleon to blend effortlessly into the background. To Lenin he was, quite simply, indispensable, which was why Lenin had installed him in place of the more lenient Lev Kamenev as chair of the Central Executive Committee, effectively making him Soviet Russia's first president and the CEC the de facto power centre of the government. Sverdlov increasingly used the CEC to circumvent open meetings of the party and thus squeeze out opposition from the Left SRs and Mensheviks, in the process strengthening his own hand. In the current increasingly tense situation over the fate of the Romanovs he was playing a key role. He was well connected with the Bolsheviks of Ekaterinburg – he'd served his apprenticeship as an underground worker in and around the Urals during 1905–6, when he had established strong links with local Bolshevik leaders. The prison camps of Siberian exile were only too familiar to him as well: he had spent three years there in 1906–9; had escaped a second term in 1910, and then had been sent to Narym, where he spent time with Stalin, before a further four years in exile in Turukhansk, where he had become firm friends with fellow exile Filipp Goloshchekin.

Sverdlov had an innate gift for judging people with extraordinary accuracy, and right now he knew who could be relied on to carry out Lenin's wishes when the final decision over the Romanovs was made. Goloshchekin was his man, and they were now in close and regular contact. It was Goloshchekin who had warned him of the weakening of security at Tobolsk; thereafter Sverdlov had given him personal responsibility for ensuring the Tsar's safety until a decision was made about his fate. From now on, control of the Imperial Family's life in Ekaterinburg, whilst seeming to emanate from the Ural Regional Soviet, was in fact closely monitored by Sverdlov and Lenin, hand in hand with Goloshchekin. And now Goloshchekin was once more in Moscow for further and final consultations with them, staying with Sverdlov in his spacious four-bedroom apartment in the Kremlin.

Over in the sitting room of the House of Special Purpose, as he added a few more lines to his letter to Sasha, Dr Botkin had no doubts about the fate in store for himself and the other occupants of the Ipatiev House:

> I am dead but not yet buried or buried alive – whichever: the consequences are almost identical . . . My children may hold out hope that we will see each other again in this life . . . but I personally do not indulge in that hope . . . and I look the unadulterated reality in the eye.

That day in Ekaterinburg another fellow medical professional had been busy, though his mission was not an altruistic one. Dr Kensorin Arkhipov, a local physician of good repute, whose house had been considered by the Ural Regional Soviet as a possible alternative venue for the Imperial Family, had been instructed, as British consul Thomas Preston had heard, to procure 400lb of sulphuric acid. Dr Arkhipov, so it seemed, had served as a medical orderly at the Ekaterinburg Military Hospital in 1916; he had not actually completed his medical studies, but this fact was ignored and a diploma issued to him anyway because of the pressing needs of the war. His fellow doctors had been wary of him – they found him wild, full of crazy ideas, unbalanced even. Nevertheless, Arkhipov did manage to make one good friend among their ranks – Yakov Yurovsky – and they had remained thick as thieves ever since.

8

'Our Poor Russia'

WEDNESDAY 10 JULY 1918

In the Oval Office of the White House in Washington, President Woodrow Wilson was grappling with a problem. What was right and feasible to do in Russia? How to provide relief to its starving masses and support for the Czech legions, whilst refraining from interfering in the country's internal affairs? Only two days earlier, Wilson had confided to his adviser Colonel Edward House that he had been 'sweating blood' over the question for many weeks now, but every time he thought he had found a solution 'it goes to pieces like quicksilver under my touch'. Meanwhile the whole contentious issue of Russia had snowballed in the world's press, and was now dominating US foreign policy, with everyone second-guessing what the President would do next. Halfway round the world and ignorant of the forces contemplating intervention in their country, the Romanovs remained impotent in the face of what they already sensed was going on outside – a situation of escalating violence. All they could do was pray that God would intervene over their beloved Russia's fate.

Public opinion on Russia in America had been galvanised since the end of June by a series of excoriating articles by US journalist Herman Bernstein, special correspondent of the *New York Herald* and the *Washington Post* (many of whose Russian dispatches were syndicated across the US and European press). Bernstein, himself a Russo-Jewish émigré who had left Russia in 1893, had recently arrived back after six months studying conditions in Russia. Prior to the Revolution he had been violently anti-tsarist and had campaigned vigorously against the persecution of Russia's Jews. In 1913 he had written an open letter to the Tsar condemning the recent wave of pogroms. Every aspiration for liberty and justice in Russia had, Bernstein wrote, 'withered in the bud'. The tsarist government had nothing but contempt for the ignorant masses who to them were so much 'human dust'.

Bernstein had therefore welcomed the Revolution as a release from the 'dark spirits of despotism and intolerance' that ruled in Russia, spending four months there in 1917. The Revolution had uprooted the 'medieval evil' of the Romanov dynasty and was Russia's great hope for the future. The 'sun of Freedom' had risen over darkest Russia at last, particularly for its oppressed Jews. But Bernstein's return to his former country a year later, to get to the truth of what was going on there, as he put it, had appalled him, and he soon went from being a friend and supporter of the 'new idea' in Russia to one of its sternest critics in the West. He had not been afraid to tell the truth about the Tsar and now asserted that he was 'not afraid to tell the truth about the tyranny of Lenine and Trotzky [sic]'. Lenin was using Russia as his laboratory, Bernstein alleged bitterly, and its people as guinea pigs for his great social experiment. He now urged American intervention: 'Russia is broken down, wretched, demoralized, and starving, and waiting for someone stronger than herself to come and pick her up.' What was needed above all was a return to a 'sane' form of government. The Russian people had lost confidence in themselves and in their desperation were even looking to Germany for a restoration of order. 'Nine-tenths of the Russian people', he was confident, 'would welcome the advent of the Allies with open arms.'

Throughout June, the high-minded President had been besieged day in, day out by a stream of influential visitors with a plethora of moral arguments and the same ultimate thought in mind – American intervention in Russia. British and French diplomats had been in constant attendance, as too had Tomas Masaryk, the respected exiled leader of the Czech independence movement; Lady Muriel Paget arrived fresh from her humanitarian work at the British Hospital in Petrograd, in her wake an assortment of Russian émigrés, former tsarist ministers and members of Kerensky's ill-fated provisional government – all of them fiercely lobbying for US support and urgent economic aid to Russia. Even Mrs Emmeline Pankhurst, the formidable former suffragette rebel and now staunch conservative, was in town, angling to give the President her pennyworth on the Russian situation. America, it seemed, was Russia's only hope of salvation. Wilson was a good and patient listener and gave everyone his ear. Bolshevism in Russia was now facing its darkest hour, he was assured; the Soviet government was politically isolated, confronted by nationwide famine and anarchy, with an inadequate Red Army to face off the German Imperial forces on its doorstep and the gathering White advance across Siberia. Many were predicting the new Soviet state's imminent demise: 'it has been a corpse for four or five weeks', US ambassador to Russia David Francis reported back to Washington, 'but no one has had the courage to bury it'. At an

impromptu party he had thrown for the American, British, French and
Italian diplomatic corps at Vologda – a railway junction halfway between
Moscow and the northern port of Murmansk – Francis had issued a
statement promising that America would 'never stand idly by and see the
Germans exploit the Russian people and appropriate to Germany's selfish
ends the immense resources of Russia'. Since 7 July he had been urging
Washington that the projected US landings in northern Russia and
Siberia be brought forward. All that was needed, so it seemed, was to
raise the Allied flags in Russia, and the people would rally to the cause
and overthrow the Soviet government.

Wilson meanwhile was finding it hard to stick to his guns and his
decision announced on the 6th to send in a limited American relief
mission only, to augment work already being done in the USA by the
Red Cross and the American YMCA. As a believer in the self-
determination of nations and the moral force of America in helping
support such aspirations, he wanted to do the right thing. Archangel was
now in British and French hands; the Czechs were holding sway along
the Trans-Siberian Railway and a small intervention force of Japanese
troops had landed at Vladivostok and was in control of Eastern Siberia
beyond Irkutsk. All of this facilitated the arrival in Russia of the projected
US mission, but Wilson was adamant that any American action should
not involve force, even though the progress of the Czech legions across
Siberia had now materially altered the situation by 'introducing a
sentimental element' into the question of American duty towards the Slav
peoples.

As a devout Presbyterian, a man of conscience and probity, Wilson was
driven by his desire to offer American solidarity with the Russian and
Czech people. It was all part of the ambitious peace plan he had initiated
in January when he had unveiled his Fourteen Points for a new world
order of peace and the establishment of a peace-making organisation to
promote it: the League of Nations. It was his sincere hope that the US
and Czech presence in Russia would provoke a spontaneous democratic
response on the part of the people of Siberia, the vast majority of whom
were anti-Communist, that would spread across Russia.

Today, 10 July, the beleaguered President could expect to be further
assaulted by even more persuasive pleas for help in Russia, for after a
meeting with his war cabinet, he was due to meet Russia's most unlikely
and most impassioned envoy: Lieutenant Colonel Mariya Bochkareva,
the 30-year-old former commander of the volunteer 1st Women's
Battalion of Death, that had served on the Eastern Front. Small, dumpy
and large-bosomed, with a round Russian face framed by close-cropped
dark hair, Bochkareva was an intimidating sight in her male army tunic,

jodhpurs and high boots along with a chest full of medals. In the West she was looked upon as Russia's very own Joan of Arc, a parallel observed by Mrs Pankhurst, who called her 'the greatest woman of the century'. Semi-literate and of stoical peasant stock, Bochkareva had been born into poverty and a large family before marrying at the age of 15 and becoming the victim of an abusive husband. She had had a tough life but remained a passionate patriot who cut to the simple truths of life, and whilst having no quarrel with the theories and social aspirations of Bolshevism, she had become appalled by what it had mutated into: a rule of terror and the mob. Back in 1914 Bochkareva had shared in the popular belief that the outbreak of war would pull Russia back from the brink of political disaster by drawing its disparate peoples together in a great tide of national unity. Determined to do her part and shame those men who were reticent about volunteering for the Front, she had in November that year sent a telegram to Nicholas II, telling him of her moral purpose and her desire to defend Russia and asking his permission to be allowed to join up. The Tsar had agreed to her request and she had initially joined the 25th Tomsk Reserve Battalion. With the permission of Kerensky's provisional government, she later organised and commanded the Women's Battalion in action in June 1917, as a response to the break-down of morale and discipline in the Russian Army. She and all her female troops had carried vials of potassium cyanide in case of capture and rape. Leading from the front, Bochkareva herself was gassed, suffered shell shock and was wounded three times – plagued ever after with pain caused by a piece of shrapnel lodged in her side. The Russian govern-ment later awarded her the St George's cross and several other honours for her bravery under fire. After being beaten up and mocked by male Russian soldiers, and narrowly missing execution by the Bolsheviks, in 1918 she had got out of Russia via Vladivostok, thanks to 500 roubles from the British consul in Moscow, intending to rally support in London for Russia's suffering masses through her contacts established with Mrs Pankhurst. Sailing across the Pacific, Bochkareva had arrived in San Francisco in June and made public appearances in New York before travelling to Washington DC, where she was sponsored by the wealthy socialite and civic dignitary Florence Harriman, a close friend of the President.

Everywhere she went Bochkareva created a furore: she stopped the traffic marching down Fifth Avenue in her military garb; people were mesmerised by her vivid accounts of her harsh childhood, her terrifying experiences in the front lines, of how she had commanded the last loyal unit to defend Kerensky's provisional government at the Winter Palace when the Bolsheviks had seized power, and, more darkly, of the later

Bolshevik atrocities she had witnessed. She was, she said, tired of the 'river of words' about Russia fuelling the Western press and wanted to see active, practical help for her country, now racked by profound moral and social internal disorder. Bochkareva had already met with former president Theodore Roosevelt, who thought her a 'remarkable woman' 'abounding in natural wisdom and determination'. On 25 June she had requested a meeting with the President, seeing him, as many did in Russia, as the embodiment of its hope and salvation. Ahead of her meeting, she had sent him a gift – a small icon of St Anne which she herself had worn at the Front; Wilson had been touched and had written a warm response.

Bochkareva's reputation as a magnetic personality and born actress, despite having to use an interpreter, went before her. Ushered into Wilson's presence at 4.30 that afternoon, she did not stand on ceremony. She was a Russian and Russians speak without inhibition, from the heart. She was highly articulate, and once she got started in her inimitable husky-voiced way she couldn't be stopped. Nor could her hapless interpreter keep pace with the torrent of words that gushed forth as Bochkareva's tongue 'went like a runaway horse', hitting the highs of passion one minute and the lows of abject despair the next, in a wild semaphore of flamboyant gestures that left the President and his aides transfixed. So impassioned were her pleas that she threw herself on the floor in floods of tears, clasping her arms tight around Wilson's knees, begging him to help poor Russia, to send food, and troops to intervene against the Bolsheviks. Her demands were extravagant – she wanted to see a combined US, French, British and Japanese force of 100,000 sent in to serve as the nucleus of a Russian fighting army of a million 'free sons of Russia' that she believed would rise up against Germany without reference to party or politics. An Allied army would, Bochkareva asserted, be met with joy by the Russian peasants and soldiers. If the Allies failed to help then she would be forced to return to Russia and tell her people that she had begged in vain and that the Allies were no better friends to Russia than the Germans.

Woodrow Wilson, a man known for his restraint and austerity, had not been able to resist this emotional tirade from Bochkareva. He sat there with tears streaming down his cheeks and did his best to assure her of his sympathy and support. A week later Bochkareva left Washington for London and an audience with King George V, leaving behind two 'legacies', as she called them, with her American friends: the story of her life, which she had dictated to the American journalist Isaac Don Levine, who translated and published it in 1919; and, somewhat alarmingly, her 15-year-old sister Nadya, for her patrons 'to keep until Russia is safe for her'. Bochkareva did not want the innocent Nadya to be exposed to the ideas of free love 'and all the other horrible things that the Bolsheviks teach'. A year later a homesick Nadya went back to Russia. Bochkareva herself clearly made an indelible impression on American sentiment, for in August 1918 Theodore Roosevelt gave $1,000 of his Nobel Peace Prize money to her 'as a token of my respect for those Russians who have refused to follow the Bolsheviki in their betrayal to Germany of Russia, of the Allies, and of the cause of liberty throughout the world'.

In all her speeches across America, Mariya Bochkareva made no reference to the fate of the Tsar who had allowed her to fight like a man. But Nicholas and Alexandra, so far away in Ekaterinburg, would have been proud of her moral fibre, her virulent anti-German sentiments and her spirited defence of Mother Russia at the White House that day. For like her, they loved Russia with a passion and still prayed daily to God to save the country from the brink of destruction. Alexandra had adopted all that was Russian with the fierce, visceral passion of a mother protecting her young: 'How I love my country, with all its faults. It grows dearer and dearer to me, and I thank God daily that He allowed us to remain here and did not send us farther away.' She constantly urged her husband and friends to keep faith in the people: 'The nation is strong, and young, and as soft as wax', she asserted. There was hope for Russia yet 'in spite of all its sins and horrors'.

But the Russia that Alexandra thought she knew was far more complex and conflicted than she ever could have imagined; her 'Russia' was a chimera, a product of her own imagination, created in isolation at Tsarskoe Selo and in exile. The idealised Russia of loyal, God-fearing ordinary people whom she and Nicholas had convinced themselves were devoted to them had never really existed; it was an abstraction. Yet when Nicholas had abdicated in March 1917 it had been in the firm belief that his sacrifice 'for the sake of the true well-being and salvation of our Mother Russia' would save the country from the violence and anarchy into which it had been descending since the February Revolution. Since childhood he had been taught to believe in the mystical relationship between tsar and people and his divine right to be master of the fate of a country that was his own personal patrimony handed down by God. He had made a solemn undertaking on the day of his coronation to act as 'little father' to his people and had entered into a sacred trust to toil unceasingly in their service, no matter that his disposition was entirely unsuited to the role.

But the hope that the God-centred Russian *narod* (nation) would respond positively, in the spirit of traditional 'Holy Russia', to his sacrifice had been smashed. The problem of Russia had been far too big for Nicholas to resolve, and the war, instead of uniting tsar and people, had only intensified the many difficulties Nicholas faced. His long-term vision of his role – like that being carved out for President Wilson – as an apostle of world peace in the coming post-war years crumbled with it.

The Russian nation – exhausted, hungry, war-weary, and perverted by centuries of cruelty, absolutism and deceit – had failed to respond to the Tsar's last-ditch gestures in 1905, in 1914 and again in 1917, just as it did in the main to the rhetoric of Bolshevism later. Despair, poverty and the dislocations of war gave birth to idleness, criminality and indifference after the first flush of hunger had goaded the masses into revolutionary action. Martial law, the suppression of a free press and courts of law and now, in the summer of 1918, the introduction of mass conscription had seen many of the new hoped-for liberties stripped away. Autocracy had been replaced by a new and insidious 'commissarocracy', as Herman Bernstein observed.

But Holy Russia – that mythical fusion of tsar, faith and people – had, under Nicholas, once enjoyed an all too brief resurgence, first during the Romanov tercentenary celebrations of 1913, when Nicholas and Alexandra had made a rare appearance *en famille*, the Tsar seeming, to British observer Bruce Lockhart, 'a small figure in the centre of the procession . . . more like a sacred ikon to be kept hidden with Oriental exclusiveness by the High Priests and to be shown to the public on feast days'. That same sense of reverence at the visible presence of a monarch who for so much of the time had remained hidden from his public came again during the heady days of mobilisation for war in July 1914. During a great sombre ceremonial on the 20th of that month, it had seemed, for one brief day, as though tsar and people were truly united in a single objective: the repulsion of the German invader. Flags had flown from every window and balcony in Russia's two great cities, St Petersburg and Moscow. Processions of the faithful had carried the Tsar and Tsaritsa's portraits through the streets, had pressed round the couple during public appearances, reaching out and kissing their clothes, their hands. Vast congregations had gathered in Russia's churches to pray, light candles and kiss the icons in a euphoria of national solidarity that had not been seen since Napoleon's Grand Armée was driven from Russia in 1812. Here at last the spirit of a great and invincible Russia depicted in Tolstoy's *War and Peace* was briefly reincarnated.

Having proclaimed his intention relentlessly to prosecute the war until the German invader was driven from the soil of the Russian motherland, Nicholas rode in a coach along the banks of the River Neva in St Petersburg to tumultuous cheers from the crowds. Later, he appeared with Alexandra on a balcony at the Winter Palace to publicly declare war on Germany and acknowledge the packed Alexander Square below. A tiny figure, dwarfed by the grandeur of the great columns of the Winter Palace on all sides, he had nevertheless inspired the swelling crowd of tens of thousands below to spontaneously kneel down and join in singing the Russian national anthem 'Bozhe, Tsarya Khrani':

> God save the noble Tsar!
> Long may he live, in pow'r,
> In happiness,
> In peace to reign!
> Dread of his enemies,
> Faith's sure defender,
> God save the Tsar!

Composed in 1833, the melody had become an integral part of Russian national identity after it was incorporated by Tchaikovsky into his *1812 Overture* in 1882. Uplifted by this profound moment of communion with his people, Nicholas had stood and wept. Russia loved him; the nation needed its *batyushka-tsar*; the people would never desert their monarch and Russia once more would be a great nation led by a great tsar. Alexandra had reiterated it time and again: the reign of their son would inaugurate a great and golden new era for the country.

A similar moment of epiphany had followed in Moscow, on 23 August, where Nicholas had attended a long and solemn service thick with the smell of incense and candles at the historic Uspensky Cathedral to pray for victory. He did so with 'a holy fervour which gave his pale face a movingly mystical expression', according to French ambassador Maurice Paléologue, who noted how Alexandra seemed physically intoxicated by the experience, her gaze 'magnetic and inspired'. Afterwards the couple joined the crowds outside to hear the cathedral's great bells pealing out a Russian message of defiance across the ancient Kremlin walls. Later that day, Nicholas acknowledged another vast, hushed crowd from the steps of the Kremlin's Red Porch, decorated with its stone lions – the place where Russia's rulers at momentous times in history had appeared before their people – recreating an almost medieval scene from an idealised Little Mother Moscow, the holy city of old, amid the glittering onion domes and spires of Moscow's ancient churches.

And so, comforted by this false image of national unity, the concerted pattern of denial continued, with Nicholas and Alexandra remaining stubbornly blind to the dramatic changes going on within the nation. Only a few months later this upsurge of xenophobia and national unity was dissipated by the devastating losses on the Eastern Front. The Russian people, whom both Nicholas and Alexandra had believed had boundless love for their tsar as the being 'from whom all charity and fortune derive', turned their backs on him, their devotion fatally undermined by the political and economic strains that, having reached a high point in 1905, had bubbled on through the Rasputin scandal and now into a disastrous war. The monarchy which Nicholas had believed was the only viable form of government for Russia's huge cross-section of races, classes and religions thereafter rapidly lost the support of the two most powerful elements that had always, traditionally, shored it up: the peasantry, called on to make the economic sacrifices to provide food and men for the Front; and the army, called on to continue fighting a war in Europe whilst revolution raged at home.

Nicholas and Alexandra, and their children too, never ceased to agonise over the fate of their 'poor Russia'. The anguish stayed with them even during their final months in Tobolsk and Ekaterinburg. If anything, it increased, for they were now completely isolated from the Russia they thought they knew. Alexandra's blind faith in miracles had never let her accept the finality of the Revolution and the Romanov removal from power. It was all a terrible mistake, a nightmare that surely would pass. All that was needed was to pray more and more fervently for God's intervention. Even when asylum for the family had been discussed in the early days after the abdication, it had been done in terms only of a temporary arrangement – until the war was over, after which the family made clear their wish to return and live in retirement in the Crimea. To be forced to leave Russia for ever would for them be a spiritual death, which other Russians – notably creative artists and writers – have also rejected. It would break their 'last link with the past, which would then be dead for ever'. The Tsar and Tsaritsa had made it clear that they would rather die in Russia than be forced to live permanently in exile, and their children shared their sentiments.

But today, 10 July, a very new and irrevocably changed Soviet Russia was about to be inaugurated at the 2,000-seater Bolshoy Theatre in Moscow, where the main auditorium was packed for the ratification of the newly composed Constitution of the Russian Socialist Federated Soviet Republic. After more than six months of preparation under Sverdlov, Lenin's government was ready to unveil a constitution that it believed would be the first in the world 'to give expression . . . to the hopes of the workers, the peasants and the oppressed and to abolish political and economic inequality once and for all'. This constitution, combined with the Declaration of the Rights of Toiling and Exploited People, approved in January 1918, set out to destroy the old bourgeois regime and the exploitation of man by man, by disenfranchising those who had so rapaciously exploited Russia – capitalists, the clergy and the aristocracy – depriving them of their civil rights, and creating a form of government where the wealth produced by the country's workers would be shared by them. Divested of 'every form of force, coercion, and oppression', the new state would set an example for the whole world and oppressed peoples everywhere.

The reality, however, was already somewhat different: the erosion of the power of the recently formed regional soviets and with it the destruction of independent political parties in Russia had begun in June with the outlawing of the Socialist Revolutionaries, anarchists and Mensheviks and the domination over them of the Bolsheviks in local government. The creation of the Cheka further fuelled the suppression of any independent political action in the regions. Since the assassination of Mirbach on 6 July, arrests and executions of political opponents had escalated across Russia's regional soviets such as Kursk, Tambov, Kaluga, Tula, Vladimir and Nizhni-Novgorod. One by one, Left SR committees in these cities were dissolved, and their representatives – and with them representation in the main of the Russian peasantry – removed. Left SRs in positions of responsibility were being driven from their posts as well as excluded from delegations to central government, and many rank-and-file party members were being arrested and interrogated. The process was further accelerated on the 10th: a telegram sent out by People's Commissar for Internal Affairs Grigory Petrovsky (who worked hand-in-glove with the Cheka) ordered provincial soviets 'immediately to take all measures [to] apprehend and detain' anyone who had taken part in the recent Left SR uprising, hand them over to military-revolutionary courts and shoot anyone who resisted.

For a brief while, the messianism of revolution and popular anger at an age-old class system based on privilege had driven the motor of change in Russia, but by the summer of 1918 it mattered little to Russia's hungry and dispossessed who now was in power. And the fate of their former tsar, now vanished from view, mattered even less. The promise of political equality laid down by the new constitution was something the hungry could not comprehend, any more than the concept of their collective responsibility to the state. It was all so new and baffling to a peasantry with no real sense of a national consciousness. Yes, a constitution and a republic were all very fine and good, they observed, provided always that there was a wise tsar too, someone to whom they could doff their caps, as they had always done. In the old days they had been taught to answer only to the tsar and to God; the idea now of answering to their newly constituted country when all most of them knew was their immediate village was beyond their comprehension. The vast majority of Russia's ordinary peasants (85 per cent of the population) were confused about the nature of this new democracy and highly resistant to the forced requisitioning of their grain which they thought the Revolution had brought them the right to keep. This was all part, they were told, of the necessary Socialist transformation of the village. But all the peasants wanted was peace and quiet, independence and the right to farm the 'three acres per soul' that the Duma had long since promised them. For a while they had been persuaded to place their faith in Lenin's 1917 promise of 'peace, bread and land' that would come once the bourgeoisie had been disarmed of its own land and property in the name of the state. But now, suddenly, the labouring masses found themselves facing the imposition of enforced labour on all, under the constitution's ominous watchword, 'He who does not work shall not eat.' It soon became clear that the land was not to be divided out equally among the peasantry but collectively worked for the nation as a whole, its produce benefiting the local communes. A new kind of official ideology, summarised in the constitution, was about to ensure that the state rather than the tsar was all, and the individual, once again, as he had been under the old feudal system, was enchained by economic slavery in a system where he counted for nothing.

The institution of so many rapid and draconian changes had meant that by July of 1918 the country's infrastructure was collapsing. Industry was in shutdown, the factories closed because of a shortage of materials; shops were boarded up, the urban food supply in crisis. The railway system had collapsed, credit had been destroyed, on top of which much of the Russian territory in the Baltic and Ukraine was occupied by the Germans. There was no firewood, no electricity, no gas, no oil for lamps. Soon there would be no candles. With supply lines disrupted, nothing was obtainable except by the card system, and with those supplies rapidly becoming exhausted, things increasingly could only be got on the black market, with hoarders realising huge profits on their goods.

Writing that day to Geoffrey Robinson, his editor at the *Times* in London, Russia correspondent Robert Wilton had no doubts of the desperateness of the situation:

I wish to say most emphatically that, unless we immediately inter- vene in Russia with a large force . . . and unless *we* establish a Russian government (on non-party lines) under a virtual dictator, who shall be backed up with all the force, military and moral, of the allied powers, the Germans will be in Moscow before the snow falls and will set up a Monarchy (Romanov or Hohenzollern) and this new authority, representing law and order, will compel and receive the adhesion of the Russian people. Russia (and Siberia) will then become German colonies and our position in India will be seriously menaced.

British interests, as ever, devolved ultimately not to royal blood ties with the Romanovs, or the interests of the Russian people, but to the security of Empire. Sixty years previously, Britain had fought a disastrous war in the Crimea for similar reasons.

In statute number 23 of its new constitution, the Soviet government had asserted that 'Guided by the interests of the working class as a whole, the [state] deprives individuals or separate groups of any privileges which they may use to the detriment of the socialist revolution.' It was now six weeks since the arrest of Count Ilya Tatishchev and Prince Vasily Dolgorukov by the Cheka as potential 'enemies of the socialist revolution'. The family had repeatedly asked about their welfare, having no idea that all this time Tatishchev had been languishing in Ekaterinburg jail. Dolgorukov, who had initially been allowed to stay in the city when he arrived at the end of April, had been arrested after compromising maps of the region showing river routes were found when his lodgings were searched. Accused of trying to plot the Romanov family's escape, Dolgorukov, together with Tatishchev, was taken by the Cheka on 10 July to a favourite killing place beyond the city's Ivanovskoe cemetery. Here a single revolver shot to the back of the head – the favoured Cheka method of execution – ended their lives, after which their bodies were thrown into a pit.

Over at the Ipatiev House the afternoon had been warm and sunny. Alexandra, although still suffering a lot of pain in her back and legs, had gone out into the garden for an hour and a half with the others to enjoy the warm air, little knowing that across the city the man who had today pulled the trigger on her loyal servant Vasily Dolgorukov was none other than Commandant Yurovsky's eager young assistant Grigory Nikulin.

9

'Everything Is the Same'

THURSDAY 11 JULY 1918

For six weeks now, day in, day out, the devoted sisters of the Novo-Tikhvinsky Convent in Ekaterinburg had made their way from the southern outskirts of the city to the Ipatiev House bringing food – eggs, flour, cream, milk, butter – for the Romanov family. They had never been allowed into the house but had had to deliver their goods to the commandant at the front door. Although they found the experience intimidating, they would not abandon their *batyushka-tsar*.

The convent had a long and eminent reputation for philanthropy; established in the late eighteenth century, it had, since 1822, been one of the wealthiest in Russia, with a complex containing eight churches set in a landscaped park with ponds, a hospital and almshouse and an orphanage for girls. The high quality of the handicrafts produced by its 900 sisters was famous: candle-making, icon-painting, needlework and embroidery. Sister Agnes, mistress of the novices who undertook the daily trip to the Ipatiev House, had instructed them to go in civilian dress – this being acceptable as they had not yet taken their vows – in order not to antagonise the Bolshevik guards, who otherwise derided them for their black nun's habits. Before his dismissal, Avdeev had regularly helped himself to the vast majority of the food, sharing it with his favourites. It was only after he was gone that Nicholas had discovered it was being systematically pilfered; yet the pilfering still went on. This morning Yurovsky had kept the Romanovs waiting for their morning inspection as he sat and tucked into the cheese brought by the nuns. He had recently told the family they would not be getting any more cream from the convent hereafter. Their meat ration was being drastically reduced too – the latest delivery, supposedly for six days, was, complained Alexandra, barely enough for the soup.

So when, after the morning inspection, three workmen arrived and began installing a heavy iron grating in front of the only open window in the Tsar and Tsaritsa's corner bedroom, this seemed yet another indicator of the tightening of the regime at the house under Yurovsky, a man whom Alexandra had taken to calling 'the ox' or 'the bull'. Nicholas was on his guard too: 'We like this man less and less', he confided to his diary. The installation of the iron grille had no doubt come about because, despite the high double palisade, Alexandra had been spotted by the external guards standing too close to the open window, trying to catch the attention of people in the large cobbled plaza, Voznesensky Square, opposite. Yurovsky had warned her not to do this, but she had ignored him. The nervousness of the guards at any attempt by the Romanovs to signal to people in the world outside had intensified since the change of regime at the house. The place might seem impregnable, but there was still the threat of attack – or even rescue.

Back in June, Avdeev had been alerted that they might need to evacuate the family due to rumours of a possible attack from anarchist extremists – their intention, though Avdeev did not of course reveal this – to murder the family out of hand. The Romanovs were told to pack and be ready to leave, but a few days later the threat had receded. Then had come the discovery, only a week or so after that, at the end of June, of a smuggled letter concealed inside the large cork stopper of a bottle of cream brought by the nuns. It was Dr Derevenko who had first requested the family be given access to these foodstuffs from the convent, and their daily delivery had inevitably been made clever use of, with messages for the family hidden in loaves of bread or scribbled surreptitiously on the paper in which food was wrapped. Derevenko at some point had been involved as an important go-between in serious plans to try and stage a rescue of the family, but he himself could not have passed notes to the family as he was always very closely watched when he came to the house to treat the Tsarevich.

A certain monarchist officer, Colonel Ivan Sidorov, one of the Tsar's former adjutants, had however sought out the doctor in Ekaterinburg in mid-June after travelling north from Odessa and through him had made contact with the nuns of the Novo-Tikhvinsky Convent, getting them to smuggle in notes in this way. It is not known whether Sidorov or some other group of loyalist officers was responsible for the letter in the cream bottle received by the family around 20 June. But Avdeev had spotted it and had handed it over to the Cheka. The letter purported to come from a group of monarchists in the city – no doubt one of several who had taken rooms in the local hotels and rooming houses under false names, where they had hatched their various hare-brained plots, singly and in groups, as they tried to find ways of contacting the Imperial Family. Some had even had the bravado to openly go and stand outside the Ipatiev House, or send in letters and gifts – all of which were confiscated.

If such plots were hare-brained, none could have been more so than that originated by Oliver Locker Lampson of the British Royal Naval Armoured Car Division sent into Russia to assist the Imperial Army in 1916. Lampson had got to know the Tsar at HQ at Mogilev, and after Nicholas's confinement at Tsarskoe Selo had deemed the opportunities for rescue very easy. Bribing the already careless guards with cigarettes, vodka and British bully beef, Lampson had planned that one of the Tsar's servants would don a false beard and cloak and take his place, Nicholas meanwhile disguising himself in a British khaki uniform that Lampson had smuggled in, shaving off his beard and walking out of the palace in front of the drunken guards. From there a field ambulance would take him to a military train and north to Archangel and a British ship to the UK. The same ploy, however, could not of course be used with Alexandra and the children; the Tsar had refused point blank to be rescued unless they could be saved too, proving himself, in Lampson's eyes, 'a true king and a true man'. The real window of opportunity for escape, had there ever been one, had been in the first two weeks of the Imperial Family's confinement at Tsarskoe Selo in March 1917. This was the convinced view of British military attaché General Wallscourt Waters, who at the time had told the War Office that 'if a fast torpedo boat and a few bags of British sovereigns should be promptly dispatched to the Gulf of Finland . . . there was a good prospect of rescue'. But it had to be the entire family; thereafter, even where the opportunities for rescue presented themselves at Tobolsk, any attempt at flight would probably have been vetoed in the end by the Tsar and Tsaritsa because of Alexey's fragile state of health.

Nevertheless, in Tobolsk, members of the Imperial entourage had had free passage in and out of the Governor's House, facilitating the passing on of plans and messages and the enlisting of the support of a powerful church leader, Bishop Hermogen of Tobolsk, as well as Petrograd supporters of Rasputin's former circle. The Tsar's aides, Count Tatishchev and Prince Dolgorukov, had been in communication with an envoy sent to Tobolsk by monarchist leaders of a National Centre group (a secret organisation of anti-Bolsheviks led by right-centre politicians) who had passed on money to assist in their escape. Other loyalists put their trust in a Russian of dubious character named Boris Solovev. Son of the treasurer of the Holy Synod and a follower of the mystic Madame Blavatsky, he had married Rasputin's daughter Mariya in 1917 in a cynical move designed to curry favour with the monarchists, and had assumed command of a rescue plan based at nearby Tyumen. He had managed to get notes through to the Tsaritsa in Tobolsk and she had approved a rescue plan fronted by Solovev and his supposed 300 officers of the

'Brotherhood of St John of Tobolsk'. Considerable amounts of money were needed, claimed Solovev, to fund the rescue, and these had been raised by means of consignments of the Tsaritsa's jewels smuggled out of the Governor's House. But not everyone trusted Solovev or his motives, and when his rescue plan failed to materialise, people started asking questions about where all the money had gone and whose side he was on: the Tsar's, the Germans' or the Bolsheviks'? Was his whole rescue plan bogus – an act of simple greed, or the first of several orchestrated attempts at deliberate provocation by the Bolsheviks to unsettle and undermine the Romanov family?

In Simbirsk, in early July, another rescue plot was hatched by a Serbian officer, Lieutenant Kappel, who had held a secret meeting at the Hotel Troitse-Spasskaya with Russian monarchists and former members of the Duma. They had at their disposal, so it is alleged, plans of the Ipatiev House drawn by the Tsar and smuggled out to Dr Derevenko, who, it was claimed, was co-operating with them in a rescue plan set for 15 July. Kappel had dispatched a monarchist captain from the Urals, Stepanov, back to Ekaterinburg to prepare plans to storm the Ipatiev House by night with a commando-style group of local officers, with the assistance of undercover Czech officers from their legion, having first created diversionary disturbances in nearby towns such as Perm. But the Ekaterinburg Cheka, by now only too well aware of monarchist plotting and intrigue in the city, arrested Stepanov as soon as he had stepped off the train. Another highly implausible plot hatched in Kiev by a former member of the Imperial entourage Aleksandr Mosolov, Prince Kochubey and the German Duke, George of Leuchtenberg, had favoured spiriting the Romanovs away to Berlin. A reconnaissance party would go on ahead to set up a base in Ekaterinburg for the family's rescue. Two officers had been sent into the city as scouts where they were to make contact with German agents already hiding out there, but when word had been passed to the Romanovs about the plan, they had vetoed any thought of rescue by Germany; as the Tsaritsa had insisted, 'I would rather die in Russia than be rescued by the Germans.'

The same fate as Stepanov's had befallen a young officer from the Imperial Guard named Captain Paul Bulygin, who had failed in early July 1918 in an ill-conceived mission, based on a false rumour he had heard that the Romanovs were about to be evacuated to Kotelnich near Vyatka. Once the family had arrived there, he and his fellow conspirators in the National Centre planned to seize weapons from the town's small Bolshevik garrison, storm the house in which they were being held and take them north by river steamer to Archangel in the Arctic. When the Romanovs failed to arrive at Kotelnich and rumours began that the Tsar had been murdered, Bulygin decided to travel to Ekaterinburg to find out what was going on. But he arrived at the city's railway station only to be recognised by a former officer who knew him and hauled off to the local jail. Here, living on salted herring and dirty bread and tortured by thirst in a cell shared with several others, he had watched in horror as night after night, one by one, his cellmates were taken away to be shot. He thought his own execution inevitable at any moment when, without explanation, he was taken from the jail and back to the station under escort and put on a train full of wounded Red Army soldiers being evacuated from the Czech Front.

The possibility of a staged rescue from within Ekaterinburg itself was not in fact as unlikely as it seemed, for the Military Academy of the General Staff of the former Imperial Army had been evacuated to the city from Petrograd in April of that year. Of its 300 officials, only a handful professed any Bolshevik sympathies. And among their ranks lurked a secret cabal of five monarchist officers led by 26-year-old Captain Dmitri Malinovsky who discussed the possibilities of rescue. With the Academy located so close to the Novo-Tikhvinsky Convent, approaches were made to the nuns to act as possible go-betweens. Dr Derevenko was also asked for a plan of the upper floor of the house – which he had seen and could readily provide. With the rapid approach of the Czechs, Trotsky had ordered the Academy to be transferred to Kazan, but only about half of the staff departed. The rest remained, declaring their 'neutrality'. Filepp Goloshchekin, however, took no chances and ensured that their activities were closely watched, and the Academy was assigned its own political commissar, a Chekist called Matveev. Nevertheless, Malinovsky and his four friends continued to plot and recruited another seven fellow officers at the Academy into their scheme. But like all the other would-be rescuers they lacked the two things most needed to further their plans: money and weapons. They could not appeal for help locally among the terrorised population and their hopes came to nothing. In the end, although as many as 37 men from the Academy were eventually involved in a rescue plot, all they were able to do was send in gifts of food via the nuns, nothing more. When the Czechs arrived at the end of July, these same 37 defected to their ranks.

We shall never know for sure the identity of the author of the first 'officer letter' received by the Romanovs at the Ipatiev House on around 20 June. Either it was genuine and indeed came from Malinovsky's group and was intercepted by Avdeev and passed on to Goloshchekin, or it was the first of four deliberate fabrications by the Cheka. If it was indeed genuine, then the Cheka were quick to spot its potential as a means of testing the Romanovs' willingness to intrigue in their own escape – in

Bolshevik eyes good enough grounds for their annihilation. And so the letter was deliberately copied and amended and passed on to the family so that any written response could be intercepted. Coming as it did through the good offices of the nuns of the Novo-Tikhvinsky Convent, the letter seemed to the Tsar and Tsaritsa trustworthy, even though it was flawed in its failure to use the correct terms of address to a tsar by a supposed loyalist. It was, nevertheless, reassuring: the family's friends on the outside had not forgotten them after all. It had arrived at a time of great despondency and offered the first tangible hope of rescue after weeks of being deprived of any letters, visits or news of the world outside. The Romanovs' 'friends', as the letter, written in red ink, announced portentously in French, 'were no longer sleeping'; the 'hour so long awaited had come'. The Bolsheviks were a clear and present danger to the family, but with the Czechs – the liberating 'army of Slavic friends' – now only 50 miles away from Ekaterinburg, Red Army troops in the city would soon capitulate. The family were told to listen out for any movement outside, to 'wait and hope' and be ready at any time – day or night – for liberation. They were to smuggle out in the cream bottle a map of the layout of their rooms with as much detail as possible. The note was signed 'from someone who is ready to die for you, Officer of the Russian Army'.

The family's cautious response, written in French by Olga in the blank space at the bottom of the letter a day or so later, warned that all their windows were sealed and that Alexey was too sick and unable to walk. They were adamant: 'No risk whatsoever must be taken without being absolutely certain of the result. We are almost always under close observation.' Another letter quickly followed on the 25th from the supposed loyal officer, talking of escape from one of the upstairs windows – an impossibility until, by coincidence or design, the Bolsheviks allowed a window to be unsealed and opened a day or so later. Would it be possible beforehand to tranquillise 'the little one' in some way so that he could be lowered down without pain? the letter asked. That same day, the 25th, the Romanovs responded with doubt and caution, giving details of the newly opened window, the location of the upstairs guards, the regular inspections, the system of alarm bells, the guards in the house across the street, the motor car always at the commandant's disposal outside. Now, too, they asked about the welfare of Dr Botkin and their servants: what about them, would they be able to come too? 'It would be ignoble of us . . . to leave them alone after they have followed us into exile', the family wrote. If they were to flee and leave them behind, could they be sure that nothing would happen to them? They were worried too about all their personal documents – letters and diaries especially – in storage crates in the outhouse. Nevertheless, they assured their rescuer officer, 'you can count on our sangfroid'. A third letter came about a day later, telling the family to prepare for a signal at night, upon which they were to barricade their door with furniture and – somewhat ingenuously – climb out of the open window by means of a rope, where their rescuers would be waiting at the bottom.

What followed seemed a flabby and ill-thought-out plan which must have set the Tsar and Tsaritsa on their guard: seven people, including a sick boy with a crippled leg, were somehow to shimmy down a home-made rope they were to contrive themselves, from the first floor to where transportation would be waiting, and a miraculous escape into hiding would follow. But what about the guards who patrolled the circuit between the two palisades, and the machine-gun placement on the ground floor that watched this area at all hours? They were highly sceptical. Be that as it may, on the nights of 25 and 26 June, the family sat up anxiously, fully dressed – the women wearing their jewels concealed in bodices – in anticipation of flight and ready for rescue. But it did not come. The waiting and uncertainty had, wrote Nicholas in his diary, 'been very trying'. The whole plan had suddenly seemed suspicious if not improbable and, clearly alarmed by this, the family had responded most emphatically on around 27 June in a letter written in crayon by the Tsaritsa: 'We do not want to, nor can we, *escape*. We can only be *carried off* by force, just as it was force that was used to carry us from Tobolsk.' Their rescuers were not to count on any active help from them; nor did they wish Avdeev and the guards who had been kind to them to suffer in any way as a result of their escape. They were now far too closely watched; if a rescue were to be attempted, then 'In the name of God, avoid bloodshed above all.'

The following night they continued to watch and wait but it was all utterly hopeless. Several days elapsed before a fourth and final letter arrived from the would-be rescuers, apologising for their slow response. The changeover of commandant and guards at the house, plus the approach of the Czechs had now made things doubly difficult. The vague promises of impending rescue seemed even more implausible now, as too did the adventure-comic instruction to 'await the whistle around midnight'. The Romanovs did not respond in the blank space provided, although they passed the letter back with a brief message in barely legible pencil on the envelope: 'Surveillance of us is constantly increasing because of the open window.' They knew this full well, for on the night of the 28th they had heard the sentry on duty below being specifically instructed to watch their every move at the window. Rescue was a chimera, as it had always been, the thought of it guaranteed only to torment and demoralise, as too was the false information contained in one of the officer letters that the family's friends 'D[olgorukov]' and 'T[atishchev]' were in safe hands. They had both already been shot.

The first letter received by the family, which Avdeev claimed to have intercepted, may have been genuine. Avdeev later stated that it had come from an Austrian army officer named 'Mahitsch'. It is possible he was referring in fact to a Major Migich, a Serbian officer and member of the Tsar's General Staff, who had come to Ekaterinburg in the entourage of Princess Helena of Serbia in June when she arrived to enquire about the fate of her own husband, now at Alapaevsk, as well as that of the Romanovs. Migich had been arrested along with several other members of Helena's entourage. The other three letters, supposedly passed on to the Tsaritsa by one of the internal guards, were clearly a deliberate fabrication, composed at the behest of the Cheka. They were dictated by a man called Petr Voikov with further input from Aleksandr Beloborodov. Voikov was a local Bolshevik who had recently been appointed People's Commissar for Food Supply in the Urals. A blond, blue-eyed intellectual with an eye for women, he had for many years lived in exile in Geneva, where he had studied chemistry and economics and had acquired the near perfect French needed to write the letters. But his handwriting was very bad, so he had dictated the letter to another loyal Chekist and Ipatiev House guard, Isay Rodzinsky. With these letters and the Romanovs' response to them in their possession, the Ekaterinburg Bolsheviks now had a smoking gun – solid 'evidence' of an escape plan and the family's willingness to conspire in one – which could be used, should they so wish, to justify the murder of the family during a possible 'escape attempt'. (Yurovsky later observed that by responding to the letters, Nicholas 'had fallen into a hasty plan by us to trap him'.) It also provided a valuable lever with the Central Executive Committee in Moscow in supporting the Ural Regional Soviet's ongoing argument that, with the Czechs approaching and the continuing threat of rescue not abating, the time had come to do away with the Imperial Family before they fell into the wrong hands.

The desperate situation in Ekaterinburg was all too apparent to British consul Thomas Preston, who on 11 July managed to get a cipher out to a colleague at the diplomatic enclave at Vologda. For 20 days he and his fellow consuls in the city had been forbidden by the Bolshevik military authorities to send or receive telegrams. Public sympathy for the Czechs now closing in on the city in a pincer movement from the south, west and east was growing, especially since the murder of 18 hostages in the city at the end of June. Since the Revolution, more than 800 local men had been reluctantly mobilised for military service, but there was now considerable opposition to this in the rural districts, with recruits refusing to fight against fellow Slavs – the advancing Czechs; nor did they want to fight in the Red Army alongside Austrian and German prisoners of war dragooned into service by the Bolsheviks. At the Verkh-Isetsk works outside the city, 4,000 old soldiers from the Front had today gathered in the public square demanding an end to military operations led by Lenin's commissars. These new men, to their mind, had no sympathies with the Russian labouring classes. The protesters were quickly dispersed and several arrested by the Cheka and threatened with shooting for their act of 'counter-revolution'. As an example to the others, five of the protesters were taken and thrown alive into a gas hole where hot slag was burned. Brutality such as this only further confirmed Preston's view that the Bolsheviks were now holding power 'exclusively by means of terrorism over [the] population'.

In the summer of 1918, the road out to the Koptyaki Forest – a dense area of ancient birch and pine forest nine miles north-west of Ekaterinburg – would take you past the straggling wooden suburbs of the low, flat city, and the stinking smoke stacks of the huge Verkh-Isetsk works, along a small local road that was crossed by the rail lines to Perm and Nizhni-Tagil. After that the going got tough. It certainly wasn't an easy place to get to by motor vehicle in July 1918 because beyond the crossings the road was little more than a muddy cart track full of puddles and potholes, surrounded by wet, peaty woodland. Nor was there much cause for anyone to wish to go there except to get to the small farming and fishing village of Koptyaki, a collection of wooden peasant huts on the shores of Iset Pond that lay beyond. There was a time when they had mined for gold here – not deep mines but shallow workings, like caves. With 10 or 12 of these old mines located in the area and now overgrown, it was a dangerous place to walk – the open workings were full of fetid silt and rainwater, and beneath that a layer of permafrost. Nevertheless, at 5 p.m. that late summer afternoon of 11 July, a mining technician, Ivan Fesenko, who had been working in the area prospecting for iron ore was idly carving his name and the date of his visit on a tall birch tree. He was sitting not far from a spot known to the locals as the Four Brothers – given its name for four tall pine trees that had once stood there, of which only two stumps remained. Nearby there were a couple of disused iron ore workings, surrounded by mounds of clayey earth, not far from a small pond the locals called Ganina Yama (Ganin's Pit).

Suddenly Fesenko noticed three men approaching on horseback in the distance. As they came nearer, he recognised one of them immediately as Commandant Yurovsky of the Ipatiev House; the other was a man called

Ermakov from the Verkh–Isetsk works; the third man looked to him like an Austrian or Magyar prisoner of war (it was probably Ermakov's close associate, a former Kronstadt sailor, Stepan Vaganov). Seeing Fesenko, the men stopped and asked him about the state of the road and access to the village of Koptyaki beyond. Could you get a lorry up there? They needed, so they said, to transport '500 poods' (about eight tons) of grain to the village. Fesenko told them he thought the road was good; you could get through by lorry. But as the men turned and rode off, he also asked himself the question: why would they want to transport such a heavy load to such a remote spot?

Back at the Ipatiev House, the guard duty book for that day was filled out, but there seemed nothing to say, except the one recurring comment of late: '*Vse obychno*'; 'Everything is the same.' In fact nothing was the same. Everything was about to change.

10

'What Is To Be Done with Nicholas?'

FRIDAY 12 JULY 1918

The pain Alexandra woke to on the sunny morning of 12 July was bad again; so bad that she could do nothing but remain in bed all day. Dr Botkin was running out of medicines and could do little to help. But he put in a formal request to Yurovsky to obtain the prescriptions he needed from Pozner, the local chemist. Maria volunteered to stay by her mother's bedside while the others went outside into the garden for their recreation periods, and spent the day reading to her – mundane Christian homilies by the religious writer Grigory Dyachenko that Alexandra loved so much and which all the family regularly shared in. Occasionally Maria's soft voice was interrupted by noises through the open window and Alexandra stilled her so she could listen. The world outside was so tantalisingly near. Dramatic changes were afoot in the city; for the last two weeks Alexandra had frequently heard the sound of troop movements, artillery had trundled past below and with it the metallic ring of horses' hooves on cobblestones and the footfalls of marching soldiers, accompanied occasionally by military bands. The Red Army was on the move, with more and more troops – many of them 'volunteer' Austro-Hungarian prisoners of war – being transported to the Front against the Czech legions. Ekaterinburg had become a chaotic transit camp, full of wounded men, who were arriving daily on crowded trains from the Front for the most rudimentary medical attention before being evacuated west. This much Alexandra knew and noted in her diary, for she had heard the guards talking about it.

But what of them – the family? How much longer would they be kept here? Something surely would happen soon and this interminable imprisonment in the Ipatiev House would come to an end. Alexandra must have nursed final faint hopes that if the longed-for rescue by Russian monarchists had now faded, then it might just be possible that the Czechs would get to the family in time. In any event, God would intervene, of that she was sure. With the afternoon punctuated by rolls of thunder and rainstorms that raged outside the iron grille of the open window in her room, Alexandra's thoughts now were increasingly preoccupied with how and when fate would take a hand. For this she was prepared, reconciled even, as were all the Romanov family.

Meanwhile, it was turning into a long, exhausting day for the loyal Bolshevik leaders of Ekaterinburg who had gathered down the road at the Amerikanskaya Hotel. Once graced by eminent visitors such as Chekhov and the scientist Dmitri Mendeleev, the hotel now resembled a military barracks, its parquet floors muddied and scuffed by the boots and equipment of the Red Army detachment based on its ground floor, whose sinister role was to carry out reprisals against local 'counter-revolutionaries'. Upstairs, the Ekaterinburg Cheka had taken over the first-floor rooms, but their plush interiors were no longer an oasis of rest to travellers on the long road through Siberia; rather a political nerve centre for men in leather jackets and forage caps, bristling with weapons, whose meetings now increasingly went on long into the night. All the local hard men of the party had now become familiar faces to the maids at the hotel: Goloshchekin; Beloborodov; Fedor Lukoyanov, a former journalist and head of the Cheka; Georgy Safarov, a close friend of Beloborodov and member of the URS's presidium; Isay Rodzinsky, who had helped fake the officer letters to the Tsar; Chutskaev from the local Soviet; Yurovsky and his assistant Nikulin – they all had their own rooms in the Amerikanskaya, though none of them lived here. Some of them seemed very young – like pasty-faced students, the maids observed – but they brought their women in with them for sex and drinking sessions, and one of the waitresses, Fekla Dedyukhina, had already taken up with the commander of the detachment downstairs. It had prompted another maid, Praskovya Morozova, to have a row with her. How could she, in all conscience, go to bed with someone who had just come back from shooting people? Dedyukhina's response had been an indifferent shrug – she didn't care – a response symptomatic of the climate in Ekaterinburg now. Nobody cared; surviving was all that mattered. A few days later, Morozova, accused of 'counter-revolutionary' behaviour, had been dismissed from her job.

On the morning of the 12th, an urgent meeting had been called at the Amerikanskaya between the Executive Committee of the Ural Regional Soviet and the Ekaterinburg Cheka. At 10 p.m. that night it was still dragging on amidst the fading imperial splendour of room no. 3 – Yurovsky's room. The potted plants, *fin de siècle* furnishings and chandeliers seemed strangely incongruous in the thickening atmosphere of cigarette smoke, sweat and political debate. The conference table had seen better days, littered as it now was with the detritus of discarded plates of food, packets of cigarettes, vodka bottles and endless glasses of tea from the Tula samovar. In the chair sat a thin and sickly-looking Aleksandr Beloborodov, president of the Ural Regional Soviet. A poorly educated former factory electrician, Beloborodov had all the qualities required of a dedicated party man: he was ambitious, hard-working and morally and ethically unprincipled. He had earned his spurs young, from the age of 14 working as a political agitator among his colleagues at the Nadezhdinsky factory and disseminating underground literature. Arrested in 1914, he served time in exile in Siberia. He had been rewarded for his services to the Revolution at the age of only 27, by being made president of the Ural Regional Soviet in April 1917. Today he had not long returned from an exhausting tour of Bolshevik forces at the Czech Front.

The object of this meeting was to give an air of revolutionary legitimacy to what was now being put to the vote by Beloborodov and his four key colleagues on the presidium of the URS: Filipp Goloshchekin; Boris Didkovsky, Beloborodov's deputy; Nikolay Tolmachev, a local political commissar who had helped organise the guard at the Ipatiev House; and Grigory Safarov, who had been a frequent visitor there.

After five days on a filthy and crowded military goods train out of Moscow, an exhausted Filipp Goloshchekin had headed straight to the meeting from Ekaterinburg's railway station, to present his colleagues with a résumé of his discussions about the Romanovs with members of the Communist Party's Central Committee. As it had turned out, because of the pressures of impending civil war, only seven of the 23 members of the Committee had been in Moscow at the time, the rest dispersed on various military and political assignments across Russia. But the three most influential of them had been in town: Lenin, Sverdlov and head of the Cheka Feliks Dzerzhinsky. The 42-year-old Goloshchekin was not nicknamed 'the eye of the Kremlin' for nothing. Filipp, or Philippe, was in fact his party name, disguising his Jewish background and his given names of Isay Isaakovich. After training as a dentist in St Petersburg, he had become a professional revolutionary. He was one of the old guard, a dedicated party man since the former Russian Social Democratic party had split into the two factions – Bolsheviks and Mensheviks – in 1903, and a vigorous political agitator during the 1905 Revolution. Like Lenin and Sverdlov, he had spent time in exile in Siberia, and had endured two years of the hellhole of the notorious Schlüsselburg Fortress during 1906–8, where many revolutionaries before him had been incarcerated by the Okhrana – the tsarist secret police. He was well known to all of the Moscow leadership in Russia and abroad, having escaped to Europe, where he had spent time in Paris with Lenin in 1909 and in Prague in 1912, on which occasion he had been chosen to serve as a member of the Central Committee. From Lenin Goloshchekin had learned the art of the loyal, professional agitator, prepared to act ruthlessly as the situation dictated. He was 'a typical Leninite . . . cruel, a born executioner', as one contemporary described him. British consul Thomas Preston found him cold and callous too – a ruthless party man. Since becoming close friends with Yakov Sverdlov in exile in Siberia, Goloshchekin's political career had been consistently promoted by his influential friend, and it was on Sverdlov's recommendation that in the spring of 1917 Lenin had hand-picked Goloshchekin to serve the party, first in Perm and then in Ekaterinburg. The quid pro quo of this was Goloshchekin's support, as a member of the CEC, for the ousting of Kamenev as chair in November that year and his replacement by Sverdlov.

Goloshchekin was 'very energetic', Sverdlov informed the Uralites, commending their new military commissar to them; more importantly, he 'holds to the party line' and would, Sverdlov knew, ensure that they did so too. As Moscow's man in the Urals Goloshchekin now had a powerful controlling influence in the local Cheka as well as on the presidium of the Ural Regional Soviet: his colleague Beloborodov had effectively been positioned as puppet president of the URS, very much under the control of Goloshchekin and Sverdlov.

The July talks in Moscow were the culmination of months of negotiation between Ekaterinburg and the Bolshevik leadership, with Sverdlov as go-between, over the fate of the Romanovs. In November 1917, Goloshchekin had had discussions with Lenin about the strengthening of Soviet power in the Urals and the need to step up the fight against the 'petty bourgeois parties' in the region. One of his first tasks after arriving in Ekaterinburg had been to lead a cadre of armed Sysert factory workers against the counter-revolutionary forces of the Cossack leader Aleksandr Dutov; some of these men later joined the guard at the Ipatiev House. Goloshchekin had quickly made his mark in the city; he held his own in the toughest, most contentious political meetings and had already initiated a local clampdown on the bourgeoisie and other anti-Bolsheviks, whom he denigrated in typical hyperbolic Leninist tones as 'supporting the White rabble displaying its poisoned fangs'. At the Communist Party Congress in February of 1918, he had intimated to his advocate Sverdlov that the transfer of the Romanovs to Ekaterinburg would be a suitable reward for his loyalty to the centre and the unpopular treaty of Brest-Litovsk. By March 1918, talks with Moscow had turned more specifically to this issue, when Goloshchekin, in the city for the 7th Communist Party Congress, had had a meeting with Lenin, in his capacity as military commissar for the Urals, about the lax security at Tobolsk and the continuing threats of a monarchist rescue. Aleksandr Avdeev and two colleagues from Ekaterinburg were later dispatched to Tobolsk by Goloshchekin to keep an eye on the situation and report back to him personally by special courier. He had returned to Moscow for further talks about the Romanovs in May. Thereafter he remained in constant touch, holding, as he did, direct responsibility for the disposition of 3rd Army forces on the Eastern Front against the Czechs and Whites. In the spring he again emphasised his concerns over the lack of efficient security measures at Tobolsk, making clear Ekaterinburg's fervent desire (raised at a meeting of the URS in February) to have the Imperial Family under its much more stringent control (Tobolsk falling under the control of a political rival, the southern Siberian Omsk regional district). Goloshchekin had promised his personal guarantee of responsibility in this respect, and Sverdlov had continued to press Ekaterinburg's case ever harder with Lenin. The latest round of talks in July between Goloshchekin and the leadership, ostensibly to discuss the defence of the Urals against the onslaught of the Czechs, had by necessity been dominated by discussion about the fate of the Romanovs.

The members of the URS meanwhile had already made up their minds, in a tense meeting held on 29 June at the Amerikanskaya Hotel, that the family should be liquidated – indeed, Left SR extremists in the city were insisting on this happening as soon as possible, accusing the Bolsheviks in Moscow of vacillation and inconsistency. When the Tsar had first arrived, radicalised workers at the Verkh-Isetsk industrial plant had announced their intention to forcibly remove him from the Ipatiev House and lynch him during the May Day celebrations; the threat of summary justice in Ekaterinburg would not go away. 'Why are you fussing over Nicholas?' the Verkh-Isetsk workers shouted at angry meetings. 'It is time to be done with it!' Either that, they threatened, or they would knock the Urals Regional Soviet 'to pieces'. Local anarchists threatened much the same: 'If you do not annihilate Nicholas the Bloody, we will do it!'

The vote on the 29th for the Tsar's execution had been unanimous and the demands of the members of the URS that the leadership pass this on to Moscow and pressure them for a decision had prompted Goloshchekin's urgent mission. He had arrived there on 3 July with a message insisting on the execution of Nicholas. Workers in the Urals, so he said, resented the fact that the Tsar and his family seemed to be living in style at the Ipatiev House as though on holiday at a country dacha with all creature comforts. It may well be too that Goloshchekin used the 'evidence' of the intercepted officer letters as a lever to show Moscow that plots to rescue the Tsar also presented a real threat, thus justifying the need to execute him. In any event, essential contingency plans needed to be made for the whole family, should the situation dramatically change and the city have to be abandoned to the Czechs. It was too late now for any evacuation to safety elsewhere: the rail lines west to Moscow from the Urals were no longer safe because of the Czech advance, and territory in the north was controlled by the Whites.

Moscow nevertheless continued to sustain a concerted web of secrecy, even within the party, about its decision on what to do with Nicholas. Lenin and Sverdlov were skilful manipulators; publicly they stuck to the official line of bringing Nicholas back to Moscow, in order to placate the Germans, who wanted the Tsar where they could keep a closer eye on him. But as for a trial – this had raised a deal of consternation in Russia: would the Bolsheviks have the nerve to bring to trial for the violation of human rights a man whose despotism paled in comparison with their own? If Nicholas were brought to Moscow, many were of the view that he would be murdered en route. Indeed, there was no judicial precedent to justify trying him for supposed 'crimes against humanity' – a term defined as early as 1915 by the Allied powers but not effectively prosecuted until the Nuremberg trials of Nazi war criminals during 1945–6. There was talk, certainly, of prosecuting the Tsar for betraying the October Manifesto of 1905 in which he set up the Duma (a body he subsequently dissolved), but the Bolsheviks would be playing a very dangerous game by attempting a trial. In seeking to imitate the justice of the French Revolution, they might well become hoist by their own petard.

Abroad, there was still talk of possible exile for the family. Herman Bernstein, home from Russia at the end of June, had been told that Nicholas was not now to be placed on trial but to be 'exiled out of Russia'; this he reported in the *New York Herald*. The former tsar was now so completely discredited in Russia that nobody feared his return to the throne, least of all the Bolsheviks. Nevertheless, in other official quarters the story was that, given the changing military situation, a trial would be held in Ekaterinburg at the end of July, with Trotsky travelling from Moscow to conduct it. The lie grew ever bigger and more complex and contradictory as July went on. Perhaps the smokescreen of a 'trial' for the Tsar was maintained to keep the fiery Trotsky's ambitions in check. Within the party there was much rivalry between Sverdlov and Trotsky, and privately Sverdlov would have liked nothing better than to see Trotsky's ambitious plans for a French revolutionary-style trial scotched.

With rumour and counter-rumour flying about, everybody was left guessing, whilst in private Sverdlov and Goloshchekin continued to discuss their own very clear final strategies for the Romanovs. The presidium of the Ural Regional Soviet should organise the practical details of the family's execution and decide the precise day on which it would take place when the military situation dictated it, and contact Moscow for final approval. Such was Sverdlov's confidence in Goloshchekin's loyalty, and in turn Lenin's trust in Sverdlov's own handling of the situation, that it was later alleged that Sverdlov had told Goloshchekin that when the situation dictated, he should 'do whatever you think fit.'

In the meantime, Lenin was kept constantly informed of the changing situation in Ekaterinburg. In his study on the third floor of the Kremlin's Senate building, the Bolshevik leader was a busy man, working yet another of his brutally hard 16-hour days. The third floor of this fine eighteenth-century neoclassical building, commissioned by Catherine the Great as the venue for her advisory council, was now the hub of the Soviet government. Lenin's office was situated at one end of the corridor from his private apartments – work thus never being more than a stone's throw from his modest living quarters, which he shared with his wife and his sister Mariya. Whilst one door from his study led directly into the conference room used by the Council of People's Commissars – the principal decision-making body in the country, now controlled by the Bolsheviks – the other led into the 'box' – the telecommunications nerve centre from where Lenin kept in close touch with the homes and offices of the Central Committee and other government officials with whom he worked in close collaboration. He was assisted in his day-to-day paperwork by his loyal, self-effacing secretary Lidiya Fotieva and an army of undersecretaries, who flitted discreetly back and forth along the Senate's echoing corridors.

Lenin's workplace was a modest office for a modest man who took no interest in his appearance and led an abstemious lifestyle – neither smoking nor drinking. He was so frugal that they called him 'the Bolshevik who has remained poor'. He had few personal possessions or pleasures other than listening to Beethoven. He didn't like emotional indulgence of any kind, and even music was something he rarely had time for these days. The Revolution and the cause of Bolshevism were his abiding passions, and such was his lack of interest in personal things that for the past 25 years, since completing his law studies, he had committed all his energy and political brilliance to promoting his socialist vision. Nothing but his already failing health would stop him.

He sat at his desk in a simple wooden armchair with a wicker back and seat. The worktop was always neatly ordered, to hand a notebook in which he made his meticulous observations and instructions and entered the names of associates and officials with whom he had appointments. Nearby stood two revolving bookstands containing all the many necessary records of party congresses and conferences and the other political reference material he constantly drew on. All the available wall space in his office was filled with further bookcases containing over 2,000 essential volumes – maps and atlases, books on economics and technology, as well as political pamphlets and magazines in various languages, all in scrupulous alphabetical order, and including the seminal works of Marx and Engels, Lenin's primary political influences, and other key French, German and Russian political thinkers who had inspired him, such as Hegel, Saint-Simon, Plekhanov, Pisarev and Belinsky.

During these July days, Lenin had a mounting pile of political pressures to juggle, and today was no exception. He adhered to a strict daily schedule: there were letters to write; decrees to draft; an endless flood of telegrams to read and send; papers and minutes of meetings to authorise and sign; Cheka reports on the activities of Left SRs and Mensheviks in the regions to monitor; discussions to hold on the direct line with various regional soviets; a delegation from Archangel to meet and talk with about the military situation in northern Russia. In between, there were to be snatched discussions on the nationalities question with Stalin before, at 8 p.m., he chaired his daily meeting with the Council of People's Commissars. It was a typical working day that went on late into the night for the man whose exceptional powers and forceful personality allowed him to demand and get centralised control over the vast apparatus he had created.

The fate of 11 people locked up in a house in Ekaterinburg came very low on his list of priorities right now, though the pressure was on him to reach a decision about their fate. With rebellion having broken out among the anarchists and Left SRs, with whom his government had, in the spring, ended its brief and uneasy collaboration, and civil war against the Whites spreading across Siberia, the Revolution was in danger of collapse. Lenin was becoming increasingly impatient; his ferocious fits of anger were unpredictable and terrifying, and when it came to acts of insurrection that threatened his intellectual master plan for the remoulding of post-revolutionary Russia, he always demanded the most swingeing countermeasures. He was relentless in his drive to resolve once and for all the class and political questions relating to the old regime, and in this respect was utterly indifferent to human suffering and did not shrink at ordering the most savage measures of revenge. He of course knew nothing of the Russian masses whose future he now dictated; after years in exile abroad he was in fact a stranger to Russia and knew the common man no better than the Tsar did. But there was nevertheless an irresistible force to Lenin's implacable revolutionary logic which made people believe that he *did* know what was best, and which took as its catchphrase 'You can't make a revolution without firing squads.' What Lenin demanded now, in a recently published pamphlet, 'The Immediate Tasks of the Soviet Government', was an 'iron proletarian discipline' in the cause of saving Bolshevism. But Lenin was also a clever tactician who had learned the Machiavellian arts of conspiracy through long years as an underground activist in exile, and he enjoyed the *schadenfreude* of subverting the intentions of the Western powers who, since Nicholas's abdication, had been lobbying for news of the Tsar. 'The West are wishful thinkers', he observed to Cheka chief Dzerzhinsky. 'We will give them what they want to think.' Prevarication was the name of the game.

Lenin would never be rushed into decision-making; he was a cold and cynical thinking machine with a sophisticated, flexible mind, and he enjoyed playing his enemies off against each other. So long as the Romanovs served a useful political purpose they should be kept alive. He had hoped for a while to use them as bargaining chips in extracting money from the Germans, such as reducing the crippling penalty of 300 million gold roubles made against Russia by Germany in the Treaty of Brest-Litovsk. But with the Ural Regional Soviet and other hardline regional soviets, such as those at Omsk and Kolomna, continuing to bombard him with telegrams demanding the execution of the Tsar, he knew that time was against him.

The idea of regicide as an act of national vengeance for crimes against the people was not a new concept in Russia. It had been born among the Russian intelligentsia back in the days of the first great eighteenth-century Russian radical Aleksandr Radishchev, who had lambasted the repressive regime of Catherine the Great and narrowly escaped execution for his outspokenness. The tradition of intellectual protest against tsarism had lived on through the poetry of Pushkin, who was exiled to the Caucasus in 1820 for publishing an 'Ode to Liberty', and Lermontov, who more openly alluded to a day of popular reckoning:

> A year will come, the year of Russia, last,
> When the monarchs' crown will be cast;
> The mob will forget its former love and faith,
> And food of many will be blood and death . . .

It reached a high point during the Decembrist revolt of 1825, when its republican leader Pavel Pestel had advocated the entire wiping-out of the royal dynasty, including its children. But it found its most extreme form in the writings of the nihilist Sergey Nechaev, who became Lenin's role model of the ideal conspirator, and whose 'Catechism of a Revolutionist', published in 1869, became the bible of the Russian revolutionary movement. Nechaevism, and its cornerstone belief that the end justifies the means, was carried forward in the hearts and minds of revolutionaries into extreme acts of political terrorism during the 1880s, culminating in the assassination of Tsar Alexander II. Lenin's own brother, Aleksandr, had been involved in a revolutionary conspiracy to assassinate Nicholas II's father, Alexander III, and was hanged at the Schlüsselburg Fortress in 1887. Lenin thus had good reason to despise the Romanovs with a vengeance, and his references to Nicholas in conversation and in his writings were always filled with the utmost venom. The monarch was 'the most evil enemy of the Russian people', 'a bloody executioner', 'an Asiatic gendarme', 'a crowned robber' who had spilt the lifeblood of Russia's workers and revolutionaries. To Lenin's mind, regicide and the liquidation of the Romanovs in the spirit of the Jacobinism of the French Revolution would show, as his colleague Trotsky later averred, that there was to be 'no going back. Ahead lay total victory or utter ruin.'

Lenin had first discussed the fate of Nicholas II soon after the Revolution, in November 1917, with other members of the Central Executive Committee of the Council of People's Commissars. On 29 January 1918 he had chaired a meeting of the council at which the question of the 'transfer of Nicholas Romanov to Petrograd in order to be brought to trial' had been discussed. This was repeated on 20 February, again under Lenin's chairmanship but with no location for the projected trial being decided upon. The leader maintained a continuing and controlling interest in the issue throughout the spring of 1918, though plans for the trial appear to have become increasingly enmeshed in a web of confusion and Soviet bureaucracy that waited on Lenin's final say-so. At the end of March the chair of the Western Siberian Soviet had telegraphed him and Sverdlov expressing his concerns about the lax security arrangements at Tobolsk, insisting that a Red Army detachment should replace the present guards. By 1 April 1918 Sverdlov knew this was becoming a serious matter and had chaired a meeting of the presidium of the CEC at which members of the special detachment at Tobolsk had reported back to him on the situation there. Around this time, Sverdlov came to the conclusion that an urgent transfer of the family was needed, away from Tobolsk to the Urals, and took effective control of the situation. Four days later he was even more categorical: the Romanovs should be handed over to the more vigilant control of his colleague Goloshchekin at Ekaterinburg. However, all the time Lenin continued to prevaricate over a decision, Sverdlov could only issue orders to reinforce the guard at Tobolsk, whilst cranking up the expectations of Ekaterinburg that they would become the Tsar's next jailers.

On 6 April a new resolution was made by the presidium of the CEC to transfer the Romanovs to the Urals. Three days later, Sverdlov, as Chair of the CEC, sent a telegraph to Goloshchekin confirming that a special commissar, Vasily Yakovlev, was being sent from Moscow to transfer Nicholas to the Urals: 'our opinion is that you should settle him in Ekaterinburg for now', he wrote, suggesting that it be in some kind of private house requisitioned for the purpose. As far as Sverdlov was concerned, Ekaterinburg was to be the end of the Romanovs' journey, but publicly he still had to contend with German demands that the Tsar be brought back to Moscow.

In order to keep all his options open, Sverdlov boxed clever: Yakovlev would be ordered ostensibly to bring the Tsar back to Moscow, thus following the government's official line, announced in the papers in April, that Nicholas would be brought to trial in the capital. The interception of Yakovlev's special train by renegade Bolsheviks in the Urals and its final detour to Ekaterinburg – acting on a tip-off from Sverdlov – would by necessity be seen as a unilateral act. Such apparent insubordination by the Ekaterinburgers would leave the central government in the clear and not answerable to German reprimands. Once Ekaterinburg had control of the Romanovs, Sverdlov knew there would be no going back; Lenin, who was still vacillating, would have to accede to their demands. The transfer of the majority of the Romanovs held captive by the Bolsheviks to locations in the Urals that summer reinforces the fact that Moscow trusted Sverdlov's Urals colleague Goloshchekin, and his right-hand man Beloborodov, to act with ruthless efficiency and keep them all safe until Lenin decided the moment had come to be rid of them. Had there been a threat to the Tsar's security on the road to Ekaterinburg, they had Moscow's permission, Beloborodov later asserted, to kill the Tsar then and there rather than lose charge of him. The inner circle of Urals Bolsheviks knew of Goloshchekin's close relationship with Lenin and Sverdlov and deferred to him. Had they been likely not to do so, Sverdlov would hardly have entrusted the Romanovs to them.

As things turned out, Yakovlev himself, sensing Moscow's double game and concerned for the safety of his charges, had become worried by the extremely threatening behaviour of the Uralites in Tobolsk and along the Trans-Siberian Railway, and had not acted according to plan. Having been ordered to bring the Romanovs back in one piece, he took his moral responsibility seriously and decided to seize control of the situation, overriding Moscow's orders and taking the train to safety further east, to Omsk. Here he had contacted Sverdlov on the direct line and asked permission to take the Tsar and Tsaritsa even further away, to the more remote Simsky Gorny district in Ufa province, where he would hide them in the mountains. Some commentators have suggested that at this point, Yakovlev, in a crisis of conscience, might even have decided to attempt to take his prisoners east to Vladivostok and out of Russia altogether.

The Uralites meanwhile were furious; having sensed a double-cross when Yakovlev skirted Ekaterinburg and took the train on to Omsk, they had immediately got on the line to Moscow, demanding his total subordination to their control. Having been promised the Romanovs, they now demanded a straight answer about what was going on and guarantees from Sverdlov and Lenin that Nicholas would be delivered to them. The detailed Biographical Chronicle of Lenin's political life shows that first Lenin (between 6 and 7 p.m.) and then Lenin and Sverdlov together (between 9.30 and 11.50 p.m.) had had direct telegraph contact with Beloborodov and Safarov about Yakovlev's change of route, at the end of which Sverdlov instructed Yakovlev (despite his conscientious warnings that 'the baggage' would be destroyed if he did so) to deliver his charges up to Ekaterinburg.

With the Romanovs now imprisoned at the Ipatiev House, Sverdlov had been upping the ante since May, regularly tabling discussion about their ultimate fate in meetings attended by Lenin. On 9 May, at a meeting of the Central Executive Committee, Sverdlov made a statement in which he outlined the government's awareness of the various plots in Tobolsk. A 'mass of documents' had been found showing that 'the flight of Nicholas Romanov was being organised', he alleged. The question of the former tsar's fate would, he promised, 'soon be taken up and settled'. At a plenary session of the CEC on 19 May, Sverdlov again emphasised that it was essential the party decided 'what to do with Nicholas', because it was well known that the Uralites were having their own independent discussions about his 'future fate'. But it is likely that Lenin remained undecided, right up until Goloshchekin's visit to Moscow in early July. He wanted to keep the Tsar alive until they had squeezed absolutely the last drop of political capital out of him. Whatever important discussions did take place, or direct orders given by Lenin, the official record – the protocols and memoranda of the CEC and the daily chronology of Lenin's official appointments – is predictably silent on the subject. The network of Bolshevik deception ensured that it remained so. Discussions must have inevitably extended to the fate of the Imperial Family, sufficient enough for the shake-up at the Ipatiev House to have been ordered by Goloshchekin before his departure and confirmed to him in Moscow by Beloborodov by telegraph. The inefficient Avdeev had been replaced by Yurovsky on 4 July, in the run-up to what was now a planned 'liquidation'.

'Liquidation': it was such an unemotional, no-nonsense word. At first it had been used to refer to the liquidation of tsarist institutions, of private property, of religion, customs and age-old habits. Then it had become an increasingly popular euphemism used by the Bolsheviks for the sup-pression and murder of political opponents; now it was being broadened even further as a cover for extensive social cleansing. Clean, quiet, efficient, scientific even, it was to become the workaday method of the newly created Cheka. In the chaos of civil war and the disruption of communications across Russia with the onward rush into organised terror, the ideals of the Revolution would finally and irrevocably lose sight of any humane boundaries of behaviour. There would be no time for acts of mercy, of singling out one victim whilst showing pity on others. Executing the Tsar alone was simply not a practical or viable proposition this late in the game. What would the Uralites then do with the women and the boy in the present escalating political situation, at a time when the Bolsheviks were barely hanging on to power? Those who had chosen to accompany the doomed monarch into exile would now have to share in his fate. It was a simple matter of expediency.

It is possible that the Soviet leadership may originally have intended to go through the motions of an open debate about the fate of the Tsar at the 5th Congress of Soviets which had opened in Moscow on 4 July, but the assassination of Mirbach and the Left SR rebellion had put paid to that. As late as the 9th there was still talk of a trial for the Tsar, according to the chair of the Petrograd Cheka Moisey Uritsky. But it was all part of a systematic policy of confusion and disinformation – even within the party itself. A trial might lend an air of fake legality to the proceedings but Lenin wanted an end to the dynasty. The time had long since passed for a proper trial to be held and he knew it. But he wanted to be sure that his name would not be in any way tainted with the killing of the Romanovs – judicial or otherwise. What is certainly clear is that it was the enigmatic Sverdlov – the man who really ran the party machinery – who pulled the strings over the final fate of the Imperial Family, in continuous direct discussion with the Urals Bolsheviks. They were Sverdlov's men, guided by discipline, fanaticism and a close observance of party diktat and dogma. And the man for job had already been appointed – Yakov Yurovsky, commandant of the Ipatiev House. He would be ably assisted in his important revolutionary task by his deputy Grigory Nikulin, a young man who only a few days ago had had no compunction about pulling the trigger on Prince Dolgorukov.

In the end it was the pressing argument of the Czech advance that won the day and the sanctioning of this ultimate act of political expediency. It was not just a matter of preventing the Romanovs falling into enemy hands but also a response to continuing pressure from Germany: if the Tsar fell into Czech hands and became a rallying point for an anti-German resurgence in Russia, then the Brest-Litovsk treaty, and with it the bolstering-up of the Soviet government, would be dead in the water. But there was an added complication. It was one thing to kill the Tsar, but foreign policy dictated that it was essential to keep any liquidation of the Romanov *family* a state secret. It would be bad politically to be seen to be killing innocent women and children, and the spilling of the Tsaritsa's German blood and by association that of her children would antagonise the Kaiser.

Be that as it may, Lenin's revolution was different: it had to show no mercy. There should be no 'living banner' – among neither the Romanov family nor their immediate relatives in Alapaevsk, around whom a White or counter-revolutionary movement could rally ordinary Russians against the Soviets. Human considerations were not part of either Lenin's or the Bolshevik mindset, only political logic. As Trotsky would later explain: 'The Tsar's family was a victim of the principle that forms the very axis of monarchy: dynastic inheritance.' For that reason alone their deaths were a necessity.

Lenin had always looked upon the House of Romanov as a very particular class enemy, as 'monarchist filth' and their dynasty a '300-year disgrace'. The Revolution demanded that they be exterminated – along with other undesirables and 'bloodsuckers': speculators, the bourgeoisie, the kulaks. It wasn't enough to cut off the head of the king alone, as Cromwell's revolution in England in 1649 had done with Charles I; revolution in Russia, according to Lenin, demanded the cutting-off of 'a hundred Romanov heads' in order to achieve the new democracy. Lenin always looked to draconian measures; he never thought in terms of individuals, only in terms of the bigger picture – entire classes and groups. For a start, it was quicker and more efficient; he was impatient to see all these class enemies wiped out wholesale, destroyed at the root. Not quite genocide but a new kind of necessary, ideological murder, in defence of the greater good of the proletariat. Under his successor, Stalin, it would be perfected on the grand scale. Eradicating the Romanovs, destroying tsarism and everything it represented was a fundamental part of Lenin's policy of 'cleansing' Russia of everything linked to the old system.

But the written record taking the chain of command and ultimate responsibility for the fate of the Romanovs back to Lenin was, from the beginning, either never made or cleverly concealed. Most likely, the decision was conveyed verbally. When it came to ordering any draconian measures, Lenin was a coward. He always operated with extreme caution, his favoured method being to issue such instructions in coded telegrams (insisting that the original and even the telegraph ribbon on which it was sent be destroyed). Elsewhere, it was by confidential notes or anonymous directives made in the collective name of the Council of People's Commissars; it is more than likely too that he often gave verbal instructions via his trusted right-hand man Sverdlov. Thus a whole host of party 'errand boys' were regularly designated to do his dirty work for him, and in all such decisions he made a point of regularly insisting that no written evidence be preserved, as recently uncovered documents in Archive No. 2 (Lenin) and Archive No. 86 (Sverdlov) as well as the archives of the Sovnarkom and the CEC have revealed. With this in mind, the 55 volumes of Lenin's enormous collected works were scrupulously censored; the memoirs of those involved in events in Ekaterinburg are also suspiciously silent, emphasising the primary roles of Sverdlov and Goloshchekin. (It is no accident either that as Jews, they were both singled out in the virulently anti-Semitic Western literature on the subject after 1918 by Sokolov, Wilton and Diterikhs, all of whom blamed Russia's woes on the Jews.) It is as though Lenin's role in the fate of the Romanovs has been airbrushed from the record. The task of Soviet historiography through 73 years of Communism would be to protect his reputation at all costs and thus ensure that no discredit was brought on the architect of the Revolution. And in this respect the Bolsheviks of Ekaterinburg played directly into Sverdlov's hands. Notorious they might be for their hot-headedness, but the men at the top in Ekaterinburg were nevertheless dedicated party men who understood only too well that the Bolshevik centre in Moscow did not and would not tolerate autonomous action. They kowtowed to a very clearly defined party hierarchy and the ultimate sanction of its indisputable despotic leader, Lenin, through his intermediary, Sverdlov. The Ekaterinburgers had no difficulty in taking personal responsibility for what was to come in order to keep the revered leader's hands clean. Indeed, it was a matter of revolutionary pride to take that responsibility upon themselves, and one which many of them traded on for years afterwards. Ekaterinburg would carry out the necessary liquidation and, in the absence of documentation to prove otherwise, would also carry the blame in the eyes of the world. Within the new Soviet Russia, the kudos for this historic act of national vengeance would be enormous.

The Ural Regional Soviet and the Ekaterinburg Cheka had thus known from early July that the liquidation of the Romanovs would be their responsibility – it was simply a matter of when, and now they were about to decide. During the day, from their stuffy meeting room at the Amerikanskaya Hotel, they had sent word to Red Army commanders at the Front for clarification of the present military situation. How much longer could Ekaterinburg hold out? The Czechs were intent on cutting the city off from European Russia. Red Army forces in the area were insufficient. As they awaited word from the Front, Yurovsky was now formally entrusted with the final preparations for the execution, codenamed, improbably, *trubochist* –'chimney sweep'. All he had to do now, as Goloshchekin assured him, was wait for the signal from Moscow.

'Absolutely No News from Outside'

SATURDAY 13 JULY 1918

Saturday 13 July brought joy to the Ipatiev House, albeit on a minor scale. It was a landmark for the Tsarevich Alexey and his delighted mother. Although Alexandra had been forced to spend yet another day lying on her bed with agonising backache, she had at least been cheered by the fact that her son at last had managed to take a bath – his first since leaving Tobolsk nine weeks previously. What joy for her that her beloved 'Baby', whose leg had been in plaster for much of the time since his arrival, and who could still not straighten it at the knee, had 'managed to get in & out alone'. Such now were the increasingly trivial highlights of the family's imprisonment at the Ipatiev House: so small, so insignificant, when all the time chaos mounted not far from their door. Down in Ekaterinburg's market, goods were now in such short supply that the trade in shoes and leather had been forbidden; these would no doubt be requisitioned for the Red Army now fighting it out against the Czechs. Protest against the increasingly oppressive Bolshevik government in Ekaterinburg still continued sporadically. Across the road from the Tsar and Tsaritsa's bedroom window, a demonstration of 'Evacuated Invalids' had been staged in Voznesensky Square by a hotch-potch of Red Army soldiers, Socialist Revolutionaries and anarchists attempting to capitalise on the absence at the Front of the majority of the city's Red Army garrison, and demanding the dismissal of the local Ekaterinburg Soviet and the transfer of control of the city to them. What few Red Guards remained quickly suppressed this mini-rebellion; a detachment of Bolshevik thugs from the Verkh-Isetsk factory, led by Petr Ermakov, had been called in to deal with it and had opened fire on the protesters. A spate of arrests and shootings of suspected counter-revolutionaries had followed that night – Alexandra herself heard several shots as she lay in bed. The city's leaders had later made use of this episode to suggest it had been a monarchist-led rebellion that threatened the security of their captives at the Ipatiev House.

In London, meanwhile, *The Times* was full of stories about 'Distracted Russia', as one leader described the country. News was 'fragmentary' and often untrustworthy, but in the West reports were now claiming that the influence of the 'Bolshevists' was waning; Lenin and Trotsky were 'undergoing an eclipse' and losing control in the regions. Their collusion with Germany was shameful; enforced conscription had brought together a raggle-taggle army mainly comprised of German POWs 'whose discipline is a farce and whose one common idea seems to be to avoid fighting at all costs'. Meanwhile, the Germans still had 47 divisions occupying Russia, from Finland in the north to the Black Sea on Russia's southern border – their objective in all regions to milk them for their economic resources, most particularly the rich grain fields of the Don valley in the south. With an Allied force gathering at Murmansk, the Czechs were now only 350 miles from Moscow and asserting themselves as a 'new power in Russia and Siberia'. They had proved 'what resolution and coherence can achieve in a Russia torn by dissensions and pillaged by the greed of its temporary masters'. Having now seized the railway across most of Siberia, the Czechs had created rallying points from which the German invasion could be checked. The last word now rested with the United States for supplies of rolling stock and railway material. President Wilson, *The Times* assured its readers, 'has been watching the Siberian situation more closely than is commonly supposed'.

Page 5 of the paper further endorsed the sense of a country about to implode. There was an ominous silence in the capital, Moscow, an atmosphere of muted feelings, the faces of passers-by so often now ingrained with a look of deep, rankling hatred. The once great neo-classical city of St Petersburg, under its new name Petrograd, was swarming with refugees. It was, according to British diplomat William Gerhardie, a 'wild, depressed, anarchic city'. Herman Bernstein noted the same desperate situation wherever he went. There was no joy on the streets of Russia any more. An anonymous report from an English nurse recently returned to England after serving for more than three years with the Russian Red Cross at the Front talked in much the same terms, of a beaten, quiescent population, 'so passive, so indifferent to famine and the fratricidal warfare around them'. 'A kind of stupor' lay on the population of Russia, she observed, the people 'bowed the head and submitted', whilst daily the Soviet powers issued endless decrees 'commanding, demanding, threatening', all of which 'were read through meekly'. Everywhere there was an outspoken contempt for human rights. With the two elemental forces of hunger and hatred at work across Russia, the people were at breaking point. Landowners had been driven from their estates, country houses pillaged and burned – not just by the Bolsheviks but by the starving and land-hungry local peasantry, now acting according to the Bolshevik diktat of 'rob that which was robbed'. The long-dormant volcano of the agrarian question had finally erupted. The old noble families of Russia were fleeing for their lives and seeking refuge in the towns, where they were forced to sweep the streets, or sell newspapers or their last possessions on corners for the price of a loaf of bread. In Moscow, Trotsky was now driving around in Nicholas II's favourite motor car, while all over Russia railway stations and even churches were filling with homeless refugees with dim, haggard eyes who had been drifting aimlessly for weeks in search of food and refuge and would remain camped out indefinitely, whole families herded together in filthy and foul-smelling conditions that spread typhus.

The Bolshevists meanwhile had announced that the hour had come to 'starve the bourgeoisie' and with them their children. Whilst workers received a healthy pound of bread a day, the ration for those people deemed to be class enemies was four ounces. With such utter despair engulfing them, Russia's former nobility and intelligentsia were openly referring to the German invasion as their only chance of salvation from the systematic victimisation they were suffering under the Bolsheviks. The Germans might at least deliver them from their own rapacious army, who even now were accosting ordinary travellers at railway stations and stealing their luggage and eatables, or ransacking homes and confiscating everything they could find, only to sell it later on Moscow's streets. 'At a wave of the hand a soldier could sell you a herring, one rouble, a pair of galoshes, 30 roubles, and a Maxim gun, 75 roubles.' Herman Bernstein concurred: there was nothing one could not get 'by bribing a commissary, from a passport to a battleship'. With industry disrupted, only the presses turning out virtually worthless Soviet paper money were still working. People asked themselves why the Allies didn't come to help the Russians in their hour of need. 'How can England look on so calmly when the existence of our country is at stake?'

How too could the English king look on knowing that his cousin Nicholas was incarcerated in Siberia awaiting an uncertain future? With the British press largely indifferent to the fate of the Romanovs, back in May of 1918, on the occasion of Nicholas's fiftieth birthday, the *Washington Post* had been the only Western paper to comment on the Tsar's desperate situation, 'neglected by his allies, his life in peril', and that it must be a source of 'great regret and compunction to Great Britain and the other powers associated with her, that no provision should have been made for his personal safety and for that of the other members of his more immediate family'. 'Today', concluded the *Post*'s correspondent, 'it is too late to save his family from without.' Too late certainly for Nicholas, and too late even for the children. Nicholas's cousin, King George V, his mind preoccupied with the Western Front, was taken up with daily gestures of solidarity with the nation, such as today attending a cricket match at Lord's in aid of the King George's Fund for Sailors, and, in the evening, accompanying Queen Mary to a special service for Woolwich munitions workers at St Paul's Cathedral. The question of the Romanov family and, more specifically, the German-born Tsaritsa, had been a political hot potato he had not wanted to handle.

Since the outbreak of war with Germany in 1914, King George had been treading on eggshells with regard to the German blood in his own line from his grandfather Prince Albert of Saxe-Coburg, as well as the German descent of his wife Mary, let alone his close family ties to his first cousin the Kaiser. Because of this, he had appeared to demonstrate a distinct loss of nerve in relation to the plight of his Russian cousin 'Nicky' and his German-born wife, despite thinking Nicholas a 'thorough gentleman who loved his country and his people'. After the Tsar's abdication the previous March, George had promised to remain his faithful and devoted friend 'as you know I always have been' in a personal telegram to Nicholas sent to Army HQ at Mogilev but (Nicholas having already returned to Tsarskoe Selo) forwarded to the provisional government. This telegram, the sole expression of solidarity from a close royal relative, was never passed on to the Tsar (nor was a telegram congratulating him on his fiftieth birthday sent by the Scots Greys, of which he was honorary Colonel-in-Chief – the British censor had intercepted it and the Foreign Office had deemed it 'impolitic' to let it get through).

George's immediate and natural impulse after the abdication had been to offer the Romanovs asylum, through the British ambassador Sir George Buchanan, no doubt influenced in part by Buchanan's urgent dispatches to the Foreign Office from the Russian capital. Since January 1917, Buchanan, a thin, dignified man with a fine moustache who performed his duties in the style of an old-school Victorian diplomatist, had been strongly urging the Tsar, with whom he was on very close terms, to liberalise his policies before it was too late. In telegram after telegram Buchanan warned London of his repeated attempts to 'bring home to the Emperor the gravity of the situation'. The dynasty would, Buchanan told the Tsar quite candidly, be exposed to danger if the present political tension was allowed to continue. Russia was, he predicted on 7 January, 'on the verge of revolution'. While Nicholas blindly dug in his heels in his fatalistic way and refused to respond to these warnings, nobody in London took note of the danger to the Imperial Family, even though diplomats were reporting open conversations by Russians in responsible positions about the possible assassination of both the Tsar and Tsaritsa.

Buchanan meanwhile had entered into urgent consultation with Pavel Milyukov, Minister of Foreign Affairs in Kerensky's provisional government. Milyukov had assured him that special measures were being taken for the protection of the Imperial Family at Tsarskoe Selo; he himself was anxious for the Tsar to leave Russia as soon as possible. Buchanan reported as much on 21 March; the provisional government would be 'most glad if our King and Government would invite the Czar to take refuge with them', so long as he remained in England for the duration of the war. The British government concurred, insisting that, publicly, the asylum proposal must be seen to be coming from the Russian government, rather than from King George. With the tenure of the provisional government increasingly precarious by the day, Milyukov and his colleagues were seriously worried about how much longer they could protect Nicholas against extremists threatening to attack Tsarskoe Selo. They wanted to be rid of the Tsar even though these groups had been pressurising them not to give him his freedom. Buchanan cabled London urgently, pressing to be given authorisation by the government to offer the Tsar asylum in England, vowing he would not be happy till the Romanovs were safely out of Russia. On 22 March, after the issue was discussed by the British War Cabinet, Buchanan received telegram confirmation that the King would be happy to receive his cousin in England. Privately George would nevertheless have preferred someone else to grasp this political nettle – such as the neutral government of Switzerland. Denmark was also suggested, but considered to be too close to Germany for comfort.

Plans meanwhile were put in motion to transport the Romanovs by special train to Port Romanov (soon to be known as Murmansk), an ice-free supply port in the Russian Arctic set up by the Allies in 1915. From here the plan was that a British warship flying the Imperial flag would take the family out under a guarantee of safe conduct through German-occupied waters, with an escort of torpedo boats. The tragedy is that such an evacuation might well have been effected quickly and before King George had had time to change his mind had not all the children been recovering from the measles, Maria having succumbed also to near-fatal pneumonia. By the time she had recovered, the provisional government, which now had put various bureaucratic delays in the way of a speedy departure, no longer had the military muscle to get the family out – either north via the Arctic or south to the Crimea. Buchanan repeatedly warned that the net around the Imperial Family was being drawn ever tighter at Tsarskoe Selo, but by now King George was having serious doubts.

The problem was Alexandra: King George disliked her and had no qualms in stating that he held her 'largely responsible for the present state of chaos that exists in Russia'. Her interference in government and her association with Rasputin had brought the Russian monarchy into such disrepute that even Buchanan was openly of the opinion that she had been 'the Emperor's evil genius ever since they married'. With King George vacillating, even the British ambassador began to doubt the wisdom of bringing the Romanovs to England. Brigadier General Waters, a former military attaché in Russia, observed at the time that the moderates in the provisional government might be 'tottering to their fall', but if bribed sufficiently might yet get the Romanovs out of Russia; unless it was done immediately, however, 'their lives were surely forfeit'.

From the moment he had abdicated, the Tsar had certainly expected to go into exile – albeit temporarily. Although he and Alexandra had both been extremely reluctant to leave, they had certainly been prepared to go England for the duration of the war, for King George V and Nicholas were on very affectionate terms. Indeed, they bore a close physical resemblance and were often referred to as 'the handsome twins'. They had been staunch friends since George had attended Nicholas and Alexandra's wedding in St Petersburg in 1894; becoming monarchs in 1894 and 1910, they had shared the same unimaginative sense of duty, were determined defenders of hereditary monarchy and equally hard-working and meticulous in dealing with government business. Disliking the formalities of royal ceremonial, both were quiet, unadventurous family men who enjoyed being at home with their children or out hunting and shooting. Assuming he would be coming to England, where he hoped to perhaps fulfil his 'life's desire and run a farm', Nicholas had looked forward to sharing in such rural pursuits with his cousin. He had busily set about sorting his books and getting his private papers in order, burning anything that might prove politically compromising, and noting in his diary on 23 March that he had been 'putting aside everything that I want to take with me if we have to leave for England'. He had also sent a request to the provisional government soon after his abdication to be allowed free passage to Murmansk as soon as the children were all recovered from their bout of measles.

George, however, although having professed himself to be 'in despair' when Nicholas had abdicated, within the space of a week had become greatly exercised by the moral and political dilemma of offering asylum to the Romanovs. He was fearful for his own rocky position as monarch, with a number of republican articles having recently appeared in the British press. With news leaking out about the offer of asylum, he was also receiving considerable amounts of hate mail about the prospect of the Tsaritsa, with her assumed pro-German sympathies, being given refuge in

Britain. He was advised however that it might now prove difficult to withdraw the invitation made to the Russian provisional government, even though additional questions had been raised about who was going to pay for the family's upkeep in Britain and where they would live. On 6 April, the King's private secretary, Lord Stamfordham, communicated the monarch's apprehensions to the Foreign Secretary, Arthur Balfour, that working men and Labour Members of Parliament were 'expressing adverse opinions to the proposal'. The fact was that the social and political climate of wartime Britain was a good deal harsher than the republican disaffection that Queen Victoria had had to face out during the 1870s, and the influence of the monarchy over politics had dwindled even further since then. With the proletariat on the march, the aristocracy in retreat, and troubles continuing in Ireland, George was convinced that the Crown was less secure than it had been in the reign of his grandmother. A series of labour disputes and strikes in the early days of his reign had convinced him and Queen Mary of a 'socialist menace to come'. Over the years, royal disquiet had grown as labour demands and strikes escalated and the living conditions of the poor deteriorated. As the war progressed, the royal couple had greatly increased their public and charitable work among the nation's poor in an attempt to counter the low public morale brought on by the continuing stalemate on the Western Front. The onset of the Russian Revolution in 1917 had for King George been a salutary warning of the dark days of social dislocation that might yet be visited on Britain; monarchies across Europe were now under threat: Portugal, Greece, Austro-Hungary, even Germany. George feared that Nicky's fall marked the imminent collapse of the whole European dynastic system. There was already much talk of a possible Labour landslide in Britain after the war and with it the advent of a Socialist administration that would 'raise the republican banner'.

Fiercely protective of his monarch, Lord Stamfordham took the bull by the horns and assumed command of the crisis, feeding the King alarming reports on the situation in Russia (deliberately inflated by Special Branch head Basil Thomson to help force the King's hand and centralise Thomson's own control of domestic intelligence); the King's anxiety levels rocketed about his promise of asylum to the Imperial Family. Stamfordham continued to crank up the tension with a succession of memoranda to the Foreign Office and Downing Street claiming that public opinion would be turned against the King. The British government meanwhile became increasingly preoccupied with how to get itself out of a delicate political situation – withdrawing its offer to the provisional government whilst simultaneously maintaining its amicable links with a valuable military ally.

And so, on 10 April, at the King's insistence, a telegram had arrived at the British embassy in Petrograd from Lloyd George's government, advising that it was no longer deemed wise for the Imperial Family to come to England. 'The British Government does not insist on its former offer', it said; indeed, it was most anxious to withdraw it, suggesting France be encouraged to offer asylum instead. (Maurice Paléologue, French ambassador in Petrograd, had in his copious and gossipy diary entries recorded little more than passing observations on the 'present sad state of the Tsar' and the 'dreadful prospects for his near future', but expressed no aspirations as to French intervention on his behalf.) Meanwhile, a variety of excuses were offered by the British to Buchanan, the most pressing being the threat of labour unrest in crucial British industries – mining, shipping, munitions – in protest at the asylum offer. There was, so Buchanan was informed, 'revolutionary talk' at Speakers' Corner in Hyde Park and a good deal of hostility to the Tsaritsa, as there was too in France, from where the British ambassador asserted that Alexandra would not be welcome, being a 'Boche not only by birth but in sentiment'. Even *The Times* was uncompromising in its hostility towards her, asking in a leader article, 'How can we tolerate this friend of Germany in our midst?' According to one Labour MP, so Buchanan's daughter Meriel later observed, the attitude in Britain was that if the Tsar was not good enough for Russia, 'he is not good enough for us'.

By 16 April, such was the King's heightened state of anxiety that Stamfordham was obliged to send a second letter to Balfour, categorically stating that the arrival of Nicholas and Alexandra in Britain 'would be strongly resented by the public and would undoubtedly compromise the position of the King and Queen'. Lloyd George was obliged to concede. His sympathies as a Liberal on the left of the party had all along been with the Revolution but nevertheless he would have supported the offer of asylum to the Romanovs had the King insisted. Yet for years afterwards both Lloyd George and Ambassador Buchanan would be vilified for their supposed failure to effect the Romanov family's rescue. Buchanan was made to fall on his sword in his memoirs and cover up the truth of the British government's failure to act, on pain of losing his pension. Bound by the Official Secrets Act, he could not reveal the truth of diplomatic moves at the time but had to go along with the official line that a handful of left-wing extremists in government, including Prime Minister Lloyd George, had pressurised the King into relenting. Meriel Buchanan never had any doubt that it was all Lloyd George's fault. In shifting the blame from her father to the Prime Minister, along with most other subsequent commentators she made Lloyd George the big bogeyman of the story. It was he who had imposed his leftist sympathies on a hapless king who, as a constitutional monarch, had had to kowtow to his Prime Minister's wishes. Official records, however, do not back up the accusations that Lloyd George was directly instrumental in preventing the Romanovs from coming to England. Indeed, he too came under pressure when writing his *War Memoirs* in 1934 to cover up the King's ignominious abandonment of the Tsar, by scrapping an entire chapter on the discussions over the asylum offer, substituting a brief comment to the effect that it was the provisional government that had scuppered the Romanovs' chances of leaving Russia by placing obstacles in the way of effecting this. In the event, for reasons of diplomatic protocol the British offer was never officially withdrawn; it was simply allowed to wither on the branch and was not pressed home by either the government or the King, in the knowledge that Kerensky's provisional government was in any event rapidly becoming incapable of effecting the family's evacuation in the face of the opposition of militant soldier and peasant deputies in the Petrograd Soviet.

Publicly, therefore, George would appear to have washed his hands of the affair in April 1917. Besides, by that summer he was far too preoccupied with the concerted democratisation of his own monarchy in order to save it, making concessions to rabid anti-German public feeling in Britain. He removed the Kaiser's honorary banner from St George's Chapel at Windsor and regretfully accepted the resignation of his First Sea Lord, Admiral Prince Louis Battenberg (a close relative of the Tsaritsa's from the royal House of Hesse), even though Battenberg was now a naturalised British citizen and soon after changed his name to Mountbatten. Yet still people were not satisfied: 'Once a Hun, always a Hun', yelled the gutter press. George was incensed that his patriotism should be in doubt: he considered himself to be 'wholly and impregnably British'. Nevertheless, such were the political pressures that on 17 July 1917, Buckingham Palace announced that the British royal family was abandoning its Saxe-Coburg name and with it all German honorifics and titles, in future to be 'styled and known as the House and Family of Windsor'. It was Lord Stamfordham who had, in a stroke of genius, come up with the Windsor surname, the choice symbolising a very obvious and emotive link with ancient British history.

But did King George in fact abandon all hope of saving his dear cousin Nicky? As late as 4 June 1917, he confided to his diary, on hearing rumours that Nicky and Alexandra might be confined in the Fortress of St Peter and Paul in St Petersburg, that if this was the case, then he feared 'he will not come out alive'. On the surface, however, the official British records were and remain silent on the matter; indeed, there is virtually no official correspondence enquiring about the plight of Nicholas II and his family during the crucial period 1917–18, though it is known that Alexandra's other sister, Victoria, married to Lord Battenberg and settled on the Isle of Wight, had also written to Foreign Secretary Balfour expressing anxiety about the safety of both her sisters and suggesting mediation by either neutral Sweden or Spain. Having also spoken to George and Mary privately at Buckingham Palace, she contacted King Alfonso of Spain, drawing yet another European royal into the political dynamic. The bonds across the royal houses of Europe, populated in large part by the children and grandchildren of Queen Victoria and Prince Albert, were many and complex. Privately, the King – and Queen Mary, who was also now making her own personal representations to King Alfonso to intervene – may well have had a crisis of conscience (as George did later over the safety of other imperilled royal relatives in Austro-Hungary and Greece). Under private pressure from his relatives, he might, in a last-minute turnaround, have sought advice on the possibility of an unofficial rescue by British secret service agents, bypassing the need for government sanction. Constitutional monarch he might be, but as head of the armed services he was, during the war, in regular contact with the War Office and its secret service operatives. Unsubstantiated suggestions have been made by Michael Occleshaw and by Tom Mangold and Anthony Summers that British agents had private meetings with the King in the spring of 1918 at which plans for a rescue were discussed. This might explain also a telegraph sent via the Foreign Office on 3 May 1918 to Bruce Lockhart, a British agent based at the British embassy in Moscow, which in rather formal, veiled terms observed that 'the King is greatly distressed by the reports which have reached him about the family's treatment [in Tobolsk]' and that 'if it were generally believed here that they were the victims of unnecessary cruelty the impression produced would be most painful'. It was thus left to the intelligence service's discretion to judge whether rescue might be viable; to do so publicly would risk not just failure but with it dangerous embarrassment to the King and the British government.

The curious fact remains that as late as November/December 1917, evidence in Canadian archives shows that money had been spent by the British in commissioning the Hudson's Bay Company at Murmansk to construct a house to accommodate the Romanov family on land near the British consulate there, should their evacuation out of Russia via the Arctic eventually be effected, suggesting that private attempts, under the control of the British military or secret service, to get the Romanovs out of Russia were still ongoing. Hudson's Bay Company records show that Allied intelligence operatives in Murmansk had been involved in building a house large enough to accommodate seven people. As late as

March 1918 a Hudson's Bay trouble-shooter called Henry Armistead, who also worked for the British secret service and whose family were well-known traders in Riga, was said to have set up a Romanov rescue bid in collaboration with a Norwegian Arctic shipping merchant, Jonas Lied, aimed at getting the family out of Tobolsk, via the River Enisei in Siberia to Murmansk. The rescue plan had still been under consideration even after the family were moved to Ekaterinburg, and might explain why British agent Major Stephen Alley had sent an undercover mission into the city in May to recce the Ipatiev House. The rescue plan he had mooted, using British agents and local Russian monarchist officers, had foundered partly because the British government would not stump up the money to fund it, but also because the Ipatiev House proved utterly impregnable and Alley's associates in Ekaterinburg too closely watched by the local Cheka.

Despite King George's apparent withdrawal of support, diplomatic and other attempts by foreign royals to obtain asylum abroad for the Romanovs date back to the Treaty of Brest-Litovsk of 3 March 1918, when King Christian of Denmark had contacted the Kaiser urging his intercession. They had continued on into 1918 from neutral Copenhagen, the Danish royal family having close links to the Dowager Empress Maria Fedorovna (Alexandra, the British Queen Mother, was the Dowager's sister, and like her, King Christian of Denmark's aunt), their lobbying bolstered by Alexandra's brother, Grand Duke Ernst Ludwig of Hesse, who had also entered the campaign. On 17 March 1918 the Kaiser had responded to King Christian's latest request, stating that he could well understand his concern and that in spite of all the painful things he and his people had suffered at the hands of his former friends the Romanovs, he could not but feel sympathy for them. However, he had to tread carefully, for any attempt he made to intercede on their behalf could be misinterpreted by his Bolshevik allies as an attempt to reinstate the Tsar. For similar reasons, Wilhelm had vetoed sanctuary in Germany for Grand Duke Kyrill Romanov and his wife, who after they fled to Coburg were obliged to move on to France. Wilhelm's opinion was that the best course of diplomatic action lay with the neutral Nordic states, such as Sweden.

From Ekaterinburg itself, the British consul, Thomas Preston, meanwhile had continued to urge his Foreign Office to try and get the Romanovs out, if only to prevent them falling into German hands, where they 'would be a trump card for a future Germanophil monarchical orientation' in Russia. The new British consul-general in Petrograd, Arthur Woodhouse, argued along much the same lines. The general view among Germany's enemies was that, should the Kaiser choose to topple the Bolshevik government, which was perfectly possible in the summer of 1918, he might well restore a puppet monarchy in a Russia reduced to a German satellite state – though not with Nicholas (who would never for one moment have agreed anyway) but rather a lesser Romanov grand duke or possibly even a regency for Alexey under Alexandra's brother, the Duke of Hesse.

The Germans had clearly been very active in their demands for the Romanovs' safety, for very good reasons. Kaiser Wilhelm had always been deeply jealous of the close relationship between King George and Nicholas and became even more paranoid about it when they became military allies against him in the war. With George failing to intercede on Nicholas's behalf, it would have been a matter of great personal satisfaction to the bombastic Kaiser to succeed where his cousin had failed, particularly as he believed the British had connived in the Tsar's overthrow in the first place, in order to prevent him making peace with Germany and pulling out of the war. In exile in the 1930s, having now also lost his own throne, Wilhelm continued to take the moral high ground, confiding to his old friend General Wallscourt Waters his readiness in 1917–18 to help the Tsar, having ordered the German Chancellor von Bethmann and his ambassador to Russia, Count Mirbach, to press the Bolsheviks hard over the issue. Prior to his murder on 6 July 1918, Mirbach had repeatedly assured Russian monarchists that the Germans had the Romanov situation in hand. He had been in regular contact with the Council of People's Commissars, reiterating to them on 10 May the expectation that the German princesses would be treated 'with all possible consideration'; he assured the Romanovs' anxious relatives that the family remained under their protection and that 'when the time comes, the Imperial German Government will take the necessary measures'.

Kaiser Wilhelm had certainly given his blessing to the British offer of safe passage by sea to England and had ordered his navy and army not to hinder such an evacuation. By the summer of 1918, with the British king out of the picture, the Germans alone, it would seem, were the only ones in a position to save the Imperial Family. Rumours had in fact abounded since the Treaty of Brest-Litovsk that a secret codicil had guaranteed that the Romanovs would be handed over to the Germans. The problem was that the Tsar and Tsaritsa would not be saved by Germany at any price. With the family now in Ekaterinburg, such German intentions that remained were no longer to do with saving the Tsar, with whom Wilhelm had always had an uneasy relationship (their links being mainly by marriage rather than blood). No: the fate of the Tsar was now a matter for the Russian people; in the end what counted were the chivalric impulses that the Kaiser still nursed to do right by his own kith and kin – Alexandra and her sister Ella, a favourite of the Kaiser's, both of the House of Hesse, and by association the four Romanov daughters. The question of Alexey as Tsarevich and heir to the Romanov throne was again a politically sensitive matter. Nor were the Imperial Family the only German royals in Russia to whom the Kaiser had to extend his protection: Maria, the widow of Grand Duke Vladimir, a princess of the House of Mecklenburg, and Elizaveta, the widow of Grand Duke Konstantin, a princess of the House of Saxe-Altenburg, were both still resident there, and the three sons of Konstantin and Elizaveta – the children of a German mother like the Romanov children – had now been incarcerated at Alapaevsk.

In May 1918 the sense of urgency increased once the Czech legions began advancing on Ekaterinburg and after false reports circulated in June of the Tsar's death. After Mirbach's murder, his replacement, Dr Kurt Riezler, was officially designated to keep up the pressure on the Bolshevik government, but during the crucial July days he was sick and out of action and it was impossible for the German government to gain any independent information about the situation at the Ipatiev House, they like everybody else being at the mercy of the Byzantine web of prevarication and disinformation spun by the Bolsheviks. Behind the scenes German agents, convinced that Lenin's government was moribund, continued to associate with monarchist groups in fomenting a counter-revolution in Russia. But if the Kaiser had given up on the Romanovs agreeing voluntarily to accept German asylum, only one option now lay open to him if he was not to lose face and be seen to be abandoning his relatives: their abduction, against their will. Rumour has it that the Swiss section of the League for the Restoration of the Russian Empire was approached in June with a plan hatched in Berlin to kidnap the Tsar and bring him to Germany. German intelligence operatives were active across the Urals and others were based in Ekaterinburg at the time under the guise of a Red Cross mission, but no conclusive evidence has come to light indicating any viable German plans for a last-ditch rescue.

In the end, all the various royal initiatives to free the Romanovs were stymied by a flabbiness of will, disunity, internal and international politics, and a conflict of political loyalties and agendas. The official German archives on the Romanov matter are, like the British ones, almost silent about the real role of the Kaiser; the Danish archives have yet to reveal any role their royal family played in the scenario. Whatever these final initiatives might have been, it was a case of too little, too late. The inability of foreign governments to take concerted action over the fate of the Romanovs played straight into the hands of the Bolsheviks, making them all ultimately the dupes of Bolshevik double-talk and phoney reassurances. In the midst of all this, the Imperial Family were reduced to the status of helpless pawns in a political game that took no account of their personal fate as human beings but only of the bigger political picture.

That evening, as a rainstorm lashed the windows, Nicholas and Alexandra retired to their room to write their diaries before bed. Alexandra noted that, in response to her repeated enquiries, they had been finally told that Nagorny and Sednev, who had been taken away from them back in May, 'had been sent out of this government', i.e. out of the jurisdiction of Ekaterinburg and Perm province. It was of course a typical Bolshevik lie; the two men were dead, shot by the local Cheka with a group of other hostages in reprisal for the death of local Bolshevik hero and commissar for labour, Ivan Malyshev, who had been captured and shot by the Whites on 23 June.

Across the city, Aleksandr Beloborodov of the Ural Regional Soviet had been on the direct wire with Moscow and the chair of the Council of People's Commissars – Lenin himself. The Ekaterinburg edition of *Izvestiya* noted the following day that their discussion had turned on a review of the tense military situation in the Urals and the security of the former tsar. Yurovsky and several others from the execution squad had been out to the Koptyaki forest again that afternoon, only this time by car; local peasants had seen them. Plans for the liquidation of the Romanovs were now well in hand.

At the White House, President Woodrow Wilson had been disappointed to miss his usual game of golf because of the rain. But after being at the receiving end of relentless lobbying by Russian sympathisers, he had relished the peace of an appointment-free day. The war on the Western Front was in its final stages; he now had time, together with his aide, Colonel House, to begin drafting his ambitious plans for a convention to establish a League of Nations in the post-war world. Its stated goal would be to preserve the integrity and political independence of large and small nations alike. Yet, puzzlingly, it would say nothing at all about the all-important defence of human rights, in particular those of prisoners of war, such as the Romanovs might be deemed to be. It would take many more deaths, particularly in Russia, and another cataclysmic world war – bringing with it a Holocaust of the Jewish people – before the United Nations charter of 1945 and the Geneva Convention of 1949 would address this pressing issue.

In Moscow a decree had been passed by the Council of People's Commissars nationalising all Romanov properties, but Nicholas of course was not to know, nor would he have cared. His only concern now was for his family, and only the smallest, most seemingly insignificant events in a tedious daily ritual had any meaning for him. Sitting at his bureau in the glow of the table lamp, he jotted down the briefest of diary entries: his son had been mobile enough that day, after weeks of enforced bed-rest, to take a bath; the weather had been warm and pleasant – years of habit meant he could not fail to record that. But the reality was that there had been no more letters from loyal officers intent on their rescue; no whistle at midnight had come. Finally Nicholas's true feelings broke through. 'Today', he noted bleakly, 'we have absolutely no news from outside.'

He had kept a diary for the best part of 36 years, but now, after almost 11 weeks imprisoned in Ekaterinburg, Nicholas Alexandrovich Romanov made his last recorded statement. All hope had finally gone.

Political exiles, Siberia, 1915. Second right is Filipp Goloshchekin, in the Bolshevik leather jacket and cap, who oversaw the Romanov murders with his friend, Yakov Sverdlov, next to him in the white shirt. Stalin is standing third from the left in the back row

Lenin in his study at the Kremlin's Senate building. From here he kept close control over the fate of the Romanovs although he ensured that his name was not associated with their fate in any official documents

Pavel Medvedev, left, head of the Ipatiev House guard and one of the key figures in the Romanov murders, poses with a Bolshevik comrade. Captured by the Whites in 1919, he died of typhus in jail

The face of a killer, Ekaterinburg, c1919. Yakov Yurovsky, back right, stands with his brothers, sister, mother and wife

The room occupied by the Tsar and Tsaritsa, which they later shared with Alexey. On 23 June, after much pleading by the family, the Ural Regional Soviet allowed one of the sealed windows to be opened

The Novo-Tikhvinsky convent, whose nuns came to the Ipatiev House each morning with gifts of milk, cream and eggs for the Imperial Family

Witnesses: the redoubtable US journalist Herman Bernstein, (*above left*), one of the first Western correspondents to report the Romanov murders. Sir Thomas Preston in 1968, (*above*); in 1918, as British Consul in Ekaterinburg, he made repeated enquiries about the Romanovs' welfare. (*Below left*) Lt Col Mariya Bochkareva travelled to Washington in July 1918 to make a personal appeal to President Woodrow Wilson (*below*) to save her beloved Russia

The coded telegram sent to Moscow on the evening of 17 July by head of the Ural Regional Soviet, Aleksandr Beloborodov, confirming that 'the entire family suffered the same fate as its head'

The Grand Duchesses' bedroom, ransacked and stripped of its valuables. On the floor are the ashes of a fire in which the guards burned possessions deemed to be of no value. The chandelier was later given to Alexey's tutor Sidney Gibbes and brought back to England

(*Left*) Petr Ermakov, who acted with ruthless savagery on the night of the Romanov murders and then proved too drunk to oversee their burial in the Four Brothers mine working in the Koptyaki Forest (*bottom*)

(*Below*) One of seven commemorative wooden churches, one for each of the Romanovs, built at Four Brothers, now known as Ganina Yama

The Church on the Blood, built in 2003 on the site of the Ipatiev House is now a place of pilgrimage for Orthodox Russians as well as being on the 'Romanov Golgotha' tourist trail

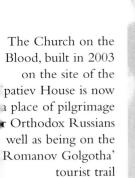

Two contemporary views, the Voznesensky Cathedral, across the road from the Ipatiev House, and the Amerikanskaya Hotel, where key decisions were made by the Ekaterinburg Cheka and the Ural Regional Soviet on the fate of the Romanovs

(*Above*) Canonised by the Russian Orthodox church as 'Holy Passion Bearers', the Romanovs are immortalised in a host of modern-day icons on sale across Russia. The iconography of an idealised family has come full circle. (*Below*) At the site of the family's first burial in the Koptyaki Forest, a mass of tall white lilies blooms every year for the anniversary of the 17 July murders

12

'Something Has Happened to Them in There'

SUNDAY 14 JULY 1918

It was a beautiful bright Sunday morning as Father Ivan Storozhev, one of two resident priests at the Ekaterininsky Cathedral over-looking the River Iset on Glavny Prospekt, got out of bed to prepare for the Sunday liturgy. Suddenly he heard a loud knock at the door. He unlocked it to find himself confronted by one of the guards from the Ipatiev House. The man, whose name was Anatoly Yakimov, was unprepossessing in appearance, with a pockmarked face and small, evasive eyes. He was unarmed and dressed in a tattered padded jacket, with a dirty old soldier's forage cap. Father Storozhev was wanted up at the Ipatiev House that morning, Yakimov informed the priest, to conduct a liturgy for the Romanovs. Storozhev was surprised; word had come from the Ipatiev House only the previous evening that his colleague Father Meledin was required for the service. But the man now standing in the doorway told him there had been a change of plan. Storozhev agreed that he would be at the house by 10 a.m. and immediately headed off to the cathedral to collect the things he needed for the service.

It had been three weeks now since the Romanovs, a profoundly pious, church-going family, had been allowed a priest in to say mass for them. To be denied the ritual of the liturgy that was so much part of their everyday lives had been agony for the family – but they had kept each other buoyed up with continuous readings from the scriptures and other sacred works, for as Russians the spiritual life was as important to them as the physical. Exhausted by their present hardships, they took great strength in religious consolation and their mutual devotion to God; it helped them transcend the uncertainty of the dangerous and unstable world they now inhabited.

This latest service had come in response to a written request made on the 11 July by Dr Botkin that a priest be allowed to celebrate *obednitsa* (liturgy without communion) with the family. At the last liturgy held for them, on Trinity Sunday, the service had been conducted by Father

Anatoly Meledin of the Ekaterininsky Cathedral, assisted by deacon Vasily Buimirov. Storozhev, who had given up a career as local public prosecutor to study for holy orders, himself had previously conducted a service – on 19 May – Father Meledin having officiated at the two subsequent services, on 2 and 23 June. On arriving at the Ipatiev House on the first occasion, Storozhev had been greatly disconcerted by the number of scruffy, heavily armed young men with hand grenades hanging from their belts who had been on duty both inside and outside the house. Commandant Avdeev's room had been a mess, a couple of slovenly men lounging around – one sleeping, the other smoking, their weapons thrown carelessly across the piano. One of the men, in soldier's tunic and breeches with a wide belt round his waist from which protruded a large revolver, Storozhev had taken to be the commandant, but no greetings or introductions had been made, the only exchange between them being the strict instruction that Storozhev should not engage in conversation of any kind with the family. In later years Storozhev regretted that he had been able only to be a passive observer of the Romanovs' situation, but he tried hard to remember every detail. The commandant himself had opened the double doors into the sitting room where the service was to take place. Here, near the connecting archway between the two halves of the room, the Romanovs had prepared a table covered with a silk cloth and icons – some old, some new, some plain, others in heavily bejewelled silver cladding, all of them arranged in meticulous order and precedence for the purpose. The Tsaritsa's most precious icon of all, the Fedorovsky Mother of God in its simple gold frame, took pride of place.

At that time, mid-May, Storozhev had been shocked at how pale, transparent even, Alexey had appeared, so tall and thin and too sick to stand, but lying on his camp bed covered with a blanket. But there was light and life still in his darting eyes, which followed Storozhev's every move with childish curiosity. Alexandra, despite appearing sickly and needing to frequently sit and rest in a chair, nevertheless looked 'majestic' – Storozhev could not deny it. She was dressed very simply, with no jewellery, but the Tsaritsa in her was still very apparent and she had taken an active part in the service. The Tsar, who had appeared calm and in good spirits, had been wearing military dress with the cross of St George pinned to his tunic. Storozhev had noticed that the four girls all had short hair. All the way through the service, Commandant Avdeev had stood in the corner by the far window keeping watch on them. The profound respect with which the family had bowed and acknowledged Storozhev as priest during the service had greatly impressed him, as too had the Tsar's deep bass voice ringing out the responses behind him and the quiet fervency with which they had all recited the prayers.

Today, from the moment of his arrival, Storozhev had again been closely watched, but he had managed to make a mental note of two things that were different about the house this time: the first was the number of 'electric wires' coming out through the window of the commandant's office (all part of the increased security at the house, the updating of its electrics and system of bells that had been going on since Yurovsky's arrival, as well as improved telecommunications). The second thing was that there was a motor car parked right up outside the front door. The commandant's room was just as dirty, dusty and disorganised as before – if not more so. Yurovsky had been sitting at his desk drinking tea and eating bread and butter. Another man – his assistant Nikulin, who practically lived in Yurovsky's room – was stretched out fast asleep and fully clothed on the truckle bed. When Storozhev asked which service they required, Yurovsky had asked him to perform the *obednitsa* (liturgy without communion) as opposed to the *obednya*, the full, and much longer, service with communion, the *obednitsa* being the truncated version often given for troops in the field when there wasn't time for more. Storozhev had been greatly disheartened by this: the Imperial Family had, to his mind, been denied the all-important 'sacrament of the Eucharist' that was their right as Christians. As he and his deacon donned their vestments for the service, Yurovsky sat there in a dark shirt and jacket, drinking his tea and watching them. Sotto voce, Buimirov began to insist to Storozhev that the family be given the *obednya*; the suggestion clearly irritated Yurovsky, who threw dirty looks at the deacon. This was what the Romanovs had asked for, he insisted; Dr Botkin himself had written it down. Perhaps the request for the shorter version of the service took into account the continuing poor health of the Tsaritsa and Tsarevich; perhaps Yurovsky, a man now in a hurry, was not prepared to allow them more.

On the surface, he behaved perfectly pleasantly towards Storozhev. Noticing the priest was rubbing his hands, which were sensitive to the cold (it was, for July, a cold day), he enquired why and was told that Storozhev had recently had an attack of pleurisy. Yurovsky became solicitous, offering his own suggestions for combating the condition and informing Storozhev that he himself had had an operation on his lungs (for tuberculosis). Throughout his and Buimirov's preparations for the service, Storozhev could not fault Yurovsky's punctilious manner. When the priest entered the sitting room, he noticed that Alexey this time was sitting in the Tsaritsa's wheelchair, and though still pale he seemed more animated than the previous time. His mother was next to him in an armchair; she seemed well enough, but was in fact exhausted, having been up all night with excruciating sciatic pain. She wore the same clothes she had worn at his previous service; the girls once more were dressed in simple dark skirts and white blouses, but their hair had grown and was now down to their shoulders. They and their father this time seemed weary and subdued. Dr Botkin and the servants, including the kitchen boy Sednev, as before joined them for the service, the tall and very proper Trupp wearing his silver-buttoned butler's jacket, carrying the censer. The table too had been precisely arranged with icons, as before. In the far corner, Yurovsky never took his eyes off them.

On the surface, Yurovsky might have imagined the service to have gone without incident, but there had in fact been profound and telling differences this time around, the significance of which Storozhev quickly noticed. The Imperial Family had not participated in the responses in the sung liturgy, as all Russians normally did. More disturbing still had been the fact that when, as part of the service, Deacon Buimirov had come to recite the traditional prayer for the dead – 'With the saints give rest, O Christ, to the soul of your servant where there is neither pain, nor sorrow, nor suffering but life everlasting' – instinct had prompted him to sing it instead, upon which the Romanovs had all silently fallen to their knees. Storozhev had sensed, in that moment, the great spiritual comfort it had given them to share in that particular prayer together. The same profound religious unity of the family was manifested again at the end of the service when Storozhev came to recite the prayer to the Mother of God, in which suffering man begs her to support him in the midst of sorrow and give him the strength with dignity to carry the cross of suffering sent down from heaven by God. At the end of the service Yurovsky allowed the Tsar and Tsaritsa to be given the sacramental bread from Storozhev as they and their servants all came forward to kiss the cross. As he turned to leave, the Romanov girls took the opportunity of their close proximity to whisper a covert thank-you to Storozhev. He noticed that there were tears in their eyes.

As he went into the commandant's office to change out of his vestments, Storozhev let out a deep sigh; overhearing him, Yurovsky laughed and asked him why. The priest made some trivial excuse about feeling unwell, to which Yurovsky jokingly responded that he should keep his windows closed so he didn't get a chill. Then his voice dropped and his tone suddenly changed: 'Well, they've said their prayers and unburdened themselves', such unexpected words, said, so it seemed to Storozhev, in utter seriousness. Thrown by the commandant's remark, he responded that he who believed in God's will always found his faith fortified through prayer. 'I have never discounted the power of religion', responded Yurovsky tartly, looking the priest straight in the eye, 'and say this to you in all honesty.' It was an extraordinary remark to come from the mouth of such a man; Storozhev responded by telling Yurovsky how grateful he was that the family had been allowed this opportunity to pray. 'But why should we prevent them?' Yurovsky said cuttingly. It was of course a specious remark; the Ekaterinburg authorities had not stopped the family praying together but certainly had severely curtailed their access to the offices of a priest. Yurovsky knew only too well that what had just taken place was effectively the Romanovs' last rites, their *panikhida*. Perhaps somewhere deep inside the mind of this hardened Bolshevik and Jewish apostate the power of his own religious roots had stirred in him, reminding him of long-forgotten moments of family prayer around the Friday night table and the profound significance to his own Jewish race of the mourners' *Kaddish* – the prayers for the dead.

When he left the Ipatiev House, Father Storozhev did so with a heavy heart. There had been about the family an intangible but overwhelming sense of doom; they were now greatly changed. The Tsar had seemed so thin, so haggard, he later recalled to a British officer in Ekaterinburg. The Bolsheviks had stripped him of his officer's epaulettes back at Tobolsk and wouldn't allow him to wear his St George's Cross any more – the one honour of which Nicholas was deeply proud and which he had always worn. Alexandra had cut his hair for him and his beard was much shorter than it had been in 20 years.

Storozhev's deacon Buimirov had sensed a profound change in the family too. The two men walked back together along Glavny Prospekt to the cathedral in silence, and then, outside the Art School building, Buimirov suddenly stopped and turned to Storozhev. 'You know, Father, something has happened to them in there.' The deacon had taken the words out of Father Storozhev's own mouth. What made him think so? The family had all seemed different somehow, Buimirov told him; the fact that none of them had sung the responses had greatly affected him. And he should know, for Buimirov, as deacon, had assisted at all five of the services held at the Ipatiev House for the Romanovs. No one from the outside world, other than Dr Derevenko, had had more access to them than he.

There are many possible explanations for this change in mood among the Romanovs, and 90 years of speculation have still not resolved it entirely. Storozhev's testimony provides one of the most valuable eye-witness accounts by an independent civilian in the final days. Bearing in mind the infrequency of the services allowed them, the uncertainty of when they might hear the liturgy again clearly had been uppermost in the Romanov family's minds, thus prompting a profound response in them.

This may well have been in part coloured by the contents of the final letter they had recently received from the supposedly loyal officers eager to rescue them. It had clearly intimated that the military endgame in Ekaterinburg was imminent. 'The hour of deliberation is approaching', it had intoned in the same cod-biblical style as the previous letters, 'the Slavic armies are advancing toward Ekaterinburg . . . The moment is becoming critical, and now bloodshed must not be feared.' The family could not fail to have been alarmed by the ominous but emphatic comment that followed: 'Do not forget that the Bolsheviks will, in the end, be ready to commit any crime.' Even without newspapers they could sense the escalating military crisis in the city; they could hear it all around them. If a last-minute rescue came now, they clearly knew and dreaded the risks. If it did not materialise, they must equally have known that if the Bolsheviks did not remove them to somewhere safe in time, their lives would be in great peril. The Czechs might come and rescue them; on the other hand, the Bolsheviks might kill them first. The thought must have crossed their minds for they had had a very long time in confinement to consider the final possible outcome of it all. So today, they had, at last, grasped the precious opportunity of a final reconciliation with God, and with their possible approaching deaths – no matter that such thoughts remained unspoken, locked up within their individual minds.

This final sense of foreboding and need for reconciliation and acceptance had not suddenly come upon them. It was a necessary part of the Romanovs' Christian faith to be prepared at all times for the life of the soul in the world hereafter. There is a popular saying, coined in the 1940s: 'the family that prays together stays together'. Retrospectively, nothing could have been more truly said of the Romanovs. Religion was the glue that had bound them tightly together through all the years of anguish, over first the Tsaritsa's collapsing health and then Alexey's near-fatal attacks of haemophilia, and now through 16 months of imprisonment, uncertainty and isolation. Toward the end of his life, the Tsarevich's tutor Sidney Gibbes recalled that if there was one thing that had impressed him more than anything else about the family, it was their religious harmony, the extent to which they were all strengthened by their Orthodox faith.

A British military observer in Russia, Lieutenant Patterson of the Armoured Car Brigade, put his finger on the power and evangelism of Russian Orthodoxy and the extent to which it was an intimate part of the nation's everyday life:

To every Ruski [sic] religion was not just a convention or a fad, but the *fabric of his life*. Old and young, rich and poor, good and bad. It was a daily revelation and solace. I don't mean just bobbing to Ikons and signing the cross and sniffing up incense. I mean that in their hearts a lamp was lit and kept trim and holy. . . they reached a depth of emotions which we westerners hardly skim.

But while Nicholas now had slipped into a negative, almost sickly state of acceptance, resigned to disaster and ready for the sacrifice that had been inevitable since the day of his birth, Alexandra had reached a new plane of calm that was more actively engaged with the preparation of the soul for heaven and the path to Christian redemption she now felt sure she was travelling. Back in March 1918, writing from Tobolsk, she had observed the overwhelming sense of reconciliation growing within the family: 'we live here on earth but we are already half gone to the next world', she had said. She had long cultivated her own mystic resignation to suffering with an all-embracing Russianness that belied her German origins and her strict Lutheran upbringing. Orthodoxy in its traditional, mystical and ritualistic sixteenth-century form instantly appealed to Alexandra's compulsive religiosity, as it had to her equally pious sister Ella when she married a Romanov in 1884. Maurice Paléologue was fascinated by the totality of Alexandra's 'moral and religious nationalisation'. She seemed a throwback to one of those old tsaritsas from the Byzantine and archaic Muscovy of Ivan the Terrible. In her propensity for profound religious exaltation, her belief in miracles and her extreme superstition, Alexandra had, by 'a process of mental contagion', absorbed the most ancient characteristics of the Russian soul, 'all of those obscure, emotional and visionary elements which find their highest expression in religious mysticism'. It had, since the moment of her conversion, been her self-designated mission to save Holy Orthodox Russia. But that was all now lost. In confinement, denied the ritual of church services, all Alexandra could do was pause and cross herself whenever they rang the church bells at the Voznesensky Cathedral opposite, their sound announcing the sacred moments for prayer during the day.

Had she been able to read it, Article 13 of the new Soviet constitution would have horrified the Tsaritsa, for it now laid down that church and state were to be separated, as too school from church, supposedly in a drive to secure for the workers 'real freedom of conscience'. From now on, every Soviet citizen had the right to take part in anti-religious propaganda, down to scrawling slogans on church walls and joining in the wholesale looting and despoliation of churches, tearing icons from their precious frames and burning them, driving priests from their congregations and overseeing the conversion of Russia's ancient churches to secular use. It was the beginning of a new state policy of militant atheism.

But Lenin's government, as too the increasingly repressive Stalinist regime that followed, failed absolutely in its underestimation of the great visceral power of religion in Russia. In the end, overthrowing the old tsarist empire proved easier than eradicating the intangible power of faith. This, at least, was one thing both Nicholas and Alexandra understood, for all their lack of empathy for other races and religions within the empire, and hidebound as they both were by the implacable, endemic anti-Semitism that tainted Russia. For them and for the multitude of observant Russians, *pravoslavie'* – Orthodoxy – was and would forever remain the repository of the last vestiges of national spiritual feeling. It was a mystical gift passed down from God to the Tsar – this 'invisible spiritual bond' Nicholas shared with the people. British agent Sydney Reilly, currently in Russia to conduct covert negotiations with the Russian Orthodox Church for its support over the Allied intervention, had no doubt that Orthodoxy was 'the one fundamental moral factor in Russian life which can be temporarily obscured, but which neither Bolshevism nor the German can destroy'. Bolshevik oppression in the first years after the Revolution brought with it for a while a backlash – a frenzy of religious observance, with people desperate for Bibles and other religious literature – but all too rapidly Russia's old religious idealism was translated into a perverted form of messianic Socialist idealism. Where once in church people called out to their 'Lord God', the mob now subverted this to cries to 'President God of the heavenly republic'. Many felt that only a Christian revival could save Russia from the dark days to come.

Meanwhile, all the Romanovs could do in confinement was submit meekly to their fate and forgive their enemies. Writing to a friend from Tobolsk earlier that year, Grand Duchess Olga had best expressed the family's sentiments:

> Father asks to have it passed on to all who have remained loyal to him and to those on whom they might have influence, that they not avenge him; he has forgiven and prays for everyone; and not to avenge themselves, but to remember that the evil which is now in the world will become yet more powerful, and that it is not evil which conquers evil, but only love.

The redemptive power of acceptance and suffering had long been inculcated in the Romanov children by their parents. Alexandra knew that the family's suffering in this world was a preparation for the next and impressed it upon her children. It is as though, in her final months, she was inviting martyrdom, her husband already long since reconciled to it.

Together as a family the Romanovs now sought to transcend the forces of irreligion that were destroying Russia. God was visiting his wrath on a sinful nation and was punishing his children. Perhaps the Romanovs felt in these final days that their sacrifice was a necessary part of it all. Perhaps, too, the Tsar, in his 16 months of passive Christian acceptance of his fate, had in some way redeemed the sins of his own deeply flawed monarchy.

Consoled and reassured by Father Storozhev's service, and confident of the resurrection to come, Alexandra spent the rest of the day lying on her bed making lace and having the scriptures read to her when the others went out for their walk. Her choice of extracts from the 12 books of the Minor Prophets offered appropriate parables for the present state of Russia. Olga and Tatiana had read to her from Hosea – a book of dark and melancholy prophecy about the sins of Israel that had brought the country great national disasters. The apocalyptic tones of chapter four seemed to mirror what was now happening in their own country – a place where there was 'no truth, nor mercy, nor knowledge of God'. In Russia, just as in Israel, 'blood toucheth blood' as the country descended into internecine strife. Russia was a land in mourning where the people had rejected 'knowledge' – i.e. religion – and were now suffering for it. Further gloom and despondency followed in the readings from Joel, which prophesied a cataclysm over a land of Israel faced with desolation, plague and famine as punishment for its sins. God soon would swoop down in vengeance and sweep it all away: 'Blow ye the trumpet in Zion, and sound an alarm in my holy mountain: let all the inhabitants of the land tremble: for the day of the LORD cometh, for it is nigh at hand.'

What vestiges of ordinary life remained in the city of Ekaterinburg seemed to be taking no account of the Day of Judgement soon to come. You could still stroll down to the summer gardens by Iset Pond and catch a performance of Ostrovsky's play *The Forest*, or go to the trotting races that afternoon at the local hippodrome at 2 p.m. or a football match at 6 p.m. But the grim reality was that the Ekaterinburg Soviet was now announcing the mobilisation of all loyal Communists in the city: two thirds of the membership of the local Urals Communist Party had joined up and were heading for the Front against the Czechs and Whites. Practically all the workers from the major factories and plants at Sysert and nearby Nizhe-Tagil and Alapaevsk were also leaving their jobs to fight.

Yurovsky, having overseen the Romanovs' *obednitsa* that morning, now had more important things on his mind: finalising where to dump their bodies after they had been killed and how to destroy as much of the evidence as possible at the same time. He had, over the last few days, been frequently in consultation with Petr Ermakov, who was in charge of the disposal squad, about finalising the location in the forest for the purpose, the mine-workings at Four Brothers seeming to be the best bet. They had to decide on the location today, it could not be left any longer, but he had to be sure that the mine was sufficiently remote and would not be discovered. As a local man Ermakov claimed to know every inch of the outlying countryside and Yurovsky had placed his trust in him.

Today Petr Voikov had accompanied Yurovsky to double-check the two clearings they had chosen where the bodies would be destroyed on a huge funeral pyre – so they anticipated – their ashes then thrown down one of the mine shafts. Voikov had been busy of late trying to get the sulphuric acid and gasoline needed for the task from the city's central supplies, Dr Arkhipov no doubt having proved unable to obtain sufficiently large quantities of sulphuric acid for his old friend Yurovsky through his own connections.

Other local Bolshevik bigwigs, including Goloshchekin, Beloborodov and Safarov, had also been out in the forest that day – having a picnic. They had even taken their women with them. According to evidence given by a local mining inspector, M. Talashmanov, they had been overheard loudly joking about what was to be done with the former Tsar and his family. Goloshchekin had been quite vocal, so it was noted, in his insistence that they had to kill all of them. But not all the others had agreed with him; there was no need to kill the Tsar, they said, he was a waste of time. But the Tsaritsa, yes, she was the guilty one. It was all her fault.

Back in the city, as the much-maligned Alexandra was stepping into a hot bath that evening at ten, the lights in room no. 3 on the first floor of the Amerikanskaya Hotel were burning bright and would do so late into the night. Once again the Ekaterinburg Cheka and the presidium of the Ural Regional Soviet were locked in urgent consultation, with Commandant Yurovsky in the chair. A report had arrived from the commanders at the Front confirming that they could not hold out much longer against the Czechs approaching from the south. Ekaterinburg had another few days at best. Yurovsky meanwhile was beginning to have serious doubts about the reliability of some of the guards from the Zlokazov works. They were not trustworthy and he was worried they might talk. Once the family were out of the way they would have to kill some of them too, to ensure secrecy. Beloborodov had immediately protested; it was a crazy suggestion, it would cause a riot in the town.

In Moscow, knowing that the situation was well under the control of the highly vigilant Sverdlov, Lenin left the city by chauffeur-driven car with his wife and sister to enjoy 24 hours of rest and relaxation at his official dacha 15 miles away at Kuntsevo. Why else would the Bolshevik leader, a man who liked to be in total control at all times, leave town at this critical moment if the Romanovs' fate had not now finally been decided at the centre?

13

'Ordinary People Like Us'

MONDAY 15 JULY 1918

Arriving at the Ipatiev House at 7 a.m. on 15 July with their daily delivery of milk, the nuns from the Novo-Tikhvinsky Convent had received a special request from Commandant Yurovsky. The next morning he wanted them to be sure to bring plenty of eggs – 50 at least, in a basket – and a quart of milk. Oh yes, and there was a written request from one of the Grand Duchesses too – for some sewing thread. As he thrust the note at them, Yurovsky hurried on. The eggs would be food for hungry men out in the forest, if all went according to plan.

Yakov Yurovsky was a busy man with murder on his mind; early that morning he had been out yet again to the Koptyaki Forest with Petr Ermakov, to discuss plans for the destruction and burial of the Romanovs' bodies after they had killed them; there would be another meeting that night at the Amerikanskaya to finalise arrangements. Petr Ermakov might look the archetypal handsome revolutionary, with his shoulder-length black hair, his aquiline nose and his sensual mouth, but he had a track record of criminality and violence as a classic Bolshevik hooligan. As a young activist, thug and thief on behalf of the party, he had been arrested and imprisoned three times by the tsarist police and was sent into Siberian exile when he offended a fourth time. He was filled with a seething hatred for autocracy which regularly boiled over into violent rages. The tsars had kept him in prison for nine of his 34 years and he wanted his revenge. Ermakov saw himself as a hard man: he'd seen a lot of people killed and killed a lot himself, he later recalled, including that summer when, as an agent for the local Cheka, he'd been involved in rounding up counter-revolutionaries in the Ekaterinburg area. He was a ruthless killer who went by the nickname of 'Comrade Mauser', but nevertheless he regarded himself as a 'softie' compared to Yurovsky.

Ermakov had seen the Tsar the day he had arrived at Ekaterinburg station: 'there wasn't a thing royal about him', he said; he could have taken him and wrung his neck then and there. The Tsaritsa, in his opinion, had looked like a 'sharp-tongued German housewife' who immediately, even at the Ipatiev House, had tried to run everything. 'But we soon fixed *her*', Ermakov later recalled with glee. He had relished the thought of the haughty former empress made to eat rations like everybody else. She had been the only one to kick up a fuss about their imprisonment. The Tsar, he said, kept quiet and smoked cigarettes all day.

The weather had started grey that morning, later turning to torrential rain, making a quagmire of the country roads around Ekaterinburg as the two men rode back to the Ipatiev House. Inside, the Romanovs had gone about their usual routine, Alexandra being read to by one or other of the girls when the others went outside, despite the rain. But there had at least been the diversion at 10.30 that morning of the unexpected arrival of four local women, sent by the Union of Professional Housemaids, to wash the floors at the Ipatiev House. It was all part and parcel of the subtle game Yurovsky was now playing with his victims, an obvious psychological ploy designed to create a sense of normality, of routine continuing uninterrupted (it wasn't the first time women had come to wash the floors), so that the doomed family should not think things were in any way different.

Mariya Starodumova, Evdokiya Semenova, Varvara Dryagina and the other, unnamed woman would be the last Ekaterinburg civilians to see the family alive. Early that morning they had washed the floors over at the Popov House where the external guard was billeted, noting that it was dirty and untidy, with sunflower seed shells strewn all over the floors. It was hard work, Evdokiya Semenova later related; the guards had 'turned their quarters into a stable with their muddy boots' and the women had had to 'scrape and scrub' to get it clean. The commander of the guard, Pavel Medvedev, had then escorted them over to the Ipatiev House. They noticed that some of the guards were foreigners – not Russians; they had to wash the floors in the basement of the house first where these men had their beds, but there were some women in the rooms with them, so they didn't do all of them.

When the cleaning women were taken up to the first floor, the Imperial Family had all been sitting in the dining room 'as though they were having a meeting' – in fact playing one of their endless games of bezique at the table, the Tsarevich sitting in the wheelchair. The family had all greeted them with smiles, the women responding with silent deep bows. They could only nod and smile, having been forbidden, like the priests the day before, to speak to the family. Yurovsky – that 'weasel' of a man, as Semenova called him – had paced up and down by the open door, watching all the time. The Grand Duchesses, she and Starodumova both remembered, had all seemed very bright and cheerful and had helped the women move the beds in their room in order to get at the floors. Evdokiya Semenova, known by her pet name of 'Avdotyushka' to her friend Starodumova, had been very excited by this once-in-a-lifetime opportunity of seeing the Imperial Family close to. A simple peasant woman with an honest heart, already sick with TB (she died not long after), she had been one of many local people still devoted to the Tsar who had sent in cakes and gifts for the Imperial Family at Easter, fearing however that the guards would keep them for themselves. She had long nursed her own naïve, romantic dreams about the family and especially the Tsar's four beautiful daughters: one would marry the King of England, another the King of France, a third the King of Germany. Like most of the ordinary Russian population she had been beguiled by those romantic publicity images of girls in white dresses. But here in the Ipatiev House, Olga, Tatiana, Maria and Anastasia did not look like princesses from fairy stories as she had imagined them; they were dressed in simple black skirts and white silk blouses – the same few clothes now left to them that they had worn the previous day. Nevertheless, Semenova had been struck by their happiness, their eyes bright, their short hair 'tumbled and disorderly', their cheeks 'rosy like apples'. In the girls' bedroom the women ventured to exchange a few comments with the Romanov daughters in low voices. When Yurovsky momentarily left the room, the irrepressible Anastasia, true to form, stuck out her tongue and cocked a snook at his back. It was a most precious experience for Semenova; every look the girls gave them was 'a gift', as she later remarked. Despite all the humiliation they were now enduring, the Grand Duchesses had seemed so vivacious, so natural. They 'breathed a love of life' and had even got down on their knees to help the women scrub the floor of their room. They had in truth welcomed this brief opportunity for physical exertion, so they whispered to them, adding that their father was 'suffering the most' for lack of it. 'We used to enjoy work of the hardest kind with the greatest of pleasure', they told the women. They had loved sawing wood with their father at Tobolsk and piling up the logs – 'Washing up dishes is not enough for us.' But although Olga was now thin and sick, Maria was still capable of hard work and was as strong as a man, they claimed. In an atmosphere of light-heartedness and camaraderie, the four girls took great pleasure in sharing a few covert jokes with these ordinary women from the outside world.

Before completing their task, Semenova managed to whisper to one of the eldest girls, 'Please God you will not have to suffer under the yoke of these monsters for much longer.' 'Thank you my dear for your kind words', the Grand Duchess had responded. 'We also hold out great hope . . .' Their faith gave them hope even now, but the strain of constantly lifting each other's flagging morale as well as that of their brother and parents was clearly taking its toll. That morning, in the face of so much desperate uncertainty, the four Grand Duchesses had demonstrated the simple good nature and profound loyalty towards each other that was their great abiding virtue and one inculcated by their parents. It had enabled them to contain their own deep fears and make of a mundane event a moment's diversion – even joy.

Semenova was, however, bitterly disappointed when she saw the Tsar and Tsaritsa: 'all my dreams evaporated in an instant', she remarked. She had grown up with an entirely rosy view of the Imperial couple, picturing them in her mind in vestments of gold, with music playing in the background and coloured drapes fluttering in the breeze, as flower petals floated down on them from above and great church bells chimed. The Tsar had been 'a figure of divinity' for her, a giant among men; the Tsaritsa too she imagined as a rosy-faced Russian beauty with a voice 'like a flute from paradise'. Now suddenly, Evdokiya Semenova discovered that her former monarchs had feet of clay. The Tsar was not the Godlike being she had imagined: what she saw that morning was 'a small and drab man, much smaller than his wife, and much simpler [in manner] than she'. He behaved like a man of the people; he was just like them and far from being a paragon of physical perfection, his hair was thinning – he had a large bald patch – and his legs were too short for his body. Alexandra, for all her paleness and physical frailty, was however still very much the proud Tsaritsa, but her eyes told Semenova how much she was suffering. As the women had moved from room to room to wash the floors, Nicholas had gently lifted and carried Alexey from bed to wheelchair to bed again. The sight of the frail and sickly Tsarevich had given Semenova profound pause for thought: here before her was the boy whom the Romanov publicity machine had led her to believe was the hope of Russia, a 'strong and flourishing cherub' as she put it, but instead what she saw was a thin, delicate child with great dark circles under his eyes, his face waxen. And even though he frequently smiled, his eyes seemed full of sadness.

Starodumova and Semenova both remembered quite clearly that at one point Yurovsky had sat down next to the Tsarevich and enquired of his health, asking the opinion too of Dr Botkin. It had seemed a most solicitous gesture to them, as it might have done to any other observer. It was of course all part of the softening-up process, but coming from a man who had trained as a medical orderly, in the knowledge of what was to come it seems particularly cruel. Did Yurovsky take pleasure or power, one wonders, from such an act – knowing that he alone was in control of the sick boy's last hours on earth? Ignorant of this fact, Semenova went away an hour and a half later convinced of one thing: the boy, in comparison to his vibrant sisters, 'was no longer of this world'. The experience had greatly moved her; she left with a love for the Imperial Family so profound, she said, that it would not leave her till the day she died. They were not the divine beings she had always supposed them to be; 'they were not gods, they were actually ordinary people like us, simple mortals'.

The women who came to the Ipatiev House that morning were never paid for their work; four days later, when they went to see Medvedev at the Popov House to collect their money, there was no one there except a few Red Army guards who were packing up to go to the Front. Then a very drunk Medvedev drove up in a troika. There was nobody at the Ipatiev House, they were told, the house was shut up. They had all 'gone to Perm'.

14

The House of Special Purpose

TUESDAY 16 JULY 1918

It was another quiet, uneventful day, the Romanov family's seventy-eighth day in the Ipatiev House. 'Baby' had a slight cold and was still weak but went out with the others in the garden in the morning. And after a week of no supplies from the nuns, there came a wonderful gift of eggs for Alexey – the boy's last supper, had he known it. The remainder of Yurovsky's requisition of 50 would be gorged later by the family's murderers out in the forest, leaving the scattered eggshells as proof to later investigators.

At around nine, while the family sat taking the same dreary tea and black bread for breakfast that every other Soviet citizen was reduced to, Beloborodov arrived at the Ipatiev House in an official car belonging to the Ekaterinburg Cheka. Soon afterwards he left with Yurovsky to attend yet another meeting of the Central Committee of the Ural Regional Soviet, followed by consultations with the Cheka at the Amerikanskaya Hotel. Yurovsky was now getting very nervous, and seemed even more so when he returned at eleven, when he went through the daily ritual of checking that the box containing the Romanovs' valuables had not been tampered with. Soon afterwards, in the privacy of his office next door, he informed his assistant Nikulin that the 'liquidation' was to take place tonight. There could be no more delays and it was paramount that they ensure that the family did not suspect anything in advance.

But had they made the right decision about how to kill them all? The simple fact was that Yurovsky, despite being utterly ruthless about fulfilling his task, had no idea how best to kill 11 people, nor had he come to grips with the logistics of disposing efficiently with that many bodies. Executing the Tsar was one thing, but to kill the whole family and their servants and manage, as instructed, to keep quiet about the fact was quite another. And then there was the added pressure of ensuring that no remains would later be found by monarchists who would exploit the ignorance of the devout among the peasantry by using them as a 'sacred miraculous relic' to rally anti-Bolshevik support.

The preferred killing method of the Cheka was to take victims out into the forest and shoot them in the back of the head; Petr Voikov suggested that they do this in the forest beyond the Verkh-Isetsk plant and then weight the bodies with lumps of metal and drop them in Iset Pond. This method might work for single victims at a time, but trying to perform an efficient execution of 11 terrified people and then, as Yurovsky was forced to take into account, prevent those involved from raping the girls or searching the bodies for jewels, might provoke mayhem. Besides, there was always the chance of local peasants stumbling on the scene – even out at that remote spot. No, the execution had to be *in situ*, in the house. Yurovsky's associates had suggested killing the family at night in their sleep – either by shooting or stabbing them. Someone even suggested putting them together in one room and throwing hand grenades in on them. But that could prove noisy and messy, and they might easily lose control of the situation. The only viable way was to get the family into a closely confined space from which they could not escape and where the noise levels from guns could be minimised. The basement rooms of the Ipatiev House were the only option. These were currently in use by the internal guards, and whichever room was selected would have to be cleared of its furniture. Yurovsky settled on one of the two rooms located furthest into the hillside into which the house had been built. It was presently occupied by the Ipatiev House machine-gun squad, led by Mikhail Kabanov, who were moved along with their beds into another room.

With the city being evacuated from the main rail station only half a mile away at the top of Voznesensky Prospekt, there was a lot of traffic passing back and forth in front of the house. The liquidation would have to be carried out late, after the traffic had died down. The hillside room would muffle the noise despite having a large arched window, which was barred and faced on to Voznesensky Lane; the double palisade would absorb some noise too. Out on the street the window and its light would not be visible. The room chosen was 25 by 21 feet, with a vaulted ceiling, large enough for 11 prisoners, Yurovsky thought; its stone walls were covered in plaster, with striped wallpaper on top of that, and should be a good buffer for any stray bullets. As too would be the wooden skirting boards. The plain wooden floor would be easy to wash clean after the event. One set of double doors opened into the room; the men would take aim at their victims from the doorway; another set of doors at the room's opposite end led into a storeroom beyond stacked full of excess furniture, but was firmly locked. In another nearby room a guard was always on duty at a Colt machine gun. There was no way out but straight into the line of fire.

At around 11.30, as Yurovsky and Nikulin finalised the plans for their hoped-for efficient 'liquidation' and the destruction of the bodies afterwards by acid and fire in the clearing chosen for that purpose, the Romanov family had their morning walk. Remaining inside with her mother, Olga helped 'arrange our medicines' – the Romanovs' code for sewing their jewels into their clothing, perhaps an indication that with the unsettled situation in Ekaterinburg the family anticipated being moved again soon and wanted to be sure the jewellery they had not given up to Yurovsky's inspection – the far more valuable strings of pearls, diamonds, rubies, sapphires and other precious gems – should remain well hidden.

While the Romanovs were sitting down to lunch at one that afternoon, over at the Kremlin in Moscow Lenin, just back from Kuntsevo, was handed a telegram from the Danish newspaper the *National Tidende*. It was asking for his comments on the latest rumours circulating abroad that the Tsar was dead; was there any truth in the story? Lenin drafted a reply denying the rumours; it was all, he asserted, 'a lie of the capitalist press' – a typical piece of Bolshevik disinformation that would be issued by Moscow over the coming weeks and months. In the event the telegram was not sent – a connection through to Copenhagen could not be made – but the evidence remains in the Russian archives.

In the afternoon Tatiana stayed indoors and read from the prophets Amos and Obadiah as Alexandra sat making lace. At around 3 p.m., the Tsar, Olga, Anastasia, Maria and Alexey went outside into the scrubby little Ipatiev House garden for what was to be the last time. One of the guards, Mikhail Letemin, saw them coming back from their walk at around four. He did not notice 'anything out of the ordinary with them', so he later recalled. As the family re-entered the house Yurovsky and Beloborodov were once again leaving it by car. A local villager saw the car out in the Koptyaki Forest at about five that afternoon. He and other peasants from the Verkhistskavo Mill had been out scything hay along the Koptyaki Road in the late summer sunshine. There were other men with Yurovsky but the man did not know who and he couldn't recall any other details, for the men in the car ordered the villagers away from the area. Another local boy encountered one of the Ipatiev House internal guard in the forest that afternoon, a man called Vaganov as he later identified him, (this was the sailor Stepan Vaganov, a sidekick of Petr Ermakov and commander of the machine-gunners of the internal guard). The boy was also ordered to turn back and go home. Yes, there were men out in the forest, he later recalled, and several cars – as many as

10 of them. He had in fact been witness to a final on-site review by the bigwigs of the Ural Regional Soviet and the Ekaterinburg Cheka in preparation for the liquidation to come.

Back at the Ipatiev House two of the external guards, Filipp Proskuryakov and Igor Stolov, who like the others had received their pay the day before, turned up for their evening shift at five, having spent the afternoon drinking at the house of a local policeman. Seeing that they were both roaring drunk and unfit for duty, commander of the guard Medvedev manhandled them into the bath house of the Popov House across the street and locked them in to sober up.

On returning to Ekaterinburg from their inspection in the forest, the Central Committee of the Ural Regional Soviet held one final, heated meeting at the Amerikanskaya Hotel, at which Yurovsky argued again, as he had earlier in the day to Goloshchekin, that he saw no reason to kill the kitchen boy Sednev, whom he wanted to send away from the house before the execution took place. During the meeting a report from the Front was discussed; the prognosis was gloomy, said Goloshchekin: hastily assembled Red Army detachments could not contend with the better-equipped Czechs and were retreating in all directions. Ekaterinburg would fall within the next three days. A 'painful silence' followed, after which it was agreed that the executions could not be put off any longer. Moscow should be contacted for the final go-ahead. A coded telegram was therefore sent by Goloshchekin and Safarov at around six that evening, addressed to Lenin in Moscow. All was ready; they were now awaiting the final signal that operation *trubochist* could go ahead.

But the lines were down and they could not get a direct connection. There was nothing for it but to send the telegram on the direct line to Petrograd instead – addressed to Grigory Zinoviev, head of the city soviet based at the Smolny Institute, and ask him to forward it on to Sverdlov with a copy to Lenin: 'Let Moscow know that for military reasons the trial agreed upon with Filipp [Goloshchekin] cannot be put off; we cannot wait', the telegraph read, the word 'trial' being code for the already agreed execution. 'If your opinion differs then immediately notify. Goloshchekin, Safarov.' Zinoviev duly forwarded the telegraph to Moscow, noting that he had done so at 5.50 p.m. Petrograd time (it was now 6.20 in Moscow and 7.50 in Ekaterinburg). The cable was not however received in Moscow until 9.22 that evening, the lines being yet again disrupted. A reply would have taken at least a couple of hours to get through to Ekaterinburg, but there is no documentary record of an answer from Moscow arriving in the city, although Yurovsky later insisted that an order from the CEC in Moscow to go ahead had been passed on to him by Goloshchekin at around seven that evening when he arrived at the Ipatiev House. What Yurovsky must in fact have been referring to was the previously drafted decree for the execution which Goloshchekin had brought back with him from Moscow, ready to pass on at the appropriate moment and to which he had now added the date and his signature.

In the late 1960s a former member of the Kremlin guard, Aleksey Akimov, claimed that Sverdlov personally instructed him to take a telegram to the telegraph office confirming the CEC's approval of the executions but with strict instructions that both the form on which it was written and the telegraph tape should be brought back by him immediately it had been sent. Because of the breakdown in the telegraph lines, it would have had to be sent via Petrograd outbound and then via Perm on the return route. At Perm, Goloshchekin already had his own men in control; all it would have needed was for them to transmit the final word from Moscow to Ekaterinburg either on the phone or via a telephonogram with the coded response, which might well have been very short, if not simply the code word *trubochist* itself.

Whether a telegram from Lenin in Moscow did actually get through and was later destroyed, the fact was that the Ekaterinburgers had already, at the beginning of July, been given the leader's agreement in principle to the execution; this latest message to the centre had been a final, perhaps nervous move to inform Lenin that they judged the time right to go ahead and wished for his final sanction. What they were about to do, Yurovsky later asserted, was, after all, to resolve a question 'of great political importance' and he was anxious that they do so 'skilfully'. The question remains, however: did the Ekaterinburgers have approval to kill *all* the family? The evidence is equivocal and one can only go by the political logic that drove Lenin and Sverdlov, the men at the centre. One might also ask whether the Ekaterinburgers, now extremely anxious to carry out the liquidation, deliberately sent their final telegram asking for approval too late that day, in the knowledge that it would not get to Moscow in time for the executions to be stopped. If the direct lines were down, the telegram would have had to go the route: Ekaterinburg–Petrograd–Moscow and then back Moscow–Perm–Ekaterinburg, and there was a two-hour time difference between the two cities. Either way, Moscow would not complain – for it was about to be saved from direct association with a highly damning political act.

At 6.10, the meeting at the Amerikanskaya broke up and Yurovsky returned to the Ipatiev House. All seemed as normal until, while the Romanovs were having dinner, something unexpected and greatly disconcerting for them happened. Yurovsky came into the sitting room to inform them that the kitchen boy Leonid Sednev should get his things together – he was leaving the house to go and see his Uncle Ivan, who had returned to the city asking to see him (Ivan was of course dead, murdered by the Bolsheviks). The family were very upset – Leonid was the fifth member of their entourage to be taken away, and none of the others had yet been returned to them. Dr Botkin as the family's spokesman went to Yurovsky's office, followed by Tatiana, who was greatly distressed, asking where Leonid had been sent, why and for how long – Alexey was already missing him terribly; it would make things so much harder for him without his company. They were assured by Yurovsky that he would be back soon. The family seemed to accept this, albeit reluctantly, so the guards later claimed, but Alexandra did not trust Yurovsky. In her diary entry that night she wondered 'whether its [*sic*] true & we shall see the boy back again!' Leonid Sednev had in fact been taken across the road to the Popov House, where he was kept that night, in earshot of what took place.

It was now 8 p.m. and the curfew was sounding over Ekaterinburg, a city now officially under a state of siege. British assistant consul Arthur Thomas, on his way back to the consulate on foot past the Ipatiev House, had been stopped by a very nervous sentry who had ordered him to the other side of the street and fired at him when he didn't move quickly enough. No one was being allowed to walk past the house; later both Thomas and Consul Preston noticed that machine guns had been placed in position on Voznesensky Square across the road from the house as well as on the roof. Local inhabitants stayed indoors, sensing something ominous was afoot. Inside the house Yurovsky was finalising arrangements for the executions. All now depended on the truck; earlier that afternoon he had ordered his chauffeur Lyukhanov– a man who had got his plum job at the House of Special Purpose thanks to his brother-in-law Aleksandr Avdeev's influence – to put in an order with the Ekaterinburg Military Garage for a truck to take the bodies away, bringing with it rolls of canvas to wrap them in. The intention was to have it parked as close to the basement entrance as possible, within the double palisade, with its engine running to mask the noise of gunshots. If the engine backfired then so much the better. As the regular change of guard came at 10 p.m. and new men arrived, the Romanovs sat upstairs reading and playing cards. Nicholas and Alexandra were enjoying a final game of bezique as the men who were to be their executioners gathered in the basement rooms downstairs.

Earlier that evening, between seven and eight, when Medvedev had just come on duty, Yurovsky had ordered him to collect all the handguns from the exterior guards. 'We must shoot *them all* tonight', so Yurovsky told him. The guns issued to the guards were old tsarist Nagants, standard issue in the Imperial Army since 1895. But they were unlikely to all have been needed for the execution. As Cheka men, the new internal guards who had been brought in especially for the job would have had their own Nagants. Yurovsky, however, was taking no chances: best to have as many weapons as possible in case any of them jammed. In the end, some of the killers had two guns; a few others were handed round to the witnesses from the Central Executive Committee of the Ural Regional Soviet, Goloshchekin and possibly Beloborodov and Safarov – just in case of trouble. Another reason for the confiscation may be that Yurovsky was so anxious about the operation that he feared some of the men of the external guard – men who had once worked inside the house and had got to know the family well, and whose reliability he had already openly doubted in a meeting at the Amerikanskaya – might prove to have last-minute sympathies for the family and try to intercede. He wasn't taking any chances and told Medvedev that although the external guards should be forewarned about the shootings, which would come after midnight, they shouldn't be told until the latest possible moment.

There was no question of using rifles for the execution – these would have made far too much noise and would have been impossible to conceal from the family in the moments before their deaths. The selection of 14 guns Yurovsky and Medvedev now chose from their entire arsenal to use that night was comprised of two Browning pistols, two American Colts and two 7.65 Mausers. The Mausers, carried by Yurovsky (who also had a Colt) and Ermakov, were relatively new models, released in 1914 and by far the most powerful of all the guns, their clips holding 10 bullets each, as opposed to the seven of the others. The remaining weapons were revolvers: one Smith & Wesson, and seven Nagants. The Belgian-made Nagants operated on the old powder system, the less acrid, smokeless nitro-powder only now being phased in for these weapons. The old black gunpowder would produce a good deal of smoke and fumes. But Yurovsky still had to decide the all-important question: who was going to kill whom. He wanted to have one killer per victim – in a moment of false humanity, the killers would later claim that they had wanted the deaths to be simultaneous so that no member of the family or their servants should see the others die. Yurovsky had originally designated 11 men to take part: himself, his assistant Nikulin, Ermakov Mikhail Kudrin, Pavel Medvedev and six others drawn from the new Cheka guards collectively labelled as 'Letts'. These latter men remain shadowy figures, their identities the subject of much discussion and controversy, among both the men who took part themselves that night and historians ever since. One thing at least is known: at this late hour

Yurovsky faced a problem. At least two of the 'Letts' – a Hungarian POW named Andras Verhas, and Adolf Lepa, himself in charge of the Lett contingent – had had cold feet. They would not shoot the girls, they said. Yurovsky sent them over to the Popov House; he could not risk men in the execution squad failing 'at that important moment in their revolutionary duty'. The execution squad was now down to probably eight or nine men.

Down in the summer gardens by Iset Pond at the bottom of Voznesensky Lane the performance of *Autumn Violins* had finished and the streets were quiet when, after ten, the family, Dr Botkin and the servants gathered together for their usual family prayers and then retired to bed. It was a mild summer's night and the sun was only just going down. It was still warm outside – 15 degrees, so Alexandra noted punctiliously. It was the final page of her diary.

In the sitting room, Dr Botkin did not immediately go to bed; he sat down to try to finish his letter to Sasha. In the distance from time to time came the sound of artillery fire on the Trans-Siberian Railway. The Czechs were now tantalisingly near, only 20 miles away on the line south to Chelyabinsk. All was quiet on the first floor of the Ipatiev House as the lights went out in the family's rooms. But in the commandant's office next door Yurovsky was in a state of escalating panic as the lights continued to blaze, men came and went and the telephone rang. Petr Ermakov, who the previous day had taken several cans of petrol out to the site in the forest as well as two buckets of sulphuric acid and a truckload of firewood, and who seemed at the time to have matters in hand, had still not turned up. Two of this evening's guard had reported for duty drunk and were out of action; two of his execution squad had bottled out, and he still hadn't given proper thought as to how the bodies would be carried out of the house and disposed on the lorry, which had been ordered to arrive at midnight.

As the hour approached and there was still no truck, Yurovsky paced his office, watching the clock and smoking incessantly, knowing full well that the sun would be up again at just after five. Summer nights in the Urals were too short for this kind of operation and everybody's nerves were on edge. Time was running out if they were to complete the liquidation under cover of darkness, but final word had still not come from Moscow. Might the commandant, for all his dutifully pragmatic attention to revolutionary duty, have had some passing *crise de conscience*, even at this late hour, about what he was about to do? In his 1922 memoir of events at the house, Yurovsky recalled that although he despised the Romanovs for what they represented and 'for all the blood of the people spilled on their behalf', they were fundamentally simple, unassuming and 'generally pleasant' people. Had he not been entrusted with their liquidation he would have had no reason to hold anything against them.

Down at the garage, meanwhile, the one-and-a-half-ton Fiat truck was only just being filled with petrol. Thanks to the chronic inefficiency and poor communications that now were beginning to characterise the entire operation, the truck was then wrongly sent off to the Amerikanskaya Hotel instead of the Ipatiev House. Realising something had gone wrong, Yurovsky's chauffeur Lyukhanov had gone down and taken charge of the vehicle himself and telephoned Yurovsky to warn him of the delay.

After further hold-ups, and a succession of urgent phone calls to the Cheka, the open-topped Fiat truck finally rattled off across the silent streets of the city. Operation *trubochist* was at last swinging into action. The truck was only minutes away, trundling up Voznesensky Prospekt, when Commandant Yurovsky got up from his chair, went out on to the landing and rang the bell at the double doors of the Romanovs' sitting room.

It was 1.30 in the morning of 17 July 1918. The Ipatiev House was now about to fulfil the 'Special Purpose' for which it had been summarily requisitioned only three months ago.

15

'The Will of the Revolution'

WEDNESDAY 17 JULY 1918

A tired and dishevelled Dr Botkin came to the door and opened it. What was the matter? he asked. Yurovsky told him that the situation in Ekaterinburg was now very unstable; the Whites were approaching and might at any moment launch an artillery attack on the city. It was dangerous for the family to remain here on the upper floor; they had to take them down into the basement for their own safety. Would Dr Botkin please go and wake the others. Yurovsky then retreated to his office, from where, through his open window, he heard the Fiat truck turn in through the palisade gates and pull up outside the house. He went downstairs and told the driver Lyukhanov to take the truck to the other side of Voznesensky Square opposite and wait.

Although the Tsar had got out of bed immediately, as though he had trained himself for the eventuality of sudden flight or rescue, the rest of the family and servants took their time getting washed and dressed, the girls carefully putting on their camisoles sewn full of gems and pearls, as they had long since prepared for under their mother's supervision. Outside in the corridor Yurovsky heard the family walking around and talking as his impatience mounted. For 40 minutes he stood listening hard at the door, his nerves jangling, trying to catch the family's reaction as they readied themselves. What were they saying? Had they any inkling of what was to come? He was about to go in and hurry them all up – something he had wanted to avoid in order not to alarm them – when one by one the Romanovs emerged on to the landing, all 'neat and tidy', as machine-gunner Aleksandr Strekotin observed, the Tsar in front with Alexey in his arms, both of them dressed in their soldier's tunics and forage caps. The girls followed in their simple white blouses and skirts, carrying pillows, bags and other small items. The Tsaritsa too was plainly dressed. None of them had their outdoor clothing on. They started asking questions but they did not seem alarmed as such; they had, after all, had false alarms before and would have known that the approaching

Czechs might have dictated their sudden evacuation at any time. Indeed, the Tsar was heard to turn and say to the servants reassuringly, 'Well, we're going to get out of this place.' If anything it was a relief for all of them. Was Nicholas being falsely reassuring, protective as he was of his family, or did he still have no true grasp of what could possibly happen to him – or them? Clearly not, for the only doubts raised by the family were trivial ones. What about their personal belongings? they asked. 'It's not necessary right now', Yurovsky reassured them, working hard to remain calm and polite as he escorted them to the stairs. 'We'll get them later and bring them down.'

It was about 2.15 a.m. when Yurovsky and Nikulin, accompanied by two of the internal guard with rifles, led the family in the semi-darkness down the steep, narrow stairs to the ground floor. Instinctively the Romanovs followed the order of precedence inculcated in them, the Tsar in front but refusing all assistance as he struggled with the burden of Alexey, who winced with pain from his bandaged leg; then Alexandra, using a stick and leaning heavily on Olga's arm, followed by the three other girls. Nikulin and Kudrin both later recalled that, as they made their way to the stairs, the family paused and devoutly crossed themselves at the stuffed mother bear and her cubs that stood on the landing – a sign of respect for the dead, thinking as they did that they were going to be leaving the house.

At this point the family's three pet dogs: Joy, Jimmy and Ortipo, must instinctively have tried to follow them and been turned back. Dogs are incredibly sensitive and would have responded to an underlying nervousness in Yurovsky and the guards. It is likely that one of the dogs came downstairs with them: Tatiana's little Pekinese, Jimmy, to whom Anastasia was deeply attached. His legs were so short that he couldn't walk up and down stairs by himself and Anastasia was in the habit of carrying him everywhere. For Yurovsky to have attempted to take the dog from her would have created an unsettling scene and set alarm bells going in the whole family's minds. Following the Imperial Family came Dr Botkin, and then bringing up the rear Trupp carrying a blanket, Demidova carrying two cushions (ostensibly for the Tsaritsa's comfort but in fact containing many of her jewels in two small boxes) and the cook Kharitonov at the rear. They all then exited the house by the door leading out into the small courtyard, re-entering by another, adjacent door leading down into the basement. Twenty-three steps – one for every year of Nicholas's disastrous reign – now led him and his family to their collective fate. As the Romanovs entered the basement rooms, one of the guards, Viktor Netrebin, noticed that even now, at this late hour, the Tsaritsa gave them a filthy look, 'as if expecting we would bow as she passed'. Both she and Olga were, he recalled, 'skin and bones', the Tsaritsa's grey hair untidy from being woken so unexpectedly. The other three girls, in contrast, were smiling and cheerful, as ever so trusting in their youth and naïvety.

But they must have been puzzled by the scene that greeted them: a bare, ill-lit storeroom with a single naked lightbulb hanging from the plaster ceiling. They did not express any alarm, but Alexandra, true to form, immediately complained. Why were there no chairs? Were they not allowed to sit down? She could not stand for long because of her sciatica, and the sick Alexey needed a chair as well. Obliging her request without showing any sign of impatience, Yurovsky sent guard Aleksandr Strekotin to fetch two, Nikulin making the acid comment under his breath as they were brought that the 'heir wanted to die in a chair. Very well then, let him have one.' Nicholas gently lowered Alexey on to his, standing protectively in front of him – was it instinct or some unspoken fear? The Tsaritsa sank gratefully into the other, the girls, thoughtful as ever, bringing their pillows for them to sit on. Even now, guard Viktor Netrebin noticed the boy's irrepressible curiosity as he sat watching 'with wide curious eyes', following every move the guards made. In a fleeting moment of sympathy Netrebin, who later admitted to being extremely nervous that night, hoped, when it came to it, that they would 'all be good shots'. In a soft voice, Yurovsky now politely asked the rest of the family and servants to take up particular places behind the Tsar and Tsaritsa, which he indicated. Like the professional photographer he once had been, he seemed to be posing his victims, as he might clients, but for something far more sinister.

Conscious of his position as Tsar and paterfamilias, Nicholas took a position in the centre of the room. He faced the open door, with Alexey to his left on a chair, both of them slightly in front of everyone else. The punctilious Botkin, in collar and tie even at this late hour, stood behind to the Tsar's right. The Tsaritsa sat in her chair to Alexey's left – in the shadows near the barred window. It had been nailed shut specially, to muffle the sound of shooting and in case of any screaming.

Maria, Tatiana and Olga stood close behind their mother in silence. Further back still, the gangly Demidova, clutching her pillows, stood beside the doors into the storeroom. They were locked because Yurovsky feared his victims would panic and try to escape any way they could. To her right, Anastasia, who had detached herself from the others, stood typically alone and, as always, defiant. Trupp and Kharitonov were just in front of Anastasia, behind Dr Botkin and leaning against the wall.

Yurovsky gazed calmly at them and then continued with his lie: the family would have to wait here until the truck came to take them to safety. Leaving them all waiting in the bare basement room for half an hour or so, he went off to check everything was ready. The family were anxious about the delay, and no doubt worried about their things, which they had left upstairs, but having lived through so many difficult, tense moments in the last 16 months they exchanged few words, not wanting to alarm each other. Alexandra broke the rules, though, whispering in English not Russian to the girls.

What the astute Dr Botkin was thinking in those moments, in light of the sanguine letter that he had been writing anticipating his own inevitable death, we cannot guess, but even at the very moment of death victims are often in denial of the fact. If any of the 11 people gathered in that room in such ominous circumstances at such a late hour had any inkling of danger it must have been he. But the thought that his Tsar might actually be *killed*, let alone his innocent family – that was impossible to contemplate.

In the guards' room next door, the killers sat hunched together, repeatedly checking their weapons, smoking cigarette after cigarette. Their nerves were running riot, their tempers rising. With the adrenalin already coursing in their veins, being Russians, they did what all Russians would do – they shared a drink or two of vodka.

The names of only five of the killers that night are known for certain. There was the swaggering alcoholic Ermakov, with three revolvers stuffed in his belt; the young, cold-blooded Nikulin; Kudrin, the factory mechanic and, as a dedicated Cheka man, a willing killer; Medvedev, a 28-year-old welder from the Sysert works and senior guard at the Ipatiev House; and, of course, Yurovsky.

Research suggests that the remaining killers were Alexey Kabanov, who manned one of the machine-gun posts in the house; Viktor Netrebin – a young and inexperienced 17-year-old Cheka man; Stepan Vaganov – Ermakov's sidekick from the Verkh-Isetsk factory, a late replacement for the Letts who had refused to kill the girls; and the most shadowy figure of all, Jan Tsel'ms, who like Kabanov had been assigned to one of the machine-gun posts. Significantly, several of the 'Letts' brought into the house by Yurovsky to be part of the execution squad had lost their nerve when it came to it, but a legend was born that night and persisted thereafter that 'Letts and Jews' were key figures in the executions when in fact this was not so; all but one of the killers were Russians and Yurovsky was a Jew by birth only.

When everything was ready, Yurovsky ordered the Fiat truck across the road to be brought round to the house. The truck arrived, with the Ipatiev House's 'official driver' Lyukhanov at the wheel. He gingerly backed the clumsy vehicle into the courtyard between the palisades, grinding its gears in the process, in order to ensure it could better pull away up the incline out of the house when fully loaded. As they watched, some of the guards might reasonably have wondered whether such a ramshackle vehicle was sturdy enough to carry 11 bodies and their escort out to the night-bound Koptyaki Forest.

With the truck now outside and gunning its engine, and the killers gathering behind him outside the door, Yurovsky prepared to re-enter the storeroom. All was silent, except for the roar of the Fiat's engine rattling the window panes. With Nikulin on his left, and Kudrin and Ermakov on his right, Yurovsky opened the double doors and entered, the rest of the execution squad crowding into the doorway behind him. What was this? A new special detachment to escort the family to their next refuge? Nicholas, Alexandra and Botkin all seemed to register Ermakov and Kudrin as being new to the house and were unnerved by their presence, as they and Yurovsky took up their positions in front of them.

'Well here we all are,' said Nicholas, stepping forward to face Yurovsky, thinking that the truck they could hear revving outside had now arrived to take them to safety 'What are you going to do now?'

His right hand clutching sweatily at the Colt in his trouser pocket, his left holding a piece of paper, Yurovsky asked the family to stand. Alexey, of course, could not and stayed where he was, as the Tsaritsa, muttering her complaints, struggled to her feet. Suddenly the room seemed to shrink in on him as Yurovsky stepped forward, brandishing his sheet of paper. It had been drafted by the presidium of the Ural Regional Soviet and given to him by Goloshchekin that day. Here, at last, was the commandant's personal moment in history. Yurovsky had rehearsed his statement many times and raised his voice in order to be heard more clearly.

'In view of the fact that your relatives in Europe continue their assault on Soviet Russia,' he began portentously, gazing straight at Nicholas, 'the presidium of the Ural Regional Soviet has sentenced you to be shot . . .'

The Tsar registered blank incomprehension; turning his back to Yurovsky to face his family, he managed an incredulous stutter – 'What? What?' – as those around him were rooted to the spot in absolute terror.

'So you're not taking us anywhere?' ventured Botkin, unable also to comprehend what had just been said.

'I don't understand. Read it again . . .' the Tsar interrupted, his face white with horror. Yurovsky picked up where he had left off:

. . . in view of the fact that the Czechoslovaks are threatening the
red capital of the Urals – Ekaterinburg – and in view of the fact that

the crowned executioner might escape the people's court, the presidium of the Regional Soviet, fulfilling the will of the Revolution, has decreed that the former Tsar Nicholas Romanov, guilty of countless bloody crimes against the people, should be shot . . .

Instinctively, the Tsaritsa and Olga crossed themselves; a few incoherent words of shock or protest were heard from the rest. Yurovsky, having finished reading the decree, pulled out his Colt, stepped forward and shot the Tsar at point-blank range in the chest. Ermakov, Kudrin and Medvedev, not to be outdone and wanting their moment of personal revenge and glory too, immediately took aim and fired at Nicholas as well, followed by most of the others, propelling an arc of blood and tissue over his terrified son beside him.

For a moment the Tsar's body quivered on the spot, his eyes fixated and wide, his chest cavities, ripped open by bullets, now frothing with oxygenated blood, his heart speeding up, all in a vain attempt to pump blood round his traumatised body. Then he quietly crumpled to the floor.

But at least Nicholas was spared the sight of seeing what happened to his wife and family. For in that moment, Ermakov had turned and fired his Mauser at the Tsaritsa only six feet away from him as she tried to make the sign of the cross, hitting her in the left side of the skull, spraying brain tissue all around, as a hail of bullets from the other assassins hit her torso. Alexandra crumpled sideways on to the floor, her warm, sticky blood and brain tissue spreading across it in a mist of steam. Next to her, poor lame Alexey, too crippled even to get up and run, sat there transfixed, clutching in terror at his chair, his ashen face splattered with his father's blood.

The other victims meanwhile had fallen first to their knees and then to the floor in an instinctive attempt to protect themselves, some of them convulsing from the trauma of flesh wounds received from bullets aimed at the Tsar and Tsaritsa that had missed, others crawling in desperation in the impenetrable smoke, trying to find a way out. Trupp had gone down quickly, his legs shattered, and was finished off by a final shot to the head. Kharitonov, his body riddled with bullets, crumpled to the floor and died beside him.

Within minutes there was such chaos in the basement room that Yurovsky was forced to stop the shooting because of the choking conditions; he did so with great difficulty, for by now the men had been overtaken by the frenzy of getting the job done. The air was thick with a nauseating cocktail of blood and bodily fluids – the faeces, urine and vomit precipitated from bodies in moments of extreme trauma. The killers were all choking and coughing from the caustic smoke of burnt gunpowder as well as showers of dust from the plaster ceiling caused by the reverberation of bullets. Their eyes were streaming too and they were all temporarily deafened by the delayed noise of the gunshots.

As Yurovsky's men staggered from the storeroom, shaking and disorientated, to gasp at the cool night air, some of them vomited. But it wasn't over. Once the deafening roar of firearms had ceased and the smoke had abated, the moans and whimpers they could hear inside made it all too apparent that they had botched the job. Many of their victims were still alive, horribly injured and suffering in agony.

Dr Botkin had already been hit twice in the abdomen when a bullet aimed at his legs had shattered his kneecaps, knocking him to the ground. From here he had lifted himself up on his right elbow and tried to reach towards the Tsar in one final, protective act. Seeing Botkin was still alive as he re-entered the room, Yurovsky took aim with his Mauser and shot him in the left temple as the doctor turned his head away in terror. His wish had been fulfilled: he had, at least, been permitted to die with his Emperor.

None of the Romanov girls – those pretty girls whom none of the guards had really wanted to have to kill – had died a quick or painless death. Maria had earlier been felled by a bullet in the thigh from Ermakov as she had pounded hysterically at the locked storeroom doors, and was now lying on the floor moaning. Her three sisters had suffered terribly, filling the room with their screams as they shrieked out for their mother, Olga and Tatiana doing what came instinctively, pressing themselves into each other's arms in the darkest corner for protection. Realising that the two older girls were still alive, Ermakov lunged at them with the eight-inch bayonet he had stuffed in his belt, stabbing at their torsos. But, drunk and uncoordinated as he was, he had trouble penetrating the girls' chests.

It was the cool and collected Yurovsky who strode though the smoke and shot Tatiana in the back of the head as she struggled to her feet to escape his approach, the brains and blood from her shattered skull showering her hysterical sister. A wild-eyed Ermakov shot Olga through the jaw as she tried to rise to her feet too and run; in her death throes she fell across Tatiana's body.

Anastasia meanwhile had taken refuge near the wounded Maria. Realising that the two youngest girls were still cowering alive in the corner, Ermakov again resorted to his bayonet and stabbed Maria repeatedly in the torso, but his weapon would not go through and Yurovsky had to step over and deliver the *coup de grâce* with a bullet to her head. Anastasia suffered horribly too: Ermakov lunged at her like a wild animal, again attempting to pierce her chest with his bayonet as he rained blows down on the helpless girl, before finally taking his gun to her head.

Yurovsky and the other killers later claimed that the bullets from the Nagants ricocheted off the layers of jewels sewn into the girls' bodices, which appear to have acted as primitive flak jackets; the bayonet thrusts failed to penetrate them too. It is more likely, however, that the force of the bullets, fired at random, simply propelled the jewels into the girls' torsos, causing numerous flesh wounds, or shattered the pearls, of which there were a great many, on impact.

Incredibly, Yurovsky now saw that the Tsarevich was still alive (for, as it later turned out, the boy too was wearing an undergarment sewn with jewels). He could not comprehend the sick boy's 'extraordinary vitality' and watched in disbelief as a shaky Nikulin spent the entire clip of bullets from his Browning on him.

But the fatally flawed blood of the haemophiliac boy still continued to pump round his body, keeping him alive when on so many occasions in the past it had nearly killed him. Yurovsky, having fired the last bullets from his Mauser, could do no better than Nikulin. Frenzied stabs by Ermakov with his bayonet again had little success at penetrating the layer of jewels surrounding the boy's torso. In the end Yurovsky pulled a second gun, his Colt, from his belt to give the dying boy the *coup de grâce* as he lay on the chair which had fallen sideways on to the floor. Alexey's body then finally slumped and rolled silently against that of his father.

Miraculously, the maid Demidova had somehow survived till now, wounded in the thigh, having fainted while those all around her were being put to death. When the shooting died down, she came to and staggered to her feet screaming, 'Thank God, I am saved!'

Immediately Ermakov turned on her with his bayonet as Demidova found superhuman strength in the face of imminent death. She had been frightened of what the Bolsheviks at Ekaterinburg might do to them all; she had said so when she left Tobolsk. And now she resisted violently, turning this way and that, fending off bayonet thrusts with her reinforced cushions – the Tsaritsa's jewels that she had so carefully protected now protecting her – until one of the assassins pulled them from her. In desperation Demidova made a final attempt to defend herself against the bayonet, hysterically swiping at it with her bare hands until she was finished off.

Yurovsky had seen plenty of death and mutilation during his time as a medical orderly in the war. He had a stronger stomach for the grisly spectacle of the basement room than most of the men there that night, and now the medical man in him took over as he went round checking pulses to make sure the victims were all dead. Ermakov meanwhile, his drunken brain reeling from this orgy of killing, staggered and stumbled and slipped as he crossed back and forth in the room, flailing at bodies with his bayonet, wreaking his personal hatred on the bullet-ridden bodies of the Tsar and Tsaritsa and cracking their rib cages.

It had taken 20 minutes of increasingly frenzied activity to kill the Romanovs and their servants. Professional marksmen given the same task would have taken 30 seconds. What should have been a quick, clean execution had turned into a bloodbath. Prior to the execution, Yurovsky had told the members of the squad who was to kill whom and to aim straight for the heart. That way there would be less blood and they would die quicker, he told them. Ermakov would later claim that they all knew exactly what they were supposed to do 'so there'd be no mistake'; he was the only one designated two targets: the Tsaritsa and Dr Botkin. But once Yurovsky had fired the first shot at the Tsar, the men behind him opened fire in a fusillade of noise, smoke and fumes, making it impossible to be certain who exactly shot whom; later accounts are confused and contradict each other. Once the killers broke from the co-ordinated firing plan, the ratio of wild, inaccurate firing became ever greater, with the men taking pot shots at each other's designated target. Many of the shots fired would have missed their targets altogether or only caused flesh rather than fatal wounds; none of them were absorbed by the wooden, plaster-covered walls as Yurovsky had hoped. With their victims panicking, screaming and crawling on the floor, the uncoordinated frenzy of the killers would have escalated. It is surprisingly easy for untrained marksmen to miss a target, even at relatively close range, if one takes into account a lack of expertise, compounded by the stress of waiting and too much to drink. Yurovsky later admitted to Nikulin's 'poor mastery of his weapon and his inevitable nerves'. Visibility would have been a major problem too: the level of smoke from the guns had rapidly fogged out the light from the one feeble electric bulb, making the room so murky that it was almost impossible for anyone to see what they were doing except by the light of momentary firearm flashes. In addition, with eight or nine killers crowded into the doorway in three rows, one shooting over the shoulder of the other, rather than spreading out across the room, many of those firing might well have been grazed by bullets or their aim skewed by the recoil from the arm of the man in front of them. Others got singed by the residue from the guns. All of the killers, within seconds of the adrenalin kicking in, would have been overtaken by that strange phenomenon of tunnel vision, when time goes into slow motion, and would not have been able to take account of the real situation in the room as a whole and act accordingly. Their victims too would have gone into a state of trauma, seeing only the barrels of the guns in front of them, until the classic fight-or-flight response took over.

Some of the old Nagants may well have jammed and proved useless because they had been loaded with the wrong bullets and the men using them were not used to handling them, thus explaining the relatively low number of bullets found here and at all three subsequent gravesites: about 57 in all out of a possible 70 bullets – roughly seven bullets per assassin from the mainly 0.32-calibre gun clips emptied that night, as subsequent investigations calculated. It has also been suggested that when the moment came, after taking revenge on Nicholas, most of the killers lost their nerve about killing the women and fired mainly at the men or above the heads of their victims, leaving the few tough nuts – Yurovsky, Nikulin and Ermakov – to kill the others.

Up in the Romanovs' quarters, the two dogs left behind had instinctively sensed danger when not allowed to accompany the family downstairs and had started whimpering the moment they were taken away. Once the shooting started down in the basement they would have barked in a frenzy of fear; and the sound of it would have been heard for some distance. Alexey Kabanov, who had left his machine-gun post in the attic to come down and take part in the killings, had run out on to the street to check the noise levels. He heard the dogs barking and also the sound of gunshots loud and clear despite the noise from the Fiat's engine; many of the neighbours later testified to hearing the shooting too. Kabanov had hurried back in and told the men to stop firing and finish their victims off with their gun butts or bayonets to reduce the noise; they should kill the dogs too.

As the smoke and fumes cleared amidst the pile of twisted bodies, the full horror of the murder scene was finally revealed. All the dead were hideously distorted, their faces contorted in their final agony and covered in blood. The bodies all had numerous bullet wounds – some of them fatal through-and-through wounds to the soft tissue, caused by the powerful, large-calibre Mausers being fired at close range – as well as bones fractured or broken by gunshots. What remained of their smoke-charred clothes was covered in blood and tissue.

Wasting no time, Yurovsky ordered any valuables from the bodies to be collected up. The assassins slipped and slithered in the glutinous, coagulating mess as they searched among the pathetically blood-soaked handbags, shoes, pillows and slippers that had fallen from their victims and now lay tumbled in disarray across the floor, and gagged at the strange and terrible smell of death that hung in the room. As they turned the bodies over, they struggled with distorted limbs to strip the jewellery from them. The Tsaritsa's gold bracelets that she never took off and which she had refused to yield to Yurovsky on the day of his arrival were yanked from her wrists, and those from her daughters too, and handed over. As Petr Voikov, who had been a witness to the killings (but who later claimed to have taken part), turned the body of one of the Grand Duchesses over, it gave out a terrible gurgling sound and blood gushed from its mouth. It was a sight to shock the hardest of stomachs. Greed inevitably prompted some of the men to pocket the valuables they found – a cigarette case here, a gold watch there – as they dragged the bodies to the doorway. Yurovsky soon got wind of this and called all the men together and threatened to shoot them if they did not take the items upstairs and leave them on his desk. Soon it was piled with 'diamond brooches, pearl necklaces, wedding rings, diamond pins and gold watches'.

Commandant Yurovsky, the agent of proletarian vengeance, had now fulfilled his revolutionary duty and he was exhausted. He went upstairs to lie down in his office for a while and recover. It was now down to Petr Ermakov to play his essential part in ensuring the efficient disposal of the bodies in the forest. But Ermakov had turned up late, and drunk (like the other guards having boozed away most of his pay the day before), and remained so for hours afterwards, his eyes bloodshot and his hair dishevelled. Could he remember the location of the site in the dark, and was he in any fit state to carry out his task at this late hour? No one seems to have given a thought beforehand as to how they would carry 11 badly bleeding bodies out to the waiting Fiat, or cope with the large bulky body of Dr Botkin, which slipped to the floor as they tried to raise it. Worse came as they moved one of the daughter's bodies – probably Anastasia's – on to the stretcher, for she suddenly shrieked and sat up, covering her face with her hands. Ermakov grabbed Strekotin's rifle and started trying to finish her off with its bayonet, but finding it impossible to penetrate her chest pulled another pistol from his belt and shot her.

Outside, the Fiat truck waited in the courtyard created between the two palisades at the north end of the house. This meant that the bodies had to be carried the long way round, through the interconnecting basement rooms from the southern end to the courtyard exit then out to the waiting Fiat. Despite the guards' crude attempts to wrap them up in sheets brought from the Romanovs' rooms upstairs, the bodies left a trail of blood across the basement and into the courtyard as the men carted them out on a crude stretcher improvised from the shafts of a sledge in the yard. Here the corpses were thrown in a jumble on to the wooden slats of the Fiat which had been covered with military cloth from the storeroom. At 6 feet by 10 in size, there was not much room for

11 bodies in the back of the truck, but someone had at least thought to put a layer of sawdust there to absorb the blood.

All this time, Goloshchekin, and other official witnesses had been hovering in the background; the guards later talked of men from the 'local soviet' or the Cheka being in attendance, but they weren't sure who. Beloborodov, as head of the Ural Regional Soviet, almost certainly would have been close by, either in the house or down the road at the Cheka HQ at the Amerikanskaya Hotel. But there was also one other essential witness, on behalf of the centre in Moscow: Aleksandr Lisitsyn of the Cheka, designated to ensure the prompt dispatch to Sverdlov in Moscow soon after the executions of the Tsar and Tsaritsa's politically valuable – and damning – diaries and letters. These would be published in Russia as soon as possible. Goloshchekin, despite being the mastermind with Sverdlov of the murders, does not appear to have had the stomach to stand and watch once the shooting started, but went outside and paced back and forth along the perimeter palisade of the house to see if anybody could hear what was going on. As the bodies were brought out to the truck he stooped down to take a look at that of the Tsar. He pondered for a moment, then turned to Kudrin, who was in charge of loading the bodies, and remarked, 'So this is the end of the Romanov dynasty, is it . . .' No, not yet; there was still much work to do in the forest before the Tsar and his family could be finally obliterated from history. Meanwhile, the last pathetic remnant of the Imperial Family's life at the Ipatiev House was brought out by a guard on the end of a bayonet – the corpse of the little lapdog Jimmy – and tossed on to the pile of bodies in the back. 'Dogs die a dog's death', hissed Goloshchekin as he stood by watching.

Yurovsky by now, however, was deeply concerned at the uncontrolled behaviour of the patently drunk and incompetent Ermakov. Earlier, knowing Yurovsky was sick with tuberculosis, Goloshchekin had suggested he need not go out to the forest to witness the 'burial'. But Yurovsky knew he would have to go with Ermakov and the others to make sure the job was done properly and the bodies didn't fall into the hands of the approaching Whites. As Ermakov, Kudrin and Vaganov climbed up into the truck, Yurovsky and Goloshchekin, leaving Nikulin in charge at the Ipatiev House, got into a nearby motor car to follow on behind them; Beloborodov and Voikov may well have accompanied them too. Three more guards rode shotgun in the open back of the truck with the bodies rolling round under their feet, as the Fiat struggled off down Voznesensky Lane, skirted the Iset Pond and then turned north-west out past the racetrack on the Verkh-Isetsk Road, heading for the Koptyaki Forest. But it was now seriously overloaded by as much as half a ton; it could barely pick up any speed and it was almost daylight.

When the shooting had finally stopped, the doors into the courtyard had been opened wide to let in the air as the men of the execution squad had stumbled out choking and coughing. One by one men from the external guard on duty that night had ventured in to view the murder scene, many of them reacting with profound horror and anger, others weeping. Several of the internal guard billeted downstairs who had heard the shootings but not taken part refused to sleep in the basement that night and had gone up to Yurovsky's room to camp out there. Even Cheka men such as these were nauseated and shocked by what had happened.

Meanwhile, Medvedev went over to the Popov House to gather a contingent of guards to clean up the floors. There was so much blood now, thick, sticky and congealing in puddles, that as the Tsarevich's tutor Gibbes was later told, they had to 'sweep it away with brooms'. The air was heavy too with the smell of gunpowder as they struggled back and forth with buckets of cold water, washing and scrubbing as best they could with sand, sawdust having been thrown down first to help absorb the puddles of blood and tissue; no doubt a few stray bullets were swept up in it as they cleared the floor. But there were blood splashes up the walls too which the men went at ineffectually with wet rags. Hardly an efficient clean-up operation and one which today would have left a cornucopia of DNA-testable clues as to who had died in that cellar, thus circumventing 80 years of speculation and baseless claims of survival.

It took two hours for the Fiat truck to crawl the excruciatingly slow nine miles out to Koptyaki. The truck's engine was noisy and its gears crunched and ground with every change, and Yurovsky was worried that it would draw attention to itself, even at this early hour. To make matters worse, he had now discovered that the incompetent Ermakov had only brought one shovel and no picks or other tools for the burials in the forest. 'Perhaps someone else had brought something with them', Ermakov ventured half-heartedly. It was now clear that the greatest moment in Russian revolutionary history was on the brink of being turned into farce.

After crossing the Perm railway line the heavily laden Fiat barely managed to negotiate a steep incline before finally getting on to the Koptyaki Road. At this point the going became even slower as the truck lurched on to what was really only a narrow, muddy rutted track leading through the forest. About half a mile further on, near crossing no. 185 on the line serving the Verkh-Isetsk works, a party of men with horses and light carts stood waiting for them across the road. They were Ermakov's outriders, 25 fellow workers and local Bolshevik thugs from the 2nd Ekaterinburg Squadron, who had turned up to be part of the burial detachment and, they hoped, of the lynch mob. They had all been drinking and had been expecting to have a bit of fun with the Romanov girls, whom they had assumed would be brought out to the forest alive. An angry scene ensued when they discovered their victims were already corpses. An exhausted Yurovsky had great difficulty maintaining control of the situation, but eventually got the men to shift some of the bodies from the truck on to the carts, one of them later claiming that he had taken the opportunity to put his hand up the Tsaritsa's skirt and finger her genitals; now, he said, he could 'die in peace'. With the mounted detachment following in the rear, the Fiat laboriously continued its journey.

A mile or so further on, not far from the Gorno-Uralsk railway line, the truck ground to a halt in an area of marshy ground as it entered the dense forest; Yurovsky ordered the men to unload all the corpses into the long wet grass so that they could try and get the truck moving again, but to no avail. Lyukhanov repeatedly gunned the engine but it rapidly overheated and he was forced to go and rouse the railway guard from her booth, near Grade Crossing 184, to get some water to cool it down. She indicated a pile of old wooden railway ties lying nearby and the men hauled these over to the Fiat and placed them across the muddy road to form a bridge. Slipping and sliding in their attempts to gain purchase in the mud, the men gave the truck an almighty push and managed to get it moving again, but the pot-holed road beyond was boggy with the heavy rainstorms of summer. When Ermakov directed Lyukhanov to turn off the road along an overgrown track in the forest surrounded by tall nettles and weeds, the vehicle lurched sideways and got stuck between two trees. They would have to give up on the truck; all of the bodies would have to be unloaded on to the carts that Ermakov's men had brought in the rear and taken on to the site by them, leaving the Fiat to be extricated later. Yurovsky placed his men on guard at the truck, under instructions to turn back any people who might pass that way, and borrowed a couple of horses from Ermakov's detachment in order to ride on ahead with Ermakov to ascertain the exact location of the burial site. Ermakov's brain was still addled by drink as he struggled to remember the precise location of the Four Brothers, somewhere amidst the tall forest that loomed over them on all sides in the dark. They had no luck, and another group of men rode off up the trail to try to find the mineshaft. Eventually, with all the bodies finally hauled from the truck and on to the rickety and inadequate carts, the ghoulish funeral cortege set off through the great watching forest to what everyone fervently hoped would be the Romanovs' last resting place.

The sun was up by the time the long line of carts came in sight of the mineshaft at Four Brothers. A group of official witnesses from the Cheka and Ural Regional Soviet, as well as an unidentified 'man from Moscow with a black beard', as some witnesses later testified, arrived soon after by car. But as the cortege came closer to the mine, Yurovsky now spotted another problem: a group of local peasants were out in the very meadow they were heading for, sitting by a fire, having camped out overnight to mow the hay along the Koptyaki Road. How on earth could they hide the bodies in secret now? Farce had turned to catastrophe. It was market day in Ekaterinburg and the peasants from nearby Koptyaki village would be heading into town to sell their fish, passing right by the meadow as the men laboured at their nefarious task. Yurovsky sent the peasants who had come to mow packing and they headed back to Koptyaki with a look of terror in their eyes. He did his best to cordon the area off, sending Ermakov's riders ahead to the village to warn its inhabitants not to venture forth, under dire warnings that the Czech legions were now very close.

With the sun coming up over the treetops and another warm July day beckoning, Yurovsky shared with his hungry men the hardboiled eggs brought the previous day by the nuns. It was all the food they were going to get that day. The men ate hastily, scattering the eggshells all around and warming themselves at the fire left by the peasants – nights in the Siberian forest are cold, even in summer. Yurovsky did not want Ermakov's rapacious cronies from the Ekaterinburg Squadron to be part of what happened next; they'd cause too much trouble trying to lay hands on the valuables that he knew were concealed about the bodies, and he ordered them back to the city. His own men from the Ipatiev House now unloaded the bodies, and began stripping and searching them. Their clothing was piled up and burned on two huge fires which belched smoke up into the blue of the early morning sky.

It was only now that Yurovsky finally discovered what he had long suspected. There were a great number of jewels hidden in three of the girls' camisoles as well as disguised under cloth buttons and fastenings; even the Tsarevich wore a jewel-filled undergarment, and his forage cap had gemstones sewn into it too. (Maria interestingly did not wear one, further confirmation, so Yurovsky thought, that the family had ceased to trust her ever since she had become too friendly with one of the guards back in May.) It was an extraordinary sight that chilly morning to see diamonds – one of eight carats and worth a fortune – as well as other precious stones spilling out on to the boggy earth from the Romanovs' torn and blood-soaked clothes. The men snatched at them with their dirty hands, pulling the clothes apart and manhandling the bodies as they ripped at them, searching frantically for anything they could find, and missing many in the process (these would be found first by curious peasants searching the site, the remainder by subsequent investigators). Much to everyone's astonishment, the Tsaritsa's corpse yielded up several rows of fine large pearls – her favourite jewellery – concealed inside a cloth belt around her waist, as well as a great thick spiral of gold wire wrapped tight around her upper arm. More touchingly, each of the children wore round their necks an amulet containing Rasputin's picture and the text of a prayer he had given them. It was hard to resist the temptation to pocket a souvenir or two, but Yurovsky's eagle eyes were on them and he took an inventory of the jewellery as the men did their work.

The corpses, many of them with hideous, gaping head wounds and broken and dislocated limbs, were now horribly mangled and ugly, their hair matted with caked blood. It was almost impossible to associate these wretched twisted bodies with the five charming, vibrant children of the official publicity. Not even the girls were pretty any more, recalled one of the men later; 'there was no beauty to see in the dead'. Then the moment came to lower the corpses of the Imperial Family and their servants down into the mine-working, one on top of the other. In death at last there was no precedence for the proud Tsaritsa. It was only then that Yurovsky discovered to his horror that the mine was far too shallow – only about nine feet deep – and that the pool of water at the bottom in which he expected the corpses to be submerged barely covered them. The smell of dissolving flesh was awful as they sprinkled acid over the tangle of bodies at the bottom of the shaft, after which Yurovsky threw down a couple of hand grenades in hopes this would make it collapse over the remains. But it didn't work – the sides were too well shored up with timber – so they covered the opening with loose earth and branches from nearby trees. But fragments of the bodies would have been blown off and scattered for later investigators to find or animals of the forest to take away, thus explaining the absence of many of the smaller bones.

It was all pointless; the suspicions of the locals had already been alerted and the site, rutted with cart tracks as it now was and trampled by men's boots and horses' hooves, would quickly be found. Worse, there was no contingency plan. Yurovsky knew he would have to start all over again with his 'troublesome corpses'; he and his men would have to come back, better equipped with picks and spades and shovels and ropes, and haul the bodies back out of the mineshaft and take them somewhere else. Leaving his own men to watch uneasily over the site and keep the

Verkh-Isetsk men, still eager to loot what they could, well away, Yurovsky headed back to Ekaterinburg. But his men were exhausted; most of them slept a sodden, fitful sleep in the long damp grass that day, while others ventured into the nearby village to get milk.

That same day back at the Ipatiev House the remaining guards, under the supervision of Beloborodov and Nikulin, had busied themselves overseeing the ransacking of the Romanov quarters and collecting up all the family's personal property – icons, diaries, letters, photographs, jewellery, clothes, shoes, fine underwear – the most valuable items being piled up on the desk in Yurovsky's office, whilst things considered inconsequential and of no value were stuffed into the stoves and burnt. Everything was to be packed into the Romanovs' own trunks from the outbuilding and taken off to Ekaterinburg railway station for dispatch to Moscow under escort by Bolshevik commissars; Cheka man Lisitsyn was already on his way back to Moscow with the diaries and letters. As the men went about their work, the local nuns arrived as usual at the front gates with a quart of milk for the family. They knocked and they stood and they waited. But nobody came. They asked the guards where the commandant was. 'Go away', the guards said, 'and don't bring any more.'

It was not long before Thomas Preston got wind of events in the Ipatiev House down the road from his consulate, though not their full and horrific details. That morning, as the men were still out in the forest burying the Romanovs, he hurried to the local telegraph office on the corner of Voznesensky and Glavny Prospekts to file 'probably the briefest and certainly the most dramatic report of my career' to Foreign Secretary Arthur Balfour in England. His text read simply: 'The Tsar Nicholas the Second was shot last night.' As he stood in line in the telegraph office a short, stumpy man approached him and snatched it from his hand. It was Filipp Goloshchekin, who proceeded to strike out the words of Preston's text, rewriting on the paper in red pencil, 'The hangman Tsar Nicholas the Second was shot today – a fate he richly deserved.' Preston recalled that he had no alternative but to let Goloshchekin's version go, though it is unlikely the telegraph ever reached London. It was the British secret agent Bruce Lockhart who was the first to hear the 'official intimation' of the Tsar's death that evening in Moscow from a commissar at the Soviet Foreign Office, and to be, as he believed, 'the first person to convey the news to the outside world'.

At the Ural Regional Soviet the members of the presidium had sat down at midday to compose their first, all-important communiqué to Moscow on the successful completion of their historic task; a copy was handed to the editor of the local paper, the *Uralskiy Rabochiy*, for publication as soon as the centre had vetted it. At 2 p.m. a formal telegram was sent to Lenin and Sverdlov informing them that in view of the proximity of the Czechs to Ekaterinburg and their discovery of a 'serious White Guard plot' to abduct the Tsar and his family (they had the documents to prove it – the officer letters to which the family had responded), 'Nicholas Romanov was shot on the night of the sixteenth of July by decree of the Presidium of the Regional Soviet'. His wife and children, it added 'have been evacuated to a safe place'. The telegram asked the centre for approval for this statement to be issued by the URS in Ekaterinburg to the public and the press, adhering to the strict instructions given them by Moscow that there should be no mention of the fate of the family. At 9 p.m. a reassuring, unofficial communiqué followed, a short coded telegram from Beloborodov, addressed to the secretary of the Council of People's Commissars, Nikolay Gorbunov (the Ekaterinburgers were conscious that nothing relating to the Tsar's death should be directly communicated to Lenin): 'Inform Sverdlov that the entire family suffered the same fate as its head.' 'Officially', Ekaterinburg now assured Moscow, 'the family will die during evacuation' from the city, their deaths becoming a meaningless statistic as just six among many casualties of the escalating civil war. Lenin and Sverdlov's hands were clean. The Revolution was off the hook. It was the beginning of a long and elaborate lie.

After Yurovsky trailed back into Ekaterinburg with his sack full of the valuables – 18lb of diamonds alone – found on the bodies out at the Four Brothers, his first duty had been to report back to Beloborodov and Goloshchekin at an emergency meeting of the presidium of the Ural Regional Soviet. No longer trusting to the bleary-eyed Ermakov's inflated claims that he knew his fiefdom of the Koptyaki Forest well, Yurovsky now decided with Goloshchekin that the bodies would first be disfigured by acid and burnt as much as possible before being reburied. Chutskaev from the city soviet told Yurovsky that he had heard of some deeper copper mines about three miles further up the old Moscow–Siberia Trakt (the road along which exiles had tramped) west of the city that might prove a more suitable location for the 11 corpses. The area was remote and swampy and a grave there less likely to be discovered. No one, however, went into the logistics of how they would reduce 11 bodies to ash by fire; nor did they have the least inkling that do so was a virtual impossibility.

It was eight in the evening of the 17th when Yurovsky, having been out on horseback to inspect the new site with a fellow Chekist,

Pavlushin, who was to help him in the burning of the bodies, got back to Ekaterinburg. En route their horses had stumbled and fallen on muddy ground, and Yurovsky had injured his leg. It was an hour before he managed to haul himself back on his horse again. He reported the latest developments to the Cheka at the Amerikanskaya Hotel and then went off to order additional trucks to be sent out to Koptyaki, whilst assigning Petr Voikov to obtain barrels of petrol and kerosene, and more jars of sulphuric acid, 15 gallons in all, and plenty of dry firewood. He also requisitioned several horse-drawn carts from the local prison to be sent out, driven by Cheka men, to assist in the removal of the bodies to the new site. Then Pavlushin announced that he couldn't come with him; he too had badly hurt his leg in the fall. Unable to get an official car to take him, Yurovsky requisitioned a horse and cart and set off back to the Four Brothers the slow way. It was now 12.30 a.m. on 18 July.

16

'The World Will Never Know What
We Did to Them'

THURSDAY 18 JULY 1918

When he arrived back in the Koptyaki Forest at about four in the morning of the 18th, Yurovsky discovered that a detachment of new men had gone ahead of him to offer their revolutionary services to the task in hand. These had been sent out from the Kusvinsky works in the city by local Bolshevik commissars; Yurovsky didn't like these men and didn't want them muscling in on his operation. He delegated some of them to watch the road and sent others to the village to warn the locals that anyone from the surrounding area trying to get through would be shot.

In the shadows of the still dark forest, by the light of flickering torches, 10 dishevelled men, like nineteenth-century grave robbers, had begun the laborious process of retrieving the bodies from the bottom of the flooded mine. Goloshchekin and some other Cheka men, including Isay Rodzinsky, had driven out by motor car to make sure the job was done properly this time. Vladimir Sunegin from the Kusvinsky detachment had been selected for the gruesome task of climbing down into the cold, flooded mineshaft to ferret out the bodies one by one. Groping around in the darkness in icy water up to his waist, he was encountering difficulties untangling the corpses in the dark, so he was joined by Grigory Sukhorukov. Finally they grabbed hold of a leg that turned out to be the Tsar's, tied ropes to it and the men at the surface hauled the body out. There, lying in the wet grass in front of them, was the lifeless, naked body of the former Tsar of All the Russias. The men could not resist this once-in-a-lifetime opportunity to take a look, and agreed that Nicholas had a very fine physique, with well-developed muscles in his arms, back and legs – and a firm backside too, so they noted.

One by one, the remaining bodies slowly twisted and turned their way to the surface at the end of ropes, after which they were laid under a tarpaulin cover. The water in the mineshaft had washed the blood from their faces and some of them were still recognisable. They were all as pale as marble lying there in the early morning light but their bodies were now badly broken by many additional post-mortem injuries from so much manhandling, and parts of limbs were missing as a result of the grenade explosion in the mineshaft. The job of pulling them up the shaft was slow and laborious; the men were getting tired and angry and hungry and Yurovsky was already worrying whether there would be time to take the bodies on to the deeper mine. He thought of digging a burial pit then and there, but when the men tried this, the ground proved too stony. At this point a peasant – a friend of Ermakov's – appeared on the scene. Yurovsky was sick of Ermakov and his 'damn friends'; they had caused one problem after another. He would have to go back to Ekaterinburg yet again to confer with the Cheka at the Amerikanskaya.

Back in the city he put in an urgent call to the military garage for a car to take him back to the forest, but it proved as unreliable as the Fiat truck and broke down on the way. Yurovsky spent an hour desperately trying to fix it but could do nothing. Realising that it was essential that he had more back-up vehicles, he started the long walk back to Ekaterinburg at a limp, his leg possibly fractured by the fall from the horse earlier that day. Fortunately he saw two riders out in the forest and prevailed on them for the use of their horses to tow his car back to the city. Here he managed to requisition another car and a single lightweight truck, which he ordered to be loaded with equipment and food, as well as blocks of concrete with which the bodies would be weighted before being submerged in the new mineshaft they would take them to. As chance would have it, he managed in the end to lay hands on a second, heavier truck which would take a detachment of Cheka men out to the Four Brothers to help move the bodies.

It was ten o'clock on Yurovsky's third night without sleep when he set off yet again for the forest. Lyukhanov and the Fiat were still parked near crossing 184; the truck was now extricated from the mud, but Yurovsky did not want to risk it getting stuck again by bringing it to the mine, so he ordered the convoy of carts on which the bodies had now been piled to rendezvous back with the Fiat at the crossing.

As dawn broke on the 19th, the procession of carts and an almost catatonic Yurovsky, who had not slept for 70 hours, slowly made their way over the treacherous boggy ground to the Fiat truck and once more transferred the bodies into it, before heading back down the road in the direction of Ekaterinburg. Time and again the men had to stop and give the truck a shove when it encountered deep ruts in the track. Then, just before they were due to swing right on to the Moscow–Siberia Trakt, the Fiat slipped and lurched and got stuck yet again in a dip in the road, near the place known as Porosenkov Log (Pig's Meadow) that they had passed on the way out to the forest. The additional truck carrying the men also ground to a halt in the mud not far behind.

Yurovsky finally gave up. They had to bury them all now, quickly, right there under the road where the truck had stalled, and they had to do it before the sun came up and before any outriders of the Czechs or the Whites, who they knew were in the area, came upon them. As the men tossed the corpses from the Fiat, Yurovsky decided to separate two of the smallest (those of Alexey and Maria) from the rest and burn them about 50 feet away, in a faint attempt to confuse anyone who might later discover the mass grave with only nine in it. The men's strength was totally spent as they grumbled and struggled to dig a grave six feet by eight in the breaking sunrise for the now bloated bodies. The grave was barely two feet deep and it filled up with peaty black water as they dug it, but finally, at seven, the Romanovs and their loyal retainers received their last ghastly funerary rites, overseen by the man who had orchestrated their deaths: thrown on top of each other, Trupp's body first, followed by the Tsar's, all of them tumbled into this small pit, their bodies doused in sulphuric acid, which fizzed and bubbled on flesh, their faces smashed to a bloody pulp with rifle butts to prevent them from being recognised. After this they were covered with quicklime and a shallow layer of boggy earth before the ground was trodden down over them and brushwood strewn around to disguise its newness.

Over at the smaller grave site, the sodden corpses of Maria and Alexey hissed and smoked on their improvised funeral pyre and were only partially burned, Yurovsky unaware that it needed as long as 50 hours to burn corpses in the open air as compared with an incinerator. Those few, pitiful charred bones of Maria and Alexey that remained were pounded to fragments with spades and tossed into their own small graves, the remaining ashes kicked around by the men in all directions 'to further blur the traces'. Finally, to disguise the location of the main grave, the men took up the pile of rotting wooden rail ties they had laid nearby on the track when the truck had stalled the day before and placed them over it. Then Lyukhanov drove the truck back and forth over the ties to make sure the earth was pressed well down and that it looked as though they had been put there long ago to reinforce the road.

By 6 a.m. on the morning of 19 July, the long and tortuous burial of the Romanovs and their retainers was finally completed. As Yurovsky drove back to Ekaterinburg from the Koptyaki Forest he felt satisfied. He had made the best of a horribly inept and botched job. The 'Imperial hangman' had been consigned to oblivion and he had fulfilled his duty to the Revolution. Pavel Ermakov would later lay claim in his lurid and self-serving memoirs to a vastly aggrandised role in the killings and the disposal of the bodies, asserting unconvincingly that they had all been destroyed on a massive funeral pyre deep in the forest. After that, so he asserted, he himself had taken a shovel and with dramatic finality had 'pitched the ashes into the air'. 'The wind caught them like dust', he said 'and carried them out across the woods and fields.'

Had this really been the final, poetic fate of the bodies of the Romanovs, Petr Voikov's confident prophecy that 'The world will never know what we did to them' might well have prevailed. The Special Detachment of the Ipatiev House may have left their victims' horribly violated bodies to rot, as highwaymen of old had been left – at a roadside without a cross or a tombstone to signify their last resting place – but 60 years later, history would finally start catching up with them. A shallow grave in Pig's Meadow would not, in the end, be the Romanovs' final pitiful resting place.

Back in Ekaterinburg, news had travelled fast. That Thursday, workers at the Verkh-Isetsk factory had been talking enthusiastically about the supposed secret execution of the Romanovs. The tongues of those who had been out in the forest with Ermakov had been wagging. It didn't take long either for rumours to filter back into the city itself. At the Opera House on Glavny Prospekt that afternoon, Goloshchekin called a meeting of Ekaterinburg's citizens at which he proudly announced that, under orders from the Ural Regional Soviet, 'Nicholas the bloody' had been shot and his family taken to another place. The Bolsheviks of the Urals were to have their moment of glory. But the crowd were angry and full of disbelief; some of them wept. 'Show us his body', they shouted.

On the evening of 18 July, Lenin had been in the midst of chairing a meeting of the Executive Committee of the Council of People's Commissars in the Kremlin when Sverdlov interrupted the proceedings, sat down behind him and whispered something in his ear. 'Comrade Sverdlov asks for the floor', Lenin told his colleagues. 'He has an announcement.' Sverdlov stood up and read out the communiqué sent on the afternoon of the 17th from Ekaterinburg that Nicholas had been executed. A show of hands was taken and a resolution passed approving the decisive action of the Ural Regional Soviet and instructing Sverdlov to supervise the composition of a suitable official press announcement, which appeared the following day in the Moscow edition of *Izvestiya*. Lenin, however, passed no comment; it was all a formality and he straight away returned to the agenda before him. Sverdlov was soon on the line back to Beloborodov in Ekaterinburg informing him of the resolution taken in Moscow and granting permission for the local paper to publish news of the Tsar's execution with the coda that 'the wife and son of Nicholas Romanov have been sent to a safe place', leaving the fate of the girls deliberately ambiguous.

Back at the Ipatiev House, senior guard Anatoly Yakimov, who had witnessed the murders on the morning of the 17th reported reluctantly for duty at 2 p.m. on the afternoon of the 18th. He was very apprehensive about entering the house after the horrors of the previous night. There was such a terrible silence upstairs, the rooms scattered with torn and fragmentary reminders of a family that had now been destroyed: buckles and fasteners, charred toothbrushes, thimbles and hairpins, porcelain dominoes and gramophone needles, strewn in all directions, as well as dozens of charred images of saints and icons and a jumble of Bibles and prayer books: *The Ladder of Paradise, Letters on the Christian Life, Of Patience in Suffering.* Among them lay perhaps the most poignant item of all, a book with a glossy blue cover bearing the monogram 'A' – Alexey's treasured copy of *Method to Play the Balalaika.*

The only sign of life that morning came from the commandant's office. Here Yakimov found Pavel Medvedev and a couple of the guards sitting, gloomy and morose, in sight of the table piled high with the Romanovs' most treasured possessions, their valuable icons, jewellery and ornamented photograph frames, all ready to be packed up and sent to Moscow.

Just then he heard a plaintive whimper. Outside, by the double doors leading into the Romanovs' quarters, sat the Tsarevich's chestnut and white King Charles spaniel, Joy, the boy's constant companion in exile, looking expectantly up at the door, his ears pricked, patiently waiting to be let in.

The Scent of Lilies

The Bolshevik commissars of Ekaterinburg could not contain their revolutionary pride for long after the murder of the Imperial Family. On 19 July the local paper announced the 'Execution of Nicholas, the Bloody Crowned Murderer – Shot without Bourgeois Formalities but in Accordance with our new democratic principles'. Although the announcement had been intended for local consumption only, word soon spread. French diplomat Louis de Robien, with the enclave at Vologda, heard the news of the Tsar's death on 20 July through a reliable contact in Moscow, who added that the centre was extremely anxious that 'it must not be known'. The diplomatic corps in Vologda went into mourning for the Tsar, in so far as they were able, as too did the local bourgeoisie, but it was September before de Robien got any of the details, from a Czech officer who had been in Ekaterinburg, and even then the story was garbled, the Tsar having been killed 'by a certain Goloshkin [sic], a Jewish dentist . . .' The names Beloborodov and Safarov were mentioned, but not a word of Yurovsky. The news of the initial finds by investigators out at the Four Brothers, as de Robien heard, seemed to indicate that the whole family had been murdered, but he felt that 'a glimmer of hope remains'.

Dutch ambassador William J. Oudendyk, who had remained in Petrograd rather than be evacuated to Vologda for his safety, had seen the official communiqué published in *Izvestiya* on 19 July reporting Sverdlov's announcement of the Tsar's execution to the Council of People's Commissars the previous day, the same day that the Bolsheviks announced that they were nationalising all confiscated Romanov properties. Oudendyk knew the report was full of untruths, but notices were already being posted up on the walls of apartment blocks around the city confirming the news. As Oudendyk boarded a crowded tram, a newspaper boy ran past announcing the death of the Tsar, but 'not a single passenger paid any attention'. Later, on the train out to

Oranienbaum, the same unnerving silence prevailed: 'it was evident that everyone was too much occupied with his own thoughts, and perhaps his conscience'.

The poet Mariya Tsvetaeva recorded much the same experience. She too heard the newsboys shouting 'Nicholas Romanov shot!' and looked around her at the people sharing her tram: workers, members of the intelligentsia, women with children. Some of them bought the paper in silence, glanced at the news story and then turned their gaze away. But everyone was too afraid; there were spies everywhere. Under the Bolsheviks, people had learned not to express their opinions in public; it might cost them their lives. Besides, the murder of the Tsar was no different from any other murder; there was now so much arbitrary brutality on the streets of Russia. But in the churches, it was a different story. The silent faithful in their thousands had gone to weep and light candles and say prayers for the souls of their former monarch and his family.

In America the news of the Tsar's murder finally broke on 21 July in the *New York Times* and the *Washington Post*, with the London *Times* following a day later, all reports buying the Bolshevik line that the Tsaritsa and the children had been spared and 'sent to a place of safety'. The Western response to this historic act was as subdued and lacklustre as that in Russia; the papers were preoccupied with blanket coverage of the 2nd Battle of the Marne, which had begun on the 15th. 'Ex–Czar Killed by Order of the Ural Soviet' jostled for space on the front page of the *New York Times* with a lead story informing readers: 'Germans Pushed Back, Allies Gain Three Miles, Now Hold 20,000 Prisoners'; the long, terrible war in Europe was finally drawing to a close. Practically all of the Western papers were hampered by having no correspondents in Siberia, or Russia for that matter, at a time when news–gathering was severely hampered by the civil war, and the disruption to the telegraph lines made things even worse. *The Times* in its obituary of the 22nd could only find praise for the Tsar's 'dogged resistance' to German oppression during the war, whilst noting that he was 'not endowed with much originality or initiative'. The *Daily Telegraph* had little to add: Nicholas suffered from an 'instability of mind and a lack of moral resolution'. The *Daily Mail* could do no better: Nicholas was 'a poor little Czar' and his life and death were 'pitiful'. But it was the illustrated weekly the *Graphic* that proved the most critical; under the dismissive headline 'The Dead Tsar', it noted that Nicholas had suffered 'a fate which he had often ordered for many of his subjects' and that his conduct during the war had found him 'completely wanting in all the qualities of statesmanship'. He had now 'gone the way of all waxworks', into the melting pot of history.

★

On Sunday 21 July, King George's aunt Princess Helena and her family arrived for lunch with the King and Queen at Windsor, only to find themselves kept waiting for an hour and a half in an anteroom. This was most unusual; the King and Queen were usually very punctual. Finally they appeared, ashen-faced, to greet Helena with the news that the Tsar had been murdered. Queen Mary made a brief note in her diary on 24 July that 'the news were [*sic*] confirmed of poor Nicky of Russia having been shot by those brutes of Bolsheviks'. It was, she said, 'too horrible and heartless'. She commiserated that afternoon with Alexandra, the Queen Mother, and Princess Victoria — the Tsaritsa's aunt and sister — over tea at Windsor, but in all their written and spoken reactions, such as they were, the British royals remained hidebound by a stiff upper lip that made their responses seem profoundly inarticulate and stunted.

The murder of his cousin Nicky was a crushing blow for the King; Mrs Asquith, wife of the Foreign Secretary, recorded that George's grief was palpable when he spoke of the vindictive and unnecessary killing of 'the poor Czar'. It was, he said, an 'abominable' act, but that was about the best he could muster. His response thereafter was to retreat into silence, apart from ordering four weeks of full mourning at court and attending a low-key memorial service on 25 July at the Russian embassy chapel in Welbeck Street. Privately, he was conscience-stricken. It was 'a foul murder', he wrote in his diary: 'I was devoted to Nicky, who was the kindest of men.' For the rest of his life George reproached himself for not having saved the Imperial Family, but that didn't stop him from making sure that his government suppressed the full grisly details of the investigation that were later forwarded to the Foreign Office from Allied HQ in Siberia. It wasn't just a matter of sparing the sensibilities of the nation, but of salving his own deep sense of responsibility.

As soon as the German government heard of the murder of the Tsar, Ambassador Riezler protested that the 'whole world would sharply condemn the Bolshevik government'. The Soviets assured him that the execution had been necessary to prevent the Tsar falling into the hands of the Czechs, but as for the Tsaritsa and the girls, yes, they might be able to arrange safe conduct for them on humanitarian grounds. With the Germans now occupying vast swathes of their territory and threatening their precarious hold on power, it was essential that the Bolsheviks continue to prevaricate. The Tsaritsa had been taken to Perm, they told Riezler, but Riezler didn't believe them. Rumours later circulated that the family had taken refuge in a monastery in Siberia. Meanwhile the Bolsheviks started suggesting various bogus trade-offs – the Romanovs in exchange for Russian POWs, or Leo Jodiches, a Polish Social Democrat leader under arrest in Berlin. But by November it was too late; the German Empire too had crumbled and the Kaiser had been forced to abdicate and go into exile. To his dying day Wilhelm denied having failed to act swiftly on behalf of his Romanov relatives, hinting at the abject failure of his cousin George: 'the blood of the unhappy Tsar is not at *my* door; not on *my* hands', he insisted.

It was left to King Alfonso and King Christian of neutral Spain and Denmark to make the last diplomatic representations on behalf of the family, not knowing that they were all already dead. The Bolsheviks played cat and mouse with Alfonso, but would not co-operate even though the King also offered refuge to the Dowager Empress and the Tsar's two sisters, Olga and Xenia, still trapped in the Crimea. Alfonso also lobbied for the release of four more Grand Dukes – Pavel, Nikolay, Georgy and Dmitry – now being held, 'for their own safety', according to the Bolsheviks, in the Peter and Paul Fortress in Petrograd. (On 28 January 1919 they were executed by firing squad in the fortress court-yard.) King Alfonso's final resort was to the Vatican. In August Pope Benedict XV put in his own pleas for the Tsaritsa and her children, backed by a personal message from Queen Mary (details of whose initiative have never been fully released). But it was all to no avail; after being fed a smooth line of disinformation and deliberate lies, the Spanish and Vatican initiatives had both petered out by the end of August. It was then that the British director of military intelligence in northern Russia cabled London, warning that reliable sources in Siberia now indicated that the whole family were dead; the news was officially communicated to the British War Cabinet on 1 September.

In the days immediately after the Imperial Family's murder, Ekaterinburg teetered on the precipice. Thomas Preston was now in considerable danger at the British consulate, with the Ural Regional Soviet becoming increasingly hostile about his perceived interference in local affairs. With the Czechs about to take the city, he had been warned that all foreigners, including himself and his family, were to be taken hostage and bartered. Receiving a tip-off that a mob was coming to get him, Preston barricaded his family into the consulate and went out to confront them. Several tins of Virginia cigarettes seemed to win them round; the crowd hadn't seen such a thing for months. Preston handed hundreds of them out as he argued about 'Britain, politics, the Revolution', until he heard shouts that the Whites were in the city suburbs, after which the crowd suddenly melted away.

Ekaterinburg finally fell to the Czechs on the night of 25/26 July after a relatively short engagement at the main Ekaterinburg railway station at the top of Voznesensky Prospekt. After a couple of days of sporadic street fighting and a second skirmish at the Mikhailovsky cemetery at the southern end of the city, the Bolsheviks finally fled. But not without having first emptied the city's banks and treasury, taking huge amounts of looted goods with them in a vast convoy of lorries that Thomas Preston heard trundling past his consulate until late into the night.

As the liberating Czechs and Whites paraded down the city streets to a rousing German march, they were greeted by waving flags and flowers thrown by the exultant population and the sound of church bells pealing. Preston had a front-row seat on the balcony of his consulate, from where he shouted, at the top of his voice, 'Long Live the Constituent Assembly' (the slogan of the Socialist Revolutionary anti-Communists). Soon afterwards, the Red Flag was hauled down and the white and green of Admiral Kolchak's new Siberian government was flying over Ekaterinburg. The city's liberation was, wrote Preston later, 'like the opening of a door into the sunshine from a huge cave in which we had been kept prisoner for nearly nine months'.

Now at last people felt safe to make their way up to the Ipatiev House, as the palisades were pulled down, to stand and stare and whisper in disbelief at what had happened there. White officers came to inspect the basement murder room and examine the last pathetic, charred and tattered remnants of the Romanov family's possessions, left scattered in their upstairs apartments. Within days an investigation was initiated under the auspices of the General Staff of the Ekaterinburg Military Academy, led by Captain D. Malinovsky, soon to be replaced by a short-lived one led by a White Russian officer, Aleksandr Nametkin. On 7 August a new White Russian investigation was set up under the presiding judge of the supreme court of Ekaterinburg, Ivan Sergeev.

In October 1918 the Ipatiev House was handed over to Czech leader General Gaida as his HQ. In January 1919 Admiral Kolchak appointed yet another investigator, General Diterikhs, to continue the investigation into the Romanov murders, but it was not until April 1919 that special investigator Nikolay Sokolov of the Omsk Regional Court began his exhaustive and historic investigation, which would take five years and accumulate photographic and eye-witness evidence filling eight volumes. It was published in French shortly after his death in 1924 as the *Enquête judiciaire sur l'assassinat de la famille impériale Russe*. Sokolov was unofficially 'assisted' in the early stages by Robert Wilton, Russia correspondent of *The Times* since 1909, who after an absence had managed to return to Russia via Siberia in October 1918 and who in 1920 serialised his own virulently anti-Semitic account of the Romanov murders in his newspaper.

Meanwhile the euphoria of liberation brought with it an orgy of anarchy and reprisal in the Urals by the retreating Bolsheviks, who tortured and murdered as they went. For all too short a while, Ekaterinburg, the strong arm of the Red Urals, became the centre of anti-Bolshevik activity in Russia, but Kolchak's White regime proved equally as repressive and brutal as the one he had ousted. Barely a year later, the Bolsheviks retook the city, as the chaos of the civil war continued.

The catalogue of Romanov murders did not end at Ekaterinburg. The big Moscow meeting in early July had taken account of the fate not only of the Imperial Family, but also of their closest relatives, as part of the systematic destruction of the dynasty. Only one day after the murders at the Ipatiev House, on the night of 18/19 July, 90 miles away at Alapaevsk, Alexandra's sister Ella, her companion Sister Barbara and the five Romanov Grand Dukes and Princes being held with them suffered an even more horrific death at the hands of the ruthless Urals Cheka. That night, men came for the prisoners at the schoolhouse where they were being held, took them by cart out into the nearby forest under cover of darkness and made them walk to the mouth of a disused mine. Here, the victims were beaten about the head with rifle butts and then one by one hurled down into the waterlogged pit. Only Grand Duke Sergey, who had struggled at the surface and been shot in the head, died quickly. Grand Duchess Ella and her companions were left to die a slow, agonising death from a combination of traumatic injury, thirst and starvation. But at least their bodies were found – only three months later.

Across Russia as a whole, the murder of the Romanovs marked the beginning of an orgy of terror, murder and bloody reprisal that would characterise the savage Russian civil war – a war which would claim 13 million lives. The signal to crank up repressive measures against counter-revolutionary activity came in August, first with the murder of the head of the Petrograd Cheka, Moisey Uritsky, and then with a failed assassination attempt on Lenin on the 30th. The rapidly expanding Cheka was now given free rein for acts of revenge; whole families of hostages, such as the wives and children of Red Army officers who went over to the Whites, were imprisoned in prototype concentration camps (created that autumn) and many were murdered. From now on the sons would be held accountable for the political sins of their fathers. Such acts of retribution escalated during the civil war and became endemic under Stalin. The cold-blooded murder of the Romanov children and with it an attempt at the systematic liquidation of the entire dynasty had been the ultimate litmus test of the amorality of Bolshevik policy. Some historians have seen it as being a turning point in the history of the twentieth century, laying the foundations for far greater acts of organised genocide later, during the Holocaust, in Africa and in Yugoslavia.

The fate of Mariya Bochkareva, the stout-hearted soldier who wanted to save her country single-handed, was typical. After making her way back to Russia via the Allied-held port of Archangel in August 1918, she tried to establish another women's battalion but came up against opposition from the Allies and Admiral Kolchak's White government. Kolchak also turned down her request to establish a women's medical battalion and sent her back to Tomsk, where she was captured by the Bolsheviks when they retook the city. Thrown into jail at Krasnoyarsk, Bochkareva was held for four months and interrogated. Finally she was taken out and shot by a Cheka firing squad on 16 May 1920; in one of the many cruel ironies that so characterise the irrationality of the times, she was condemned as an 'enemy of the peasant-worker republic'.

There was at least one happy outcome – Alexey's Spaniel Joy, who had run away from the house in terror as the bodies were being taken away after the murders and then returned to wait patiently for his master, was later found at the home of guard Mikhail Letemin. A member of the Allied Intervention Force, Colonel Paul Rodzianko, took Joy back to the British Military Mission based at Omsk, where Alexandra's former lady-in-waiting, Baroness von Buxhoeveden, visited him. The dog seemed to recognise her, although he was now almost blind. At the end of the campaign, Rodzianko took Joy home to England with him, where he lived out his life at the colonel's stables near Windsor Castle.

As for the men who were directly complicit in the murders of the Imperial Family, they largely escaped punishment for their crimes in the immediate months after the murders, such being the dislocations of the civil war period. Late in 1918, Stepan Vaganov fell victim to summary peasant justice: he was set upon and murdered, not for his part in the Romanov killings, but for his participation in local acts of brutal repression by the Cheka. Pavel Medvedev was captured by the Whites in Perm in February 1919. During his interrogation he denied taking part in the murders in order to try and save his skin, but soon afterwards caught typhus and died in prison. Yakov Sverdlov, the mastermind, a man who clearly had been positioning himself as Lenin's successor, remained at the centre of the Communist Party machinery until his untimely death in March 1919 during the flu pandemic. Petr Voikov worked in the Soviet Commissariat for Foreign Trade until posted as ambassador to Warsaw in 1924, where he was assassinated by a Russian monarchist on 7 July 1927 in revenge for his role in the Romanov murders.

But in the end, the great maw of the Revolution began to consume its own: Georgy Safarov of the presidium of the URS joined the leftist opposition to the Bolsheviks in the late 1920s and lost all his government posts. Arrested as a Trotskyist in 1927, he was expelled from the party and then reinstated; it was the beginning of Stalin's drive against the old guard. In 1934 Safarov was arrested again and in 1942 was shot. The war years were a favourite time for the disappearance of Stalin's political opponents, their deaths being lost in the vast fog of war casualties. Safarov's colleague Aleksandr Beloborodov held a succession of political posts until he too was expelled from the party as a Trotskyist in 1927. Released in 1930, he went the same way as Safarov: repentance, rehabilitation and ultimate rearrest. He was shot in the cellars of Moscow's notorious Lyubyanka prison in 1938. The same fate awaited Beloborodov's deputy Boris Didkovsky, who became a career Bolshevik until he too was shot at the height of the Stalinist purges in 1938.

For a while Filipp Goloshchekin rode the wave of favour with Moscow, and was rewarded for his loyalty to the centre in the liquidation of the Romanovs with a seat on the Central Committee of the Communist Party in 1924. He also held a key position at the Moscow headquarters of the Cheka and its successor organisations. A bisexual, he had a relationship with Nikolay Ezhov, the man who later headed Stalin's secret police, the NKVD, during the most ferocious period of the purges. But Goloshchekin's life as a career politician ended in 1941 when Stalin finally caught up with him. He was arrested in June and shot that October in an NKVD prison in Kuibishev (now Samara), and like all the other victims of Stalin's terror was consigned to an unmarked grave. In this at least there was some justice.

Petr Ermakov, amazingly, survived unscathed in Ekaterinburg after the murders, despite the arrival of the Whites. He fought in a Red Army battalion in the Urals during the civil war, after which he returned to Ekaterinburg to work for the militia and later in the prison camp system in the Urals area. He was pensioned off in 1934 as not being up to his position of responsibility; no doubt by now the alcohol had got to him. Unlike the other killers he was given no awards or advancements and because of that grew bitter and began to inflate his role, not just in the Romanov murders but in the Revolution itself. In 1934 he took part in a deliberately stage-managed act of misinformation when he was set up by the secret police to meet US traveller and journalist Richard Halliburton, in Russia hungry for a scoop about the Romanov murders. Halliburton proved a very willing dupe, taken in completely by the sight of the supposedly terminally ill Ermakov as he listened to his highly bowdlerised 'deathbed confession', a story which was widely disseminated in Halliburton's *Seven League Boots* of 1936.

Ermakov had the good fortune to die in his bed – in Ekaterinburg in 1952. As too did the man at the centre of it all, Yakov Yurovsky. After leaving Ekaterinburg three days after the murders, he reported to Lenin on the events of that night and soon after was rewarded with an appointment to the Moscow City Cheka. He returned to Ekaterinburg in 1919 to head the Cheka there after the city was retaken, but was something of a pariah when visited in 1920 by British army officer Francis McCullagh. People looked and whispered when Yurovsky passed on the street; there went 'the man who murdered the Tsar', they told each other. Even the Bolsheviks shunned him, so McCullagh was told, and it was hard to square the sight of the now scrawny, red-eyed, nervous man in carpet slippers with a mass murderer. In 1920 Yurovsky returned to Moscow, where he held a succession of key economic and party posts and fattened out like the good well-fed apparatchik he became – in middle age looking not unlike Stalin. Death at the age of 60 spared him the inevitable bullet in the back of the skull from the NKVD, his daughter Rimma already having been sent to the Gulag in 1935 (she was released 20 years later).

Fortunately for him, Yurovsky, whose health had always been bad, died of a gastric ulcer in the comfort of the Kremlin Hospital in 1938, having donated the guns with which he killed the Imperial Family to the Museum of the Revolution and leaving three different and valuable accounts of the events of July 1918. In a final letter to his children, he reminisced on his revolutionary career and how 'the storm of October' had 'turned its brightest side' towards him. He had met and served Lenin, and Lenin's men after him, and he considered himself to be 'the happiest of mortals', a loyal Bolshevik to the end.

In 1964, the 70-year-old Grigory Nikulin was persuaded to take part in a radio interview conducted by the son of fellow killer Mikhail Kudrin. But he did so grudgingly and refused to be drawn into any more than superficial detail. 'There's no need to savour it', he grunted. 'Let it remain with us. Let it depart with us.' Shortly afterwards, the only other survivor, Alexey Kabanov, confirmed what Nikulin told Kudrin's son that day – that it was Kudrin who had killed the Tsar and not Yurovsky. 'The fact that the Tsar died from your father's bullet was something every worker in the Ural Cheka knew at the time.' Whether that was true or not we shall never know. What really happened that night at the Ipatiev House was, from the very first, distorted by a systematic web of official lies, confusion, poor memory and disinformation, fuelled by the deliberate feeding to gullible Western reporters of entirely spurious stories about the fate of the family. By October 1918 the first intrepid American journalists were making their way to the city, travelling in from Vladivostok with the American intervention forces. Carl Ackerman of the *New York Times* arrived first and was elated to land what he thought was a massive scoop about the Tsar's final hours. He hastily dispatched it to the paper in December 1918 and it was syndicated across America. It told a lurid tale of the Tsar's midnight execution by firing squad, in a state of collapse, propped up against the firing post, the text accompanied by a drawing of a distraught Tsaritsa and Alexey at the killers' feet, begging for mercy. The story, related by the Tsar's 'personal servant', a man called 'Parfen Dominin', who had supposedly been with him in the Ipatiev House, was hardly credible. It has been suggested that it came from the elderly Chemodurov, who had fallen sick in May and had been taken from the house to the local hospital, but had since become senile. To the jaundiced eye of any New York newspaper editor, however, it was great copy.

Ackerman, hundreds of miles away in Siberia, was not to know that he had been duped, but the redoubtable Herman Bernstein was a lot more circumspect. He was a highly experienced Russia correspondent and was not fooled by Bolshevik lies and duplicity. Arriving in Siberia in October 1918, he headed for Ekaterinburg and straight for Judge Sergeev's office in search of the truth. By now Bernstein had heard six different versions of the Tsar's fate: he had been burned to death in the forest; killed by a bomb on the outskirts of Ekaterinburg; shot in the Ipatiev House; murdered in a secret passage leading from the house as he tried to escape; spirited away by Russian officers to Germany; or had escaped with his family in disguise as poor refugees and was now living in hiding in the Ural mountains. Bernstein reported back at length in a leader story for the *Washington Post* and the *New York Herald* in February 1919, but could come to no solid conclusions about the fate of the family except to state that the citizens of Ekaterinburg were largely indifferent to the Tsar's fate. As one cab driver observed to him, 'Who cares about the Czar? I am better off than he is now, dead or alive.' Bernstein came away frustrated by the mystery in which the whole story had become shrouded but convinced that either way it was the end of the monarchy. A liberal Russian officer had put it to him best:

The Tsar is dead – whether he is dead or alive . . . Russia is a land of accident. Russia freed herself by accident. Russia lost her freedom by accident. Russia may regain it by accident. But of one thing I am certain, Whether the Tsar was killed or not, the Tsar business is dead in Russia.

It may well have been so in Russia, but in the West the 'Tsar business' was far from over. On 12 September 1918, the *Daily Express* in London claimed to have 'unquestionable information' that the Tsaritsa and her four daughters had been murdered, a story confirmed by other sources in December. Nevertheless, over the next four years the Soviets persisted in denying that they were dead, killed on the same night as Nicholas. As late as April 1922, Soviet Foreign Minister Chicherin was still giving out the official line to the *Chicago Tribune*, in a story reproduced in the London *Times,* that Lenin's government was not entirely clear about the fate of the Tsar's family, blaming it on the Czechoslovak occupation of the city which had prevented the immediate 'circumstances of the case' from being cleared up. As far as Chicherin was concerned, 'The Tsar was executed by a local soviet without the previous knowledge of the Central Government.' As for the girls, he had read in the papers somewhere 'that they are now in America'.

Meanwhile, in Berlin in 1920, the Anastasia cause célèbre had broken and would keep the press and the Romanov family exercised for many decades to come. Claims of Anastasia's miraculous survival and the promotion across Europe of the mysterious 'Anna Anderson' were a gift horse for the Soviets. They were only too happy for the émigré Russian community to be at each other's throats as they split into two camps for and against Anderson's claim and squabbled over the few pathetic charred remnants found by Sokolov's investigation at the mineshaft at the Four Brothers: tiny fragments of bone, part of a severed female finger, Dr Botkin's upper dentures and glasses, corset stays, insignias and belt buckles, shoes, keys, pearls and diamonds and a few spent bullets. As the Anastasia claim gathered pace in the courts and in the émigré enclaves of Europe and America, the hunt for the Romanovs' bodies went cold. By 1924 and the death of Lenin, all hopes of a proper investigation vanished as Ekaterinburg, renamed Sverdlovsk, entered a new, tougher era.

In August that year, the American dancer Isadora Duncan, down on her luck and past her best, undertook a tour of the Russian provinces. Finding herself lumbered with a week's engagement in Ekaterinburg, she immediately sent an impassioned plea to her agent to get her out of there as quickly as she could. 'You have no idea what a living nightmare is until you see this town', she wrote. 'Perhaps the killing here of a *certain* family in a cellar has cast a sort of Edgar Allen Poe gloom over the place – or perhaps it was always like that. The melancholy church bells ring every hour, fearful to hear.' Even six years on, the Romanov murders cast a pall over the city – 'Its psychosis seems to pervade the atmosphere', wrote Duncan. Under the Soviets, Sverdlovsk became a dirty, tough place of heavy industry, munitions and scientific technology, a city with iron in its soul, dominated by the vast Uralmash machine plant. For the best part of 70 years it remained a closed city, its one brief claim to fame coming in 1962 when the American U-2 pilot Gary Powers was shot down here during a spying mission. In the post-Imperial era, its tsarist statuary was replaced by Bolshevik heroes; its magnificent eighteenth-century Ekaterininsky Cathedral was torn down in 1930. Imposing Stalinist civic buildings rose up in its place – notably the government offices that today house the Ekaterinburg Duma. Meanwhile, many of historic Ekaterinburg's fine old neoclassical mansions were allowed to fall into disrepair and large swathes of its traditional wooden houses were demolished wholesale to make way for grim new Soviet apartment blocks.

As for the Ipatiev House itself, after the Bolsheviks recaptured Ekaterinburg in 1919 it was used as a Red Army officers' mess, a notice over the door proclaiming the triumph of Soviet enlightenment over the dark hegemony of the tsars. In 1927 it was converted to a Museum of the Revolution, then in the early thirties it became an agricultural school. In 1938 it was deemed an appropriate venue for an Antireligious Museum, to which apparatchiks came in coachloads, posing for their photographs in front of the bullet-damaged wall in the cellar where the Romanovs were shot and stabbed to death. And then suddenly, in 1938, Stalin issued a clampdown on all discussion of the Romanov murders. In 1946 the Sverdlovsk party archives took the house over and finally, in 1974, it was listed as a Historical Revolutionary Monument.

By now, stories had been getting back to Moscow about the increasing numbers of pilgrims arriving in Ekaterinburg to pay homage at the Ipatiev House to the murdered Imperial Family. In 1975, with the sixtieth anniversary of the Romanov murders due in 1978, Leonid Brezhnev's Politburo decided to take action. A closed session agreed that the Ipatiev House was not of 'sufficient historical significance' and ordered its destruction. A secret directive was passed down the line to the local party chair, Boris Eltsin. Finally, in September 1977, the house was demolished and its site covered with asphalt. In his memoirs, published in 1990, Eltsin admitted that 'sooner or later we will be ashamed of this piece of barbarism'. Even so, the pilgrims kept coming, albeit surreptitiously, conducting their own private moments of remembrance on the mournful, barren site.

In 1979 the Koptyaki Forest finally began to yield up its secrets, when in May an Ekaterinburg-born amateur sleuth, Aleksandr Avdonin, after years of covert evidence-gathering and a study of the primary evidence, located the shallow grave under the rotting railway ties with the help of film-maker Geli Ryabov. Together they had secretly made a topographical survey of the Koptyaki Forest in order to define where precisely the grave was located; a secret dig took place on 31 May at which they discovered three skulls and a selection of bones, which they yanked at random from the ground without keeping any kind of documentary or archaeological record. They later reburied the skulls, having taken plaster casts of them, but were forced to sit on their story for 10 years until the presidency of Mikhail Gorbachev brought with it the era of *perestroika*, when Ryabov told his story to the *Moscow News*. The remains of the Romanovs and their servants were disinterred in a hasty 'official exhumation' that further trashed the site, destroying precious evidence. Then began the long, tortuous process of identification, at a time when DNA testing was in its infancy, as scientific experts in Britain and America began to squabble among themselves and the Anastasia camp continued, still, to talk of miraculous escapes.

Meanwhile, in Ekaterinburg after the collapse of Communism in 1991, a simple wooden cross was erected to mark the site of the Ipatiev House until funds could be raised to build a huge new cathedral there. By the time the Church on the Blood had its official opening in 2003, the Romanovs had been officially canonised by the Russian Orthodox Church and a monastery commemorating them had been founded out at the Four Brothers, now better known as Ganina Yama. On 17 July 1998, the eightieth anniversary of the murders, the remaining, scattered descendants of the dynasty gathered in St Petersburg for the solemn reburial of the remains of all but two of those murdered at the Ipatiev House. The bodies of Alexey and Maria had yet to be found, and still the controversy raged over whether the skeletal remains identified and interred in St Petersburg as Anastasia's were really hers or in fact Maria's.

It took another amateur group of local enthusiasts – members of Ekaterinburg's Military Historical Club – to finally achieve, in the summer of 2007, what previous official investigators and a whole host of weekend amateur diggers had failed to do for 90 years – locate the lost remains of Alexey and Maria. The team based their search on a close study of the statements made by Yurovsky about the location of the final graves, under the aegis of Ekaterinburg's Institute of History & Archaeology. On 29 July, a few shards of bone, nails, bullets and fragments of ceramic vessels (the jars that had contained the sulphuric acid) were located in two small bonfire sites not far from the main grave site on the Koptyaki Road.

Ekaterinburg today is becoming hostage to big business as it rushes headlong towards a market economy. More and more of its neglected historic buildings are being torn down to make way for offices and expensive apartment blocks. Gift shops, fast food and the most fashionable of Western clothes are now available at shopping malls such as Vainer Street, where the ear is assaulted by tinny and obtrusive disco music. Here the foreign businessman can get an excellent three-course '*biznes lanch*' for as little as 350 roubles (about £7). The Amerikanskaya Hotel is still there; dusty, tatty and disconsolate. But it's not a hotel any more. Western travellers seeking the creature comforts they expect now head for the newly built Park Inn on Malysheva.

Out at Ganina Yama, where Yurovsky oversaw the hasty consignment of the bodies to the mineshaft that first night, the air in July is heavy with the rich, cloying smell of lilies. On the 17th, the anniversary of the murders at the Ipatiev House, the site is covered with huge ranks of these tall white flowers that sway gently in the humid air. In the traditional Russian iconography of mourning, they have been planted here to symbolise the restored innocence of the soul at death. This once lonely site is now the Monastery of the Holy Tsarist Passion Bearers. The actual grave site – a couple of miles away in the forest glade where Ryabov and Avdonin found the remains in 1979 – was until recently marked only by a simple wooden cross and some plastic flowers. Some 60 metres beyond it lie the two small pits where the last pathetically few burnt remains of Maria and Alexey were found.

Standing in front of the bank of lilies at Ganina Yama – a quiet, atmospheric spot where the pilgrims tread softly and unobtrusively – one gets an overwhelming sense of the emotional dynamic of a story that, for the faithful, has now been set in stone as a national tragedy encapsulating everything that Russia has lost. Elsewhere on the site there is a strangely unreal quality about the fairytale architectural ensemble of seven picturesque churches built Russian-style of pine wood without a single nail. With their dainty curves and arches, their malachite green roofs and delicate golden cupolas and spires, each church is the personal shrine for a member of the Romanov family. But their beauty seems somehow too contrived, too new, too perfect, making the overall effect uncannily that of a Disney-style Russian theme park.

The politics behind the creation of this – the Russian Orthodox Church's official commemoration of the Romanovs – are complex. Its construction is also in fundamental conflict with considerable ongoing dissent within the Church itself about whether or not the bones actually discovered in the forest are those of the Romanovs at all, for which reason, when they were interred in St Petersburg in 1998, they were referred to by the priest conducting the service as being of 'Christian victims of the Revolution' rather than the Imperial Family. Perhaps now with the final discovery of the remains of Maria and Alexey (at the time of writing, still pending the results of DNA tests) that omission will be rectified. Be that as it may, the Russian Orthodox Church now has an overriding control over Ganina Yama's burgeoning tourist industry, its influx of pilgrims, its gift shop full of garish icons, and its official tour guides, just as it does at that other major place of Romanov pilgrimage, Ekaterinburg's Church on the Blood. In the summer of 2007 the All-Russia Conference of Tourism laid down plans for the inception of an official 'Romanovs Royal Tourist Route', taking in the cities of Tobolsk, Tyumen, Ekaterinburg, St Petersburg and Kazan. The inevitable commercialisation of the Imperial Family as a valuable asset in Russia's burgeoning market economy is now at hand. And with it the possibility of defending the truth of their story from an onslaught of inaccuracy, sentiment and hagiography rapidly recedes. As the Romanov gifts and souvenirs proliferate, so too the unstoppable and growing interest in the Romanov legend at home and in the West becomes ever more covered in a coat of saccharine. The mushrooming of the Romanov tourist industry has done little to throw new light on the events of July 1918, merely adding further obscuring layers, like varnish, over time, to an old icon.

It is only in the dappled shadows of the still rough opening in the ground where the scent of the lilies overwhelms the senses that something intangible on the heavy summer air brings with it a moment of epiphany. In breathing in the sickly aroma, one catches the sense of an enduring romantic tragedy that transcends – if not defies – all the logic of political and historical argument. Here there is an eerie silence, broken only by the occasional softly spoken prayer of the faithful, who stand and look, and sometimes weep. With the sunlight gently filtering down through the birch trees and catching the gold of their great long stamens, the lilies stand like dozens of living white headstones, memorials to innocent young lives cut short.

Back in 1998, travel writer Colin Thubron noted on a visit to a far less commercial Ekaterinburg that the whole Romanov story was already drowned in a 'mist of holiness'. That mist has now become an inundation. As time goes on, it is the sanitised commercial image of the Romanovs as saints and 'Holy Passion Bearers' that will increasingly prevail, no matter what historians may argue, or the archives yield up to us. Ganina Yama is the obligatory place of pilgrimage for any Russian believer, and the high point for any foreign tourist visiting what Russian tour websites now call 'The Romanov Golgotha'. The legend has simply become irresistible; too powerful, too emotive, forever perpetuated in the hearts and minds of the many thousands of sincere believers who find their way here. Indeed, their numbers are increasing so rapidly that soon the very basic infrastructure at Ganina Yama, as well as the overstretched facilities at the Church on the Blood, will not be able to cope, inundated by an influx of pilgrims and seekers after God – the needy, the hopeful, the despairing – who now see in their reverence for the martyred Imperial Family a way of atoning for the past, for the depredations of 73 years of Communism, for the loss of Russian national and spiritual identity. For them it is a way of building hopes for the restoration of faith, and with it a better life.

Attempting, as one inevitably does on contemplating the lilies of Ganina Yama, to imagine the true events of that violent and chaotic night in July 1918, it is those inescapably romantic, evocative images of the Imperial Family that inevitably twist and turn into view. No matter how hard one tries to resist, they nag at one's consciousness . . . a boy in a sailor suit . . . girls in white dresses . . . untainted, murdered children . . . a devoted family destroyed . . . all of them now forever young, forever innocent and, as they all so fervently wished for in their many prayers, 'At Rest with the Saints'.

Note on Sources

This book is a synthesis and retelling of a large number of Russian and English sources, many of the former published in Ekaterinburg (and Sverdlovsk, under its Soviet name) and difficult to access in the West. It is not a political history, nor does it set out to evaluate the reign of Nicholas II or his vices and virtues as a monarch. It seeks to tell the story of the Romanov family within the dynamic of those extraordinary last 14 days. For this reason, with the predominance of material coming from difficult-to-locate Russian-language sources, and also by virtue of the nature of the story's telling, it was decided to write this book without the intrusion of footnotes. The priority was to create a strong historical narrative that did not enter into academic digression or interrupt the story with debate about contentious issues. There are, of course, many controversial points of interpretation in the story of the Romanov murders, but in the end this book, as much as any other on a real, historical topic, is a subjective one, based on my own evaluation of the material available to me. At all times I have stayed with historical truth in so far as it has been possible to substantiate the facts in the face of much contradictory material, but there have, inevitably, been moments when I have had to take my own leaps of faith as a historian and come to my own conclusions.

There is a vast wealth of material, both written and visual, on the Romanov family, but one has to treat much of the written record with caution. Many contemporary memoirs by members of the Imperial Court are little more than unbridled hagiography based on extremely personal, subjective views of the family; similarly, in the years since the Romanovs were canonised, a welter of sentimental literature – both in Russia and among the now huge Russian Orthodox émigré community – has sought to detach the family as real people from the context of their story and their very violent times, and present them as plaster saints, above criticism. And whilst much revisionist literature on the political career of Nicholas II now concentrates on pointing the finger at his treatment of the Jews and the endemic tsarist anti-Semitism in which he was brought up, there is, at the polar opposite of this, a strong anti-Semitic strain to many books about the murder of the Romanovs from the 1920s onwards (notably those of the early investigators Melgunov, Diterikhs, Wilton and Sokolov). Some of these seek, in an often extremely distasteful manner, to emphasise the Jewishness of many of the leading Bolsheviks of the day (not just those involved in the murders) and take this as a stepping-off point for blaming all of Russia's woes, from the Revolution to the murders in Ekaterinburg, on a darkly seditious Jewish cabal. The simple fact is that with the strong traditional value placed on knowledge and learning within the Jewish faith, education has always been a priority; hence the large numbers of Russian Jews who by default were drawn into the intellectual elite of the Russian revolutionary movement.

It is thus something of a minefield steering one's way through the two opposing camps of the sycophantically pro-tsarist and violently anti-Jewish and anti-Bolshevik sources relating to the Romanov story. It prompted me, as much as possible, to stick as closely as I could to those sources written nearest to the time of the events themselves by people who were there, in Russia. This related in particular to early accounts of Lenin and the Soviet leadership before they were tainted by Stalin's post-1924 cult of the personality that created a Leninist hagiography that even today has barely been dented. This was very much the line taken by Professor Ivan Plotnikov, who urged me when I met him in July 2007 to go back to the earliest accounts I could find, in particular those of Yakov Yurovsky, and stay as much as I could with them.

At the beginning of this project I made the decision not to spend precious research time, on a very limited budget, going over the extensive Russian archival sources on the subject; these have been very well picked over by a host of other scholars and are now largely available. Practically all the seminal material relating to the regime at the Ipatiev House, members of the execution squad and eyewitnesses to the murders and burials in the forest has now been republished in a range of Russian collections – sources such as Alekseev (1993), Aksyuchits (1998), Buranov & Khrustalev (1992), Ross (1987), a valuable collection of very rare testimony, Nikulin & Belokurov (1999), Lykova (2007), as well as the Tsar's diaries for the period (Zakharov, 2007). In English, King & Wilson (2003) have done much ground-breaking work, as too Steinberg & Khrustalev (1995) in making primary sources available. Instead, I decided to take a lateral approach to the story, exploring new and unseen eyewitness accounts of the situation in Siberia in 1918 and in Ekaterinburg itself, written by American and British observers who were there at the time or soon after – either as diplomats, or independent journalists, or with the Allied Intervention Forces (see list of Archival Sources). In particular the eyewitness accounts of the British consul in

Ekaterinburg, Thomas Preston (he did not inherit his baronetcy of Beeston St Lawrence, as Sir Thomas, until after the events in this story), had, I felt, been seriously underrated and underused. His full typescript memoirs in the Leeds Russian Archive contain much valuable detail not included in the published version *Before the Curtain*, as too do his extensive official memoranda and reports in the Public Record Office at Kew and the article he wrote for the *Daily Telegraph* to commemorate the fiftieth anniversary in 1968. Other hunches turned up unexpectedly interesting material: the Belusov letter from the archives of the British and Foreign Bible Society at Cambridge came after I discovered that Ekaterinburg had been home to a major depository for the Society's onward dissemination of religious literature across Siberia. The archive of the outstanding Russianist and historian Sir Bernard Pares, who was in Siberia after the Romanov murders, also threw up some valuable nuggets of information. Similarly, a search in the much underrated Tyrkova-Williams collection of revolutionary and civil war pamphlets printed in Russia – many of them so extraordinarily rare that the surviving copies are unique to this collection – threw up Debogory-Mokrievich's fascinating account of the Bolsheviks in Perm and Ekaterinburg 1917–18.

Pride of place, however, must go to the now forgotten Herman Bernstein – a Russian-born Jew and US Russia correspondent for the *New York Herald* and the *Washington Post*. I flew to New York to conduct an entirely speculative search of his archive and I was not disappointed. It is an absolute treasure trove of material – letters, photographs, articles and newspapers cuttings charting Bernstein's passionate love–hate relationship with Russia during his numerous trips there, his contact with many distinguished Russians and several variant accounts of his visit to Ekaterinburg and his interview with Judge Sergeev and other eyewitnesses. The archive charts Bernstein's own personal journey from violently anti-tsarist, as a leading critic of the Jewish pogroms in Russia, through ecstatic welcome of the Revolution as the big New Idea, to bitter disillusion and anger at the Bolshevik abuse of human and civil rights during the civil war. Bernstein's invaluable archive, whilst being somewhat haphazard in its organisation and often in a very poor state (crumbling newspaper cuttings, often undated and unattributed), deserves much wider recognition and study.

In the West, it was Robert K. Massie's *Nicholas and Alexandra*, first published in 1967, that set the Romanov industry on a roll that has at times so romanticised the story as to lose all perspective on the real, flawed characters of Nicholas and Alexandra. I must therefore commend the enormous labour of love that is Greg King and Penny Wilson's *The Fate of the Romanovs*, which is exhaustive in its attention to detail and absolutely invaluable in its accessing of eyewitness testimony from Russian archives. Whilst I have come to my own often different conclusions, *The Fate of the Romanovs* is an absolutely indispensable source, which I recommend to any reader wishing to follow the story further – particularly in terms of the Sokolov investigation, the later rediscovery of the grave in the Koptyaki Forest and the whole contentious issue of identification of the remains. It is a matter of great regret that King and Wilson's Romanovs magazine *Atlantis: In the Court of Memory* is now sadly defunct and also seemingly unavailable in any British library.

Ultimately, though, I have to single out Professor Ivan Plotnikov in Ekaterinburg, whose work, as far as I can ascertain, has until now been entirely overlooked in the West, no doubt because it is all in Russian and has only been published in Ekaterinburg and is thus extremely difficult to get hold of. The professor is an outstanding expert on Urals history, particularly during the civil war, and in his *Gibel' Tsarskoy Semi* (2003) he has summarised his exhaustive research in obscure Russian provincial archives that no Westerner would have a hope of accessing. As I write, the professor is working on an ambitious four-volume account of the murder of the Romanovs, which will draw on his extensive archive and a lifetime's research. I sincerely hope that his frail health will allow him to complete it. Meanwhile, the recent work of Lyudmila Anatol'evna Lykova has filled in a few more valuable parts of the archival jigsaw and is also to be commended to any Russian speaker wishing to read more.

My interest in the Romanovs does not of course end here; I shall continue to monitor new material becoming available with great interest in hopes of perhaps returning to the story or some aspect of it at a later date. I will therefore be only too happy to respond to enquiries from readers wishing to know about any specific references consulted in the writing of this book. I would also greatly value hearing from readers with any new or interesting information of their own to offer, so do please contact me via my website, www.helenrappaport.com, or c/o my publishers:

Hutchinson
The Random House Group
20 Vauxhall Bridge Road
London SW1V 2SA

Bibliography

Archival Sources

Herman Bernstein, 'The Murder of the Romanoffs' (dated Ekaterinburg, November 1918), TS RG 713/3335A (a fuller version of his newspaper articles), Herman Bernstein papers, Yivo Institute, Center for Jewish Studies, New York

Margaret Bibikova papers, Liddle Collection, RUS 03, Leeds University Library

Mr Bjelousoff (K. Belousov) letter from Ekaterinburg, 11 January 1919, in Papers of the British and Foreign Bible Society, Cambridge University

Sir Charles Eliot, 'Fate of the Russian Imperial Family', report in FO 371/3977, Public Record Office, Kew

Lloyd George papers, Parliamentary Archives, London

Charles Sidney Gibbes papers, Bodleian Library, Oxford

Stephen Locker Lampson, 'Nothing to Offer but Blood', TS biography of Oliver Locker-Lampson, in Liddle Collection, RUS 30, Leeds University Library

Sir Bernard Pares, 'Siberian Diary, January–October, 1919', Sir Bernard Pares Papers, School of Slavonic and East European Studies, London, PAR/6/9/2

— Report on Bolshevik Atrocities in Siberia, PAR/6/9/4

— Report of Frances McCullagh, PAR 6/15/1

Lieutenant Patterson RNA, 'Armoured Car Brigade in Russia 1916–17', TS memoirs, Liddle Collection, RUS 30, Leeds University Library

Sir Thomas Preston papers, Liddle Collection, RUS 37, Leeds University Library

Sir Thomas Preston diplomatic correspondence from Ekaterinburg and reports on Siberia, in FO 538/1, PRO Kew (some published in 'A Collection of Reports . . .', 1919, below)

Sir Thomas Preston, 'Witness Statements in English, French and Russian sworn before HM Consul at Ekaterinburg giving details of Pillage and Murders committed by Bolsheviks', FO 538/1, PRO Kew

Paul J. Rainey, 'General Observations on the Situation in Russia', c.

September 1918, Paul James Rainey papers, Wichita State University, Kansas, MS 88-07

Colonel Paul Rodzianko, 'Account of the Murdering of the Tsar and His Family by the Bolsheviks at Ekaterinburg', in FO 371/3977, PRO Kew

Herbert Galloway Stewart photograph collection, Bradford Media Museum

Tyrkova-Williams Collection, British Library

Robert Wilton papers, Geoffrey Dawson papers, *Times* Newspapers Limited Archive, News International Limited

Newspapers 1917–18

Chicago Daily News
Chicago Tribune
New York Herald
New York Times
The Times
Washington Post

Primary Sources

Aksyuchits, Viktor, *Pokayanie: Materialy pravitel'stvennoi kommissii po izucheniyu voprosov, svyazannykh s issledovaniem i perezakhoroneniem ostankov rossiiskogo Imperatora Nikolaya II i chlenov ego sem'i*, Moscow: 'Vybor', 1998

Alekseev, Venyamin, *The Last Act of a Tragedy: New documents about the Execution of the Last Russian Emperor Nicholas II*, Ekaterinburg: Urals Branch of Russian Academy of Sciences Publishers, 1996

— *Gibel' tsarskoy sem'i: mify i real'nost', novye dokumenty o tragedii na Urale*, Ekaterinburg: Bank Kul'turnoi Informatsii, 1993

Alexander, Grand Duke, *Once a Grand Duke*, New York: Cosmopolitan Book Corp., 1932

Alexandrov, Victor, *The End of the Romanovs*, London: Hutchinson, 1966

Alferev, E. E., *Pis'ma tsarskoy sem'i iz zatocheniya*, Jordanville, NY: Holy Trinity Monastery, 1974

Anichkov, Vladimir P., *Ekaterinburg–Vladivostok (1917–1922)*, Moscow: Russkii Put', 1998

Avdeev, A., 'Nikolay Romanov v Tobol'ske i Ekaterinburge', *Krasnaya Nov'*, 1928, no. 5, pp.185–209

— 'His Jailer Tells of the Czar's Last Days', *New York Times*, 15 July 1928, p.4

Benckendorff, Count Paul, *Last Days at Tsarskoe Selo*, London: Heinemann, 1927

Bernstein, Herman, '6 Versions of Czar's Fate', *Washington Post*, 16 February 1919

Besedovsky, Grigory, *Revelations of a Soviet Diplomat*, London: Williams & Norgate, 1931

Biryukov, Evgenii, *Ipat'evskii Dom*, Ekaterinburg: Izd. SV-96, 2003

Bokhanov, Alexander, et al., *The Romanovs: Love, Power and Tragedy*, Italy: Leppi Publications, 1993

Bonetskaya, N. K., *Tsarskie deti*, Moscow: Izdatel'stvo Sretenskogo Monastyrya, 2004

Botkin, Gleb, *The Real Romanovs, As Revealed by the Late Czar's Physician and His Son,* London: Putnam, 1932

Buchanan, George, *My Mission to Russia and Other Diplomatic Memories,* 2 vols., London: Cassell & Co., 1923

Buchanan, Meriel, 'The Grand Duchess Olga Nicholaievna', in Meriel Buchanan, *Queen Victoria's Relations,* London: Cassell, 1954

Bulygin, Captain Paul, *The Murder of the Romanovs: The Authentic Account by Captain Paul Bulygin,* London: Hutchinson, 1935

Bunyan, James, *Intervention, Civil War and Communism in Russia, April–December 1918: Documents and Materials*, Baltimore: Johns Hopkins Press, 1936

Buranov, Yu., *Pravda o Ekaterinburgskoi tragedii: sbornik stat'ei*, Moscow: Russkii Vestnik, 1998

— *Tainy i istorii: ubiitsy tsarya. unichtozhenie dinastii*, Moscow: Terra, 1997

— and V. Khrustalev, *Gibel' imperatorskogo doma 1917–18*, Moscow: Progress, 1992

Buxhoeveden, Baroness Sophie, *The Life and Tragedy of Alexandra Fyororovna*, London: Longmans, Green & Co., 1928

— *Left Behind: Fourteen Months in Siberia during the Revolution*, London: Longmans, Green & Co., 1929

Bykov, P. M., *Poslednie dni Romanovykh*, Moscow: Gosudarstvennoe Izdatel'stvo, 1930

— *The Last Days of Tsardom*, London: Martin Lawrence, 1934

— *Rabochaya revolyutsiya na Urale: epizody i fakty*, Ekaterinburg: Gos. Izd, Ural'skoe Oblastnoe Upravlenie, 1921

'A Collection of Reports on Bolshevism in Russia' (abridged edn.), Parliamentary Paper, Russia No. 1, London: HMSO, 1919

Debogory-Mokrievich, V. K., '14 mesyatsev vo vlasti bol'shevikov Permskie uzhasy,' Pamphlet, Ekaterinburg, 1919, in Tyrkova-Williams Collection, British Library

Diterikhs (Dietrichs), General Mikhail, *Ubiistvo tsarskoy sem'i i chlenov doma Romanovykh na Urale*, Vladivostok: Voennoi Akademii, 1922

Elchaninov, A. G., *Nicholas II: Czar of Russia*, London: Hugh Rees, 1913

Figes, Orlando, *A People's Tragedy: The Russian Revolution 1891–1924*, London: Jonathan Cape, 1996

Fomin, Sergey, 'Ipat'evskii Dom (khronika)', in Markov (2002)

Fuhrman, Joseph T., ed., *The Complete Wartime Correspondence of Tsar Nicholas II and the Empress Alexandra, April 1914–March 1917*, Westport, CT: Greenwood Press, 1999

Gilliard, Pierre, *Thirteen Years at the Russian Court*, London: Hutchinson, 1921

Golikov, Georgii Nazarovich, *Vladimir Il'ich Lenin – Biograficheskaya khronika 1870–1924*, volume 5 (1918), Moscow: Izd. Politicheskoi Literatury, 1975

'Historic Photographs of the Ex-Emperor of Russia Taken July 1917', *Illustrated London News*, 11 August 1917, pp. 146–7

Ioffe, Genrikh, *Revolyutsiya i sud'ba Romanovykh*, Moscow: Respublika, 1992

— 'V sushchnosti ya uzhe umer', *Literaturnaya Gazeta*, 1 September 1993, p. 13

Jagow, Dr Kurt, 'Die Schuld am Zarenmord: Eine Antwort an Paléologue', *Berliner Monatshefte* vol. 13 (1), May 1935, pp.363–401

Kerensky, A., *The Catastrophe: Kerensky's Own Story of the Russian Revolution*, New York: D. Appleton & Co., 1927

— 'The Road to the Tragedy', in Bulygin (1935)

Kheifets, Mikhail, *Tsareubiistvo v 1918 godu: versiya prestupleniya i fal'sifitsirovannogo sledstviya*, Moscow: Festival, 1992

King, Greg, *The Last Empress: The Life and Times of Alexandra Fedorovna, Tsarina of Russia*, London: Aurum, 1996

— and Penny Wilson, 'Fate of the Romanovs: An On-Line Resource, including previously unpublished historical documents', at http://www.kingandwilson.com/FOTRresources/index.htm

— *The Fate of the Romanovs*, Hoboken, NJ: John Wiley, 2003

Kozlov, V. A., and V. M. Khrustalev, *Poslednie dnevniki imperatritsy Aleksandry Fedorovny Romanovoi, Fevral' 1917 g. – 16 Iyulya 1918*, Novosibirsk: Sibirskii Khronograf, 1999

— *The Last Diary of Tsaritsa Alexandra*, intro. Robert K. Massie, London: Yale University Press, 1997

Kuznetsov, V. V., *Taina pyatoi pechati. Sud'ba tsarya – sud'ba Rossii*, St Petersburg: Derzhava 'Satis', 2002

Landau-Aldanov, Marc, *Lenin*, New York: Dutton 1922

Latyshev, A. G., *Rassekrechennyi Lenin*, Moscow: 'Mart', 1996

Lieven, Dominic, *Nicholas II. Twilight of the Empire*, London: Pimlico, 1993

Lunacharsky, Anatoly, 'Yakov Mikhailovich Sverdlov', in *Revolutionary Silhouettes*, London: Penguin, 1967

Lykova, Lyudmila Anatol'evna, 'Neizvestnyi otvet tsarskoy sem'i na pis'mo "ofitsera". Iyul' 1918 g. Ekaterinburg', *Otechestvennye Arkhivy*, 2006, no. 2, pp. 39–44

— 'V. I. Lenin i sud'ba tsarskoi sem'i', *Istoricheskii Arkhiv*, 2005, no. 5, pp. 3–9

— *Sledstvie po delu ob ubiistve rossissskoi imperatorskoi sem'i: istoreografi̇cheskii i arkheografi̇cheskii ocherk*, Moscow: Rosspen, 2007

Maliyutin, A. Yu., *Tsesarevich: dokumenty, vospominaniya, fotografi̇i*, Moscow: Vagrius, 1998

Markov, Sergei, *How We Tried to Save the Tsaritsa*, London: Putnam's, 1929

— *Pokinutaya tsarskaya sem'ya, 1917–18, Tsarskoe Selo–Tobol'sk– Ekaterinburg*, Moscow: Palomnik, 2002

Maslakov, V. V., ed., *Ekaterinburg: entsiklopediya*, Ekaterinburg: Izdatel'stvo 'Akademkniga', 2002

Massie, Robert K., *Nicholas and Alexandra*, London: Gollancz, 1968

Matveev, P. M., 'Tsarskoe Selo–Tobol'sk–Ekaterinburg: Zapiski i vospominaniya o Tobol'skom zaklyuchenii tsarskoi sem'i', *Ural'skii Rabochii*, 16 September 1990

Maylunas, Andrei, and Sergei Mironenko, *A Lifelong Passion: Nicholas and Alexandra, Their Own Story*, New York: Doubleday, 1997

McCullagh, Francis, *Prisoner of the Reds: The Story of a British Officer Captured in Siberia*, London: John Murray, 1921

Mel'gunov, S. P., *Sud'ba imperatora Nikolaya II posle otrecheniya: istoriko-kriticheskie ocherki*, Paris: La Renaissance, 1952

Mel'nik (Botkina), Tatiana, *Vospominaniya o tsarskoi sem'e i ee zhizni do i posle revolyutsii*, Belgrade: Vseslavyanskii knizhnoi magazin, 1921

Mossolov, Alexander, *At the Court of the Last Tsar*, London: Methuen, 1935

Nepein, Igor, *Pered rasstrelom: Poslednie pis'ma tsarskoi sem'i . . . 1917–18*, Omsk: Knizhnoe izdatel'stvo, 1992

Nikolaus, F. von B., *Poslednii tsar: konets Romanovykh . . . po neopubliko-vannym nemetskim istochnikam*, Petrograd: 'Edinenie', 1918

Nikulin, M. P., and K. K. Belokurov, *Poslednie dni Romanovykh: dokumenty, materialy, sledstviya, dnevniki, versii*, Sverdlovsk: Sredne-Ural'skoe Knizh. Izd., 1999

O'Conor, John F. (trans. and comm.), and Nicholas A. Sokolov: *A Translation of Sections of Nicholas A. Sokolov's 'The Murder of the Imperial Family'*, London: Souvenir Press, 1971

Ofrosimova, S. Ya., 'Tsarskaya sem'ya (Iz detskikh vospominanii)', *Bezhin Lug*, no. 1, 1995, pp.146–7

Pagannutsi, P., *Pravda ob ubiistve tsarskoi sem'i,* Jordanville: Svyato-Troitskii Monastyr', 1981

Paléologue, Maurice, *An Ambassador's Memoirs, 1914–1917,* London: Hutchinson, 1973

Pankratov, Vasili, 'With the Tsar in Tobolsk', in Steinberg & Khrustalev (1995)

Pipes, Richard, *The Russian Revolution 1899–1919,* London: Fontana Press, 1992

Platonov, Oleg, *Ubiistvo tsarskoi sem'i,* Moscow: Sovetskaya Rossiya, 1991

— *Ternovyi venets Rossii: Nikolai II v sekretnoi perepiske,* Moscow: Rodnik, 1996

Plotnikov, Ivan F., 'Lenin i poslednii rossiiskii imperator. Rol' Tsentra v reshenii sud'by tsarskoi sem'i', *Glavniy Prospekt,* no. 27, 10–16 July 1997

— 'Goloshchekin i ko. Kto, kogda i kak realizoval ustanovku Tsentra na unichtozhenie tsarskoi sem'i v Ekaterinburge', *Glavniy Prospekt,* no. 28, 17–23 July 1997

— entries on Ermakov, Goloshchekin, Sokolov, Sverdlov, in *Ural'skaya istoricheskaya entsiklopediya* (2000)

— entries on Avdeev, Beloborodov, Botkin, Voikov, Goloshchekin, Ermakov, Ipatiev, Lukoyanov, Safarov, Sverdlov, Chutskaev, Yurovsky in Maslakov (2002)

— *Gibel' tsarskoi sem'i: Pravda Istorii,* Ekaterinburg: Sverdlovskaya Regional'naya Obshchestvennaya Organizatsiya 'Za dukhovnost' i nravstvennost'', 2003

— *Plotnikov Ivan Fedorovich: Bibliograficheskii ukazatel',* Ekaterinburg: Izdatel'stvo Ural'skogo Universiteta, 2005

Preston, Thomas, *Before the Curtain,* London: John Murray, 1950

— Affadavit on murder of the Romanovs, 22 January 1960, in Vorres (1964)

— 'Last Days of the Tsar', *Sunday Telegraph,* 14 July 1968, p. 7

Prochaska, Frank, 'George V and Republicanism, 1917–1919', in *Twentieth-Century British History,* 10 (1), 1999, pp. 27–51

Radzinsky, Edvard, *The Last Tsar: the Life and Death of Nicholas II,* London: Hodder & Stoughton, 1992

Radziwill, Catherine, *Nicholas II, the Last of the Tsars,* London: Cassell & Co.,1931

Ross, Nikolay, *Gibel' tsarskoi sem'i: materialy sledstviya po delu ob ubiistve tsarskoi sem'i' ,* Frankfurt am Main: Posev, 1987

Rose, Kenneth, *King George V,* London: Phoenix Press, 1983

Ryabov, 'Prinuzhdeny vas rasstrelyat'', *Rodina* nos. 4 and 5, 1989, pp. 85–95 and 79–92

Semchevskaya, E., 'Vospominaniya o poslednikh dnyakh velikikh knyazei v gorode Ekaterinburge', in *Dvuglavyi Orel*, 15 (28), June 1921, pp. 27–32

Serbia, Princess Helena of, 'I Was at Ekaterinburg', in *Atlantis Magazine: In the Courts of Memory*, vol. 1, no. 3, 1999

Shcherbatov, A. P., *Pravda na proshloe*, Moscow: Izdatel'stvo Stretenskogo Monastyrya, 2005

Skrobov, S. V., *Dom Ipat'ev: Istoricheskoe i arkhitekturnoe opisanie*, Ekaterinburg, privately printed, 2003

Slater, Wendy, *The Many Deaths of Nicholas II: Relics, Remains and the Romanovs*, London: Routledge, 2007

Sokolov, Nicholas, *Ubiistvo tsarskoi sem'i*, Berlin: Slovo, 1925

Sonin, L. M., 'Otmazka Lenina', in Sonin, *Zagadka gibeli tsarskoi sem'i*, Moscow: Veche, 2006

Speranski, Valentin, *La 'Maison à destination spéciale'* , Paris: J. Ferenczi et Fils, 1929

Spiridovich, Alexander, *Les derniers années de la cour de Tsarskoe Selo*, 2 vols., Paris: Payot, 1928

Steinberg, Mark D., and Vladimir M. Khrustalev, *The Fall of the Romanovs*, London: Yale University Press, 1995

Sverdlova, Klavdiya, *Yakov Mikhailovich Sverdlov*, Moscow: Molodaya Gvardiya, 1960

Ural'skaya istoricheskaya entsiklopediya, Ekaterinburg: Akademkniga, 2000

Voiekov, Vladimir, *S tsarem i bez tsarya*, Minsk: Harvest, 2002

Volkov, A. A., *Okolo tsarskoi sem'i*, Moscow: Chastnaya Firma 'Ankor', 1993

Vorres, Ian, *The Last Grand Duchess*, London: Hutchinson, 1964

Vyrubova, Anna, *Memories of the Russian Court*, New York: Macmillan, 1923

Waters, Brigadier W. H. Wallscourt, *Secret and Confidential: The Experiences of a Military Attaché*, London: John Murray, 1926

— *Potsdam and Doorn*, London: John Murray, 1935

Wilton, Robert, and George Gustav Telberg, *The Last Days of the Romanovs*, London: Thornton Butterworth, 1920

Wortman, Richard, *Scenarios of Power: Myth and Ceremony, Russian Monarchy,* vol 2., Princeton, NJ: Princeton University Press, 2000

Yurovsky, Yakov, 'Zapiski Ya. M. Yurovskogo o rasstrele tsar'skoi sem'i i sokrytii trupov' (Russian text of his 1920 account of the murders), in Buranov & Khrustalev (1992)

— 'Slishkom vse bylo yasno dlya naroda: Ispoved' palacha' (Russian text of his 1922 account), *Istochnik*, 1993 (0), pp. 107–17

— 'Iz rasskaza Ya. M. Yurovskogo o rasstrele tsarskoi sem'i na soveshchanii starykh Bolshevikov v g. Sverdlovske' (Russian text of his 1934 account), in Buranov & Khrustalev (1992)

Zaitsev, Georgy, *Romanovy v Ekaterinburge. 78 dnei. Dokumental'noe povestvovanie*, Ekaterinburg: Izdatel'stvo Sokrat, 1998

Zakharov, I., ed., *Dnevnik Nikolaya Romanova*, Moscow: Zakharov, 2007

Secondary Sources

Ackerman, Carl W., 'Is the Czar Dead? Six Chances in Ten that He Was Executed by the Bolsheviki', *New York Times,* 23 February 1919, p. 62

— *Trailing the Bolsheviki: 12,000 Miles with the Allies in Siberia*, New York: Scribner's, 1919

Alexander, Robert, *The Kitchen Boy: A Novel of the Last Tsar*, New York: Penguin, 2003

Allshouse, Robert H., *Photographs for the Tsar: The Pioneering Photography of Sergei Mikhailovich Prokudin-Gorskii commissioned by Tsar Nicholas II,* London: Sidgwick & Jackson, 1980

'Annual Reports': Siberia, British and Foreign Bible Society, 1917–20

Ashton, Janet, '"God in All Things": The Religious Beliefs of Russia's Last Empress and Their Personal and Political Context', at www.alexanderpalace.org/palace/godinallthings.html

Baedeker, Karl, *Baedeker's Russia 1914*, reprinted London: Allen & Unwin, 1971

Baker, Ray Stannard, *Woodrow Wilson: Life and Letters*, Vol. VIII, *Armistice: March 1–November 11, 1918*, London: William Heinemann, 1939

Barkovets, A., and V. Tenikhina, *Nicholas II: The Imperial Family*, St Petersburg: Abris Publishers, 2002

Becvar, Gustave, *The Lost Legion,* London: S. Paul & Co., 1939

Benaghy, Christine, *An Englishman at the Court of the Tsar,* Ben Lomond, CAL: Conciliar Press, 2000

Bernstein, Herman, 'Nicholas, If Dead, Slain While Going to Trial by Reds', *Philadelphia Inquirer*, 29 June 1918

—'The Bolsheviki: The World Dynamiters', pamphlet, New York, 1919, in Herman Bernstein Archive

— 'Bernstein Has Changed His Mind about Bolsheviki', *New York Herald*, 24 June 1918

Bochkareva, Maria, *Yashka, My Life as Peasant, Officer and Exile*, trans. Isaac Don Levine, NY: Frederick A. Stokes, 1919

Bryant, Louise, *Six Months in Red Russia*, London: Journeyman Press, 1982

Buchanan, Meriel, *Petrograd, City of Trouble, 1914–1918*, London: W. Collins, 1919

— *Recollections of Imperial Russia*, London: Hutchinson, 1923

— *Diplomacy and Foreign Courts*, London: Hutchinson, 1928

— *The Dissolution of an Empire*, London: John Murray, 1932

— *Ambassador's Daughter*, London: Cassell & Co., 1958

Chekhov, Anton, *Pis'ma,* vol. 4, *Yanvar' 1890–Fevral' 1892*, Moscow: Nauka, 1976

Cherniavsky, Michael, *Tsar and People,* New Haven CT: Yale University Press, 1961

Clarke, William, *The Lost Fortune of the Tsars: The Search for the Fabulous Legacy of the Romanoffs*, London: Orion, 1996

Clay, Catrine, *King, Kaiser, Tsar: Three Royal Cousins Who Led the World to War*, London: John Murray, 2007

Coudert, Amalia, 'The Human Side of the Tsar', *Century Magazine*, vol. LXXII, 1906

Crawford, Rosemary and Donald, *Michael & Natasha: The Life and Loves of the Last Tsar of Russia*, London: Weidenfeld & Nicolson, 1997

Danilov, Yuri, *Na puti k krusheniyu: ocherki iz poslednego perioda russkoi monarkhii*, Moscow: Voennoe Izdatel'stvo, 1992

'The Dead Tsar', *Graphic*, vol. 98, 27 July 1918, p. 88

Dehn, Lili, *The Real Tsaritsa*, London: Thornton Butterworth, 1922

Dillon, E. J., *The Eclipse of Russia*, London: J. M. Dent, 1918

Dmitriev-Mamonov, A. I., and A. F. Zdziarski, *Guide to the Great Siberian Railway (1900),* rev. John Marshall, London: David & Charles, 1971

Dorr, Rheta Child, *Inside the Russian Revolution*, New York: Macmillan, 1917

Duncan, Irma, and Allan Ross MacDougall, *Isadora Duncan's Russian Days*, London: Gollancz, 1929

Eager, Margaret, *Six Years at the Russian Court*, London: Hurst & Blackett, 1906

Essad-Bey, Mohammed, *Nicholas II: Prisoner of the Purple*, London: Hutchinson, 1936

Eudin, Xenia, et al., eds., *The Life of a Chemist: Memoirs of Vladimir N. Ipatieff*, London: Oxford University Press, 1946

'The Fate of Nicholas II', *Illustrated London News,* vol. 153, 27 July 1918, p. 97

Ferro, Marc, *Nicholas II, The Last of the Tsars*, New York: Oxford University Press, 1993

Fic, Victor, *The Collapse of American Policy in Russia and Siberia, 1918*, New York: Columbia University Press, 1995

Fisher, H. H., ed., *Out of My Past: Memoirs of Count Kokovtsov*, London: Oxford University Press, 1936

Francis, David R., *Russia from the American Embassy April 1916–November 1918*, New York: C. Scribner's Sons, 1921

Gelardi, Julia, *Born to Rule: Granddaughters of Victoria, Queens of Europe*, London: Headline Review, 2006

Gerhardie, William, *The Romanovs: Evocation of the Past as a Mirror of the Present*, London: Rich & Cowan, 1940

Grabbe, Count Alexander, *The Private World of the Last Tsar; In the Photographs and Notes of General Count Alexander Grabbe*, London: Collins, 1985

Greece, Prince Michael of, *Nicholas and Alexandra: The Family Albums*, London: Tauris Parke Books, 2002

Halliburton, Richard, *Seven League Boots*, London: Geoffrey Bles, 1936

— *Richard Halliburton, His Story of His Life's Adventure; As Told in Letters to His Mother and Father*, London: G. Bles, 1941

Handbook for Travellers to Russia, Poland and Finland, London: John Murray, 1893

Harcave, Sidney, trans. and ed., *The Memoirs of Count Witte*, Armonk, NY: M. E. Sharpe, 1990

Harriman, Mrs J. Borden, *From Pinafores to Politics*, London: George Allen & Unwin, 1933

Harris, James, *The Great Urals: Regionalism and the Evolution of the Soviet System*, Ithaca: Cornell University Press, 1999

Hennessy, James Pope, *Queen Mary, 1867–1953*, London: Phoenix Press, 2000

Hill, Captain George A., *Go Spy the Land: Being the Adventures of I.K.8 of the British Secret Service*, London: Cassell, 1932

Hoare, Samuel, *The Fourth Seal: The End of a Russian Chapter*, London: William Heinemann, 1930

Hough, Richard, *Louis and Victoria, the First Mountbattens*, London: Hutchinson, 1974

'How Czar and Entire Family Were Slain . . .', *New York American*, 10 June 1923

Hughes, Michael, *Inside the Enigma: British Officials in Russia 1900–1939*, London: Hambledon Press, 2000

Hynes, E. L., *Letters of the Tsar to the Tsaritsa 1914–1917*, London: John Lane, 1929

Judd, Dennis, *The Life and Times of George V*, London: Weidenfeld & Nicolson, 1993

Kasvinov, M. K., *Dvadtsat' tri stupeni vniz*, 2nd edn., Moscow: Mysl', 1987

Kennan, George, *Siberia and the Exile System 1845–1924*, 2 vols., London: James R. Osgood, 1891

— *Soviet–American Relations, 1917–1920*, vol. 2, *The Decision to Intervene*, Princeton, NJ: Princeton University Press

King, Greg, and Penny Wilson, eds., *Atlantis Magazine: In the Courts of Memory*, 5 vols., 1999–2004

Kiste, John Van der, and Coryne Hall, *Once a Grand Duchess: Xenia, Sister of Nicholas II*, Stroud, Gloucs: Sutton, 2004

— *Kaiser Wilhelm II: Germany's Last Emperor*, Stroud, Gloucs: Sutton, 1996

— *The Romanovs: 1818–1959*, Stroud, Gloucs: Sutton, 1998

Kleinmichel, Countess, *Memories of a Shipwrecked World: Being the Memoirs of Countess Kleinmichel*, London: Brentano's, 1923

Kruchinin, A. M., *Padenie krasnogo Ekaterinburga*, Ekaterinburg: Belaya Rossiya, 2005

Kudrin, U. V., *Dnevniki imperatritsy Marii Fedorovny (1914–1920, 1923 gody)*, Moscow: Varius, 2005

Kurth, Peter, *Tsar: The Lost World of Nicholas and Alexandra*, London: Little, Brown & Co., 1995

Lansdell, Henry, *Through Siberia*, London: Sampson, Low, Marston, Searle & Rivington, 1882

Lasies, Joseph, *La tragedie Siberienne: le drame d'Ekaterinbourg*, Paris: L'edition Française Illustrée, 1920

Lavrinov, Valery, *Ekaterinburgskaya eparkhiya: sobytiya, lyudi, khramy*, Ekaterinburg: Ural'skii Universitet, 2001

Leggett, George, *The Cheka: Lenin's Political Police*, Oxford: Clarendon Press, 1981

'Lenin, Orator, Writer and Dictator', *New York Times*, 9 July 1922

Levine, Isaac Don, *Eyewitness to History: Memoirs and Reflections of a Foreign Correspondent for Half a Century*, New York: Hawthorn Books, 1973

— *The Russian Revolution*, London: John Lane, 1917

Lincoln, W. Bruce, *Red Victory: A History of the Russian Civil War*, London: Cardinal, 1991

Lockhart, R. H. Bruce, *Memoirs of a British Agent*, London: Putnam, 1932

Luk'yanin, Valentin, and M. Nikulina, *Progulki po Ekaterinburgu*, Ekaterinburg: Bank Kul'turnoi Informatsii, 1998

Lutyens, Mary, ed., *Lady Lytton's Court Diary 1895–1899*, London: Rupert Hart-Davis, 1961

MacKenzie, Frederick A., *Russia before Dawn*, London: T. Fisher Unwin, 1923

Mangold, Tom, and Anthony Summers, *The File on the Tsar*, rev. edn., London: Orion, 2002

Maples, Dr William R., and Michael Browning, *Dead Men Do Tell Tales*, New York: Doubleday, 1994

Marye, George Thomas, *Nearing the End in Imperial Russia*, London: Selwyn & Blount, 1929

Massie, Robert K., *The Romanovs: The Final Chapter*, London: Cape, 1995

McNeal, Shay, *The Secret Plot to Save the Tsar: New Truths Behind the Romanov Mystery*, New York: Perennial, 2003

Meakin, Annette B., *Russia: Travels and Studies*, London: Hurst, 1906

Meier, I. L., 'Kak pogibla tsarskaya sem'ya', Los Angeles: Soglasie, 1956

Mendel, Arthur P., ed., *Paul Miliukov: Political Memoirs 1905–1917*, Ann Arbor: University of Michigan Press, 1967

Miller, Lyubov, *Tsarskaya sem'ya: zhertva temnoi sily*, Moscow: Velikii Grad, 2005

Mohrenschildt, Dimitri von, 'The Early American Observers of the Russian Revolution, 1917–1921', *Russian Review*, 3(1), Autumn 1943, pp. 64–74

Morrow, Anne, *Cousins Divided: George V and Nicholas II*, Stroud, Gloucs: Sutton, 2006

Nadtochii, Yu, *Ubiitsy imenem revolyutsii: dokumental'naya povest' o poslednikh dnyakh zhizni Nikolaya II i ego sem'i*, Tyumen: Uralskiy, 1994

Nansen, Fridtjof, *Through Siberia: The Land of the Future*, London: Heineman, 1914

Nielson, Keith, *Britain and the Last Tsar: British Policy and Russia 1894–1917*, Oxford: Clarendon Press, 1995

'No Chance to Save Russia Through the Bolsheviki Says Herman Bernstein', *New York Herald*, 4 July 1918

Occleshaw, Michael, *Armour Against Fate: British Military Intelligence in the First World War*, London: Columbus, 1989

— *The Romanov Conspiracies*, London: Orion, 1993

— *Dances in Deep Shadows: Britain's Clandestine War in Russia 1917–20*, London: Constable, 2006

Orekhov, Dmitri, *Podvig tsarskoi sem'i*, St Petersburg: 'Nevsky Prospekt', 2001

Ossendowski, Ferdinand A., *Lenin, God of the Godless*, London: E. P. Dutton & Co., 1931

Oudendyk, William J., *Ways and By-Ways in Diplomacy*, London: Peter Davies, 1939

Paley, Princess, *Memories of Russia 1916–1919*, London: Herbert Jenkins, 1925

Pares, Bernard, *My Russian Memoirs*, London: Cape, 1931

— *The Fall of the Russian Monarchy: A Study of the Evidence*, London: Cassell, 1988

Radziwill, Catherine, *The Intimate Life of the Last Tsarina*, London: Cassell, 1929

— *The Taint of the Romanovs*, London: Cassell, 1931

Ramm, Agatha, *Beloved and Darling Child: Last Letters between Queen Victoria and Her Eldest Daughter, 1886–1901*, Stroud, Gloucs: Sutton, 1990

'Reported Assassination of the Tsaritsa and Her Daughters', *Illustrated London News*, 21 September 1918, p. 327

'Revolution in Petrograd', *Illustrated London News*, 14 April 1917

Rivet, Charles, *The Last of the Romanovs*, London: Constable, 1918

Robien, Louis de, *Diary of a Diplomat in Russia 1917–1918*, London: Michael Joseph, 1969

Robins, Raymond, *Raymond Robins' Own Story*, New York: Harper Brothers, 1920

Rodzianko, Count Paul, *Tattered Banners*, London: Seeley Service & Co., 1939

Romanovsky-Krassinsky, HSH The Princess, *Dancing in St Petersburg: The Memoirs of Kschessinska*, London: Gollancz, 1960

Ross, Edward Alsworth, *Russia in Upheaval*, New York: Century Co., 1918

Roumania, Marie of, *The Story of My Life, Marie Queen of Roumania*, 3 vols., London: Cassell, 1934–5

Russell, Charles Edward, *Unchained Russia*, New York: D. Appleton & Co, 1918

'Russian Revolution and the Overthrow of the Tsar', *Illustrated London News*, 24 March 1917

Salisbury, Harrison E., *Black Night, White Snow: Russia's Revolutions 1905–1917*, London: Cassell, 1977

Sazonov, Serge, *The Fateful Years 1906–1916*, London: Jonathan Cape, 1928

Service, Robert, *Lenin, A Biography*, London: Pan Books, 2002

Shavel'sky, Georgy, *Vospominaniya poslednego protopresvitera Russkoi armii i flota*, 2 vols., New York: Izdatel'stvo imeni Chekhova, 1954

Shepherd, Gordon Brook, *Iron Maze: The Western Secret Services and the Bolsheviks, 1917–1921*, London: Pan, 1998

Solzhenitsyn, Alexander, *November 1916: The Red Wheel, Knot II*, London: Cape, 2000

Stopford, Albert, *The Russian Diary of an Englishman, Petrograd 1915–1917*, London: Heinemann, 1919

Sydacoff, B. von, *Nicholas II: Behind the Scenes in the Country of the Last Tsar*, London: A. Siecle, 1905

Thomas, Herbert, 'Cambourne Engineer in Russia: In Room Where Czar Was Murdered', *Cornishman and Cornish Telegraph*, 21 January, 1920, p. 2

Thubron, Colin, *In Siberia*, London: Chatto & Windus, 1999

Townend, Carole, *Royal Russia: From the James Blair Lovell Archive*, London: Book Club Associates, 1999

Trotsky, Leon, *Dnevniki i pis'ma*, Moscow: Izdatel'stvo Gumanitarnoi Kul'tury, 1994

Vassili, Count Paul (Catherine Radziwill), *Behind the Veil at the Russian Court*, London: Cassell, 1913

Volkogonov, Dmitri, *Lenin: A New Biography*, London: Free Press, 1994

Vyrubova, Anna, *The Romanov Family Album*, intr. Robert K. Massie, London: Allen Lane, 1982

W. B. (a Russian), *Russian Court Memoirs, 1914–1916*, London: Herbert Jenkins, 1917

Walsh, Edmund A., 'Last Days of the Romanovs', *Atlantic Monthly*, vol. 141 (3), March 1928, pp. 339–54

— *The Fall of the Russian Empire: Story of the Last Romanovs and the Coming of the Bolsheviki*, London: Williams & Norgate, 1929

Ward, John, *With the 'Die-Hards' in Siberia*, London: Cassell, 1920

Warwick, Christopher, *Ella, Princess, Saint and Martyr*, Hoboken, NJ: John Wiley, 2006

Washburn, Stanley, *On the Russian Front in World War I: Memoirs of an American War Correspondent*, New York: Robert Speller & Sons, 1982

'Waves of Slander Engulfed the Deposed Tsar's Children . . .', review of Vasily Pankratov's 'Five Months with the Romanoffs', *New York Herald*, 9 March 1919

'Weighed Czar's Fate: Bolsheviki Warned by Huns at Brest Not to Try Him', *Washington Post*, 29 July 1918

Weiner, Leo, *An Interpretation of the Russian People*, London: McBride, Nast & Co., 1915

Welch, Frances, *The Romanovs and Mr Gibbes*, London: Short Books, 2002

— *A Romanov Fantasy: Life at the Court of Anna Anderson*, London: Short Books, 2007

Wenyon, Charles, *Four Thousand Miles Across Siberia*, London: Robert Culley, 1899

Whittle, Tyler, *The Last Kaiser: A Biography of William II*, London: Heinemann, 1977

Wiener, Leo, *An Interpretation of the Emperor Nicholas II As I Knew Him*, London: Arthur L. Humphreys, 1922

Williams, Arthur, *Through the Russian Revolution*, London: Labour Publishing Company Ltd., 1923

Wilton, Robert, *Russia's Agony*, London: Edward Arnold, 1918

Windt, Harry de, *From Pekin to Calais by Land*, London: Chapman & Hall, 1892

Yakovlev, Alexander, *A Century of Violence in Soviet Russia*, New Haven, CT: Yale University Press, 2002

Yashchik, Timofey K., *Ryadom s imperatritsei: vospominaniya leib-kazaka*, St Petersburg: Nestor-Istoriya, 2004

Yeltsin, Boris, *Against the Grain: An Autobiography*, London: Cape, 1990

Yermilova, Larissa, *The Last Tsar*, Bournemouth: Parkstone/Planeta, 1996

Young, Kenneth, ed., *The Diaries of Sir Robert Bruce Lockhart*, vol. 1, *1915–1938*, London: Macmillan, 1973

Zeepvat, Charlotte, *The Camera and the Tsars: The Romanov Family in Photographs*, Stroud, Gloucs: Sutton, 2004

— *Romanov Autumn: Stories from the Last Century of Imperial Russia*, Stroud, Gloucs: Sutton, 2000

Zinovieff, Sofka, *Red Princess: A Revolutionary Life*, London: Granta Books, 2007

Zlokazov, L. D., and V. B. Semenov, *Staryi Ekaterinburg: gorod glazami ochevidtsev*, Ekaterinburg: IGEMMO 'Lithica', 2000

Index